VIOLENCE IN FRANCOPHONE AFRICAN & CARIBBEAN WOMEN'S LITERATURE

Violence *in* Francophone African & Caribbean *Women's* Literature

CHANTAL KALISA

University of Nebraska Press
Lincoln and London

Acknowledgments for the
use of copyrighted material
appear on page viii, which
constitutes an extension
of the copyright page. ♾

Library of Congress Cataloging-in-Publication Data
Kalisa, Chantal.
Violence in Francophone African and Caribbean women's literature/
Chantal Kalisa.
p. cm.
Includes bibliographical references and index.
ISBN 978-0-8032-1102-5
(cloth: alk. paper)
1. African literature (French) — Women authors — History and criticism.
2. Caribbean literature (French) — Women authors — History and criticism. 3. Violence in literature. I. Title.
PQ3980.5.K36 2009
840.9'9287 — dc22
2009024323

Set in Galliard.
Designed by Nathan Putens.

Contents

Acknowledgments

A study of violence is difficult to undertake. I would like to recognize the many scholars, family members, and friends who made it easier. I am grateful to the anonymous reviewers for their astute comments that strengthened this study as well as to Ladette Randolph, Kristen Elias Rowley, and Joeth Zucco at the University of Nebraska Press for their invaluable guidance in bringing this book to publication.

I am particularly indebted to Anne Donadey, Jeanne Garane, and Dean Makuluni for their insightful observations and continuous involvement in my scholarship. For their support over the years, I wish to recognize Jacques Bourgeacq, Sandra Barkan, Rosemarie Scullion, Janet Altman, Louise Jefferson, Charles Stivale, Michael Giordano, Marshall Olds, Thomas Carr Jr., Gerise Herndon, Margaret Jacobs, Joy Ritchie, Josias Semujanga, and Odile Cazenave. I also thank all my colleagues at the University of Nebraska–Lincoln for their consistent encouragement.

My heartfelt gratitude goes to members of the Interdisciplinary Genocide Studies Center (IGSC) in Kigali, Rwanda, most notably Rangira Béatrice Gallimore, Jean-Pierre Karegeye, Erik Ehn, and Roberta Levitow, whose engagement with issues of genocide, violence, justice, and reconciliation continue to shape my own arguments. Special thanks go to Christopher Steinke for his contributions.

Most of all, I would like to acknowledge the invaluable support of family and friends. As always, loving thanks go to Jacob, Daniel, and Stephen Witte for their patience and understanding.

An earlier version of chapter 1 appeared as "Black Women and Literature: Revisiting Frantz Fanon's Gender Politics" in the *Literary Griot* 14.1–2 (Spring–Fall 2002): 1–22. A condensed version of chapter 2 appeared in a short article entitled "Colonial Violence and Trauma in the Works of Michèle Lacrosil and Ken Bugul," *International Journal of Francophone Studies* 3.1 (2000): 59–64. The section of chapter 4 entitled "Space, Violence, and Knowledge in Gisèle Pineau's *L'espérance-macadam*" appeared in an earlier version under the same title in the volume *Discursive Geographies: Writing Space and Place in French / Géographies Discursives: L'écriture de l'espace en langue française*, edited by Jeanne Garane (Amsterdam: Rodopi, 2005), 103–17.

VIOLENCE IN FRANCOPHONE AFRICAN
& CARIBBEAN WOMEN'S LITERATURE

Introduction

Geographies of Pain

By sharing a history dominated by the violent disruptions of slavery, colonialism, and latent neocolonialism, African and Caribbean peoples belong to what Françoise Lionnet calls "geographies of pain."[1] Caribbeanist Jack Corzani identifies various forms of this historical violence. Physical violence manifests itself in the enslavement and killing of Africans and in the dispossession of their continent; in the fights between masters and slaves, between colonized and colonizers, and among colonizers themselves; in abolitionist struggles; and in several postcolonial revolutionary wars (Corzani 15). Figures such as the soldier or the policeman symbolize the violence used to maintain colonial regimes in Africa and the Caribbean. The physical violence with which Europeans conquered Africans was accompanied by what Corzani calls a "politic of transculturation," or what Gayatri Spivak identifies as "epistemic violence" — that is, the cultural violence in the dehumanization of slaves; the imposition of the colonizers' language, religion, and customs; enforced assimilation; and political dependence. Slaves and the colonized experienced a mixture of physical and cultural violence through unbearable work conditions, mutilations, and executions. In the context of the Caribbean, Corzani suggests that violence and terror together "served as matrix to the formation of Creole people" (16). As for Africa, contemporary forms of violence generated by civil conflicts and political unrest continue to dominate literature and the world media. Natural disasters and politics combine with history to explain the pervasive climate of violence in these lands, where violence existed in the past, persists in the present, and threatens the future.

Although gendered violence plays a significant role in African and Caribbean literary creativity, critics have devoted little work to this complex subject. *Violence in Francophone African and Caribbean Women's Literatures* fills this void in the study of African and Caribbean women's literatures at a time when women writers from these regions are making extraordinary efforts to explore how old and new forms of violence affect the female gender. This work examines the many ways in which women write about violence to break the silence imposed on them by society and to challenge readers with their gendered perspectives on violence. By comparing women's literary works from different spatial and temporal areas, it thoroughly addresses different types of violence, including its colonial, familial, and linguistic manifestations as well as war-generated violence linked to dictatorships and genocide. In the book I evaluate known and relatively new writers in terms of current intellectual concerns with violence and its effect on women. These include the Caribbean writers Michèle Lacrosil, Simone Schwarz-Bart, Gisèle Pineau, and Edwidge Danticat, and the African writers Ken Bugul, Calixthe Beyala, Nadine Bari, and Monique Ilboudo. Edwidge Danticat is part of a generation of novelists who write from exile in a language other than French but whose work reflects their francophone origins. She lives in the United States and writes in English, yet the Haitian world she creates is not unlike the one found in the fiction of her compatriots. I have also involved the work of the male writers Sembène Ousmane and Frantz Fanon for their unique perspective on the relationship between violence and gender.

Critics have often approached violence in African and Caribbean literatures through what is considered "public" discourses of violence about the history of slavery and colonialism as well as the postcolonial era of corruption and dictatorships. In this work I demonstrate that not only are women absent or poorly represented in this public discourse of violence but also that critics often ignore the "private" or "intimate" violence associated with women or interpret it only in a metaphorical sense. For women writers, literature offers a privileged medium through which they attempt to resolve the tension between historical or external forms of violence associated with colonialism and postcolonial conditions and internal forms of violence that result from unfair cultural, social, and political rules based on gender. While they clearly aim to write gender within commonly validated, authenticated forms of violence, women are particularly interested in lifting taboos over traditionally silenced discourses about domestic and intimate violence. Their writings often examine the effects of rape, sexual violence, and physical and physiological abuses on women. In so doing, they remove intimate violence from its private and domestic sphere and interweave it with public discourses of violence. As Calixthe Beyala explained in an interview, "I do not see how a political scene is less shocking than an erotic scene. A woman sold or prostituted; a dictator who goes in the street, meets a man and shoots him in the head. They are exactly the same thing; one should not separate the two worlds. The human being is deeply touched in the spirit [. . .] there is no special rule for a man and disrespect for a woman. Ateba [a female character] is no different from a political prisoner" (Matateyou 609).

Feminist work on gendered violence has dismantled the dichotomous relationship between the so-called private and public worlds, replacing it with the violence continuum (Jacobs 5). I selected novels that not only describe a wide range of forms of violence but also illustrate the unmaking of the oppositional dynamic by representing gendered violence on a continuum. This continuum is also evident in the link between historical and contemporary manifestations of violence. I argue that women choose to write explicitly about violence because they want to denounce and expose violence against women. Writing is also an opportunity for women to participate in knowledge production about the difficult subject of gendered violence.

Many factors have prompted African and Caribbean women novelists to write about violence. The wave of democratization that swept the African continent in the late 1980s exposed an identity crisis that gave rise to continuous conflict. At the same time, these political changes gave African women the opportunity to raise awareness of violence against women and children. Additionally, two events in 1994 forced scholars to rethink gendered violence and its consequences: the collapse of apartheid in South Africa — one of the longest cases of state-sponsored violence — and the genocide of Tutsis in Rwanda. Currently, scholars recognize that the process of peace and reconciliation in post-conflict situations cannot occur without addressing women's rights. Subsequent to the Tutsi genocide, the United Nations' International Criminal Court for Rwanda established rape — the ultimate form of violence — as a crime of genocide. In their study of family violence in the Caribbean, Paula Morgan and Valerie Youssef rightly assert that slavery and colonialism are at the root of how we see gendered violence in contemporary Caribbean societies. While they were violent toward men and women both, these systems created, to a certain extent, a situation that put black women in positions where they were vulnerable to abuse by black men (10). But theorists of the Creolist movement — Jean Bernabé, Patrick Chamoiseau, and Raphaël Confiant — encouraged Caribbean peoples to look not at external sources of violence but inward, within their insular conditions, giving the foremost attention to internal sources of oppression. An analysis of violence must also consider the function of domestic factors and behaviors on the continuum of violence. The events and conditions that forced Africans and Caribbean peoples to examine themselves have helped women writers, whose texts have traditionally concentrated on the so-called domestic issues, rise to prominence since the mid-1980s.

While scholars have devoted little attention to violence and specifically gendered violence in Francophone women's literature, *Francophone African and Caribbean Women's Literatures* nonetheless builds on a few scholarly books that have been published in English in recent decades. These include books on African women such as Irène Assiba D'Almeida's *Francophone African Women Writers: Destroying the Emptiness of Silence* (1994); Odile Cazenave's *Rebellious Women: The New Generation of Female African Novelists* (2000, English translation of her 1996 *Femmes rebelles*); Nicki Hitchcock's *Women Writers in Francophone Africa* (2000); and Kenneth Harrow's *Less Than One and Double: A Feminist Reading of African Women's Writing* (2001). However, all these books focus solely on sub-Saharan African writings, and they all present broad, various themes and discourses that define the writing of Francophone African women as well as the relationship between African and Western feminism in terms of what it means for these women to write and "speak out." Except for Cazenave, who devotes a section on the language of violence and presents it as a catharsis for women's suffering, the subject of violence is skirted. Renée Larrier's *Francophone Women Writers of Africa and the Caribbean* (2000), Valérie Orlando's *Of Suffocated Hearts and Tortured Souls* (2003), and, more recently, Mildred Mortimer's *Writing from the Hearth: Public, Domestic, and Imaginative Space in Francophone Women's Fiction of Africa and the Caribbean* (2007) are closer predecessors to *Violence in Francophone African and Caribbean Women's Literatures* for two reasons. First, their authors opt for a comparative approach to African and Caribbean women writings that I also adopt. Second, the authors choose a specific aspect of these literatures instead of presenting general themes. Larrier follows oral traditions in which women are speaking subjects, Orlando pinpoints the theme of madness in selected novels, while Mortimer focuses on the delineation of the domestic space as an alternative arena. Yet none of these books focus on discourses of violence.

Defining (Gendered) Violence

Most people agree that "violence" is difficult to define. Scholars define the term differently according to their field of study. Psychologists and psychiatrists study the concept in the area of behavioral sciences in order to describe physiological aspects of human aggression. Historians analyze causes and effects of violent events within a particular society. Sociologists study violence as it occurs between people. Currently, social scientists worldwide are actively engaged in a debate over family and gender violence. On the African continent, the debate over violence centers on peace research – an effort to end violence due to national, racial, religious, linguistic, ethnic, or tribal differences. Kumar Rupesinghe suggests, for instance, that "violence plays the same organizing role in peace research as poverty in political economy or illness in public health" (16–17). Jean-Marie Domenach argues that when scholars define violence, they rely on a certain historical, geographical, or ideological point of view; "what we call 'violence,'" he contends, "gradually came to be understood from three main points of view: (a) the psychological aspect, an explosion of force assuming an irrational and often murderous form; (b) the ethical aspect, an attack on the property and liberty of others; and (c) the use of force to seize power or to misappropriate it for illicit ends" (28).

This definition – which accounts for psychological, moral, and physical aspects of the concept – fails to mention other components of violence widely studied in important works such as René Girard's *La violence et le sacré*. Using classic examples of violence from the Bible and Greek tragedies, Girard differentiates between "sinful" violence, like the fratricide of Abel by Cain, and the violence practiced in religious rituals, such as sacrifices used to expiate condemned or sinful violence. In the essay "Critique of Violence," Walter Benjamin makes a different kind of distinction between what he considers to be the two main approaches to violence: natural law and positive law. Under natural law, violence is a vital natural means. In other words, "violence is a product of nature, as it were a raw material, the use of which is in no way problematical, unless force is misused for unjust ends" (Benjamin 278). However, under "positive law" violence is considered a product of history. Benjamin contends that forms of violence are usually distinguishable based on whether they are sanctioned or unsanctioned, legitimate or illegitimate (278). The interpretation of similar violent acts may vary depending on whether a specific society rationalizes or condemns them. These definitions provide useful insights into different approaches to the concept of violence, especially how societies may choose to condemn or condone violence according to their interests. In patriarchal societies, for example, women are often the victims of permissible acts of violence.

While it is difficult to find a unique definition for the concept of violence, it is easier to recognize its numerous manifestations. Rather than focus on the problematic search for a satisfying definition of the term, I will elaborate on specific forms of violence in Caribbean and African history. These forms have been useful to my study of the representation of gendered violence in selected novels. For scholars considering the question of violence, the work of Frantz Fanon has been particularly important. Fanon, a psychiatrist from Martinique, was closely involved with the Algerian nationalist movement during the Franco-Algerian War in the 1950s. He gave an account of his experience in the 1959 *L'An V de la révolution algérienne* (*Studies in a Dying Colonialism*, 1965), later republished in 1968 under the title *Sociologie d'une révolution* (*Sociology of a Revolution*). He had a major influence on prominent Third World revolutionary figures such as Fidel Castro and Ché Guevara. Today, he is considered to be one of the most important theorists of African decolonization, specifically because of his critically acclaimed 1961 book *Les damnés de la terre*

(*Wretched of the Earth*). He also wrote extensively on the colonial experience of the French Caribbean in the well-known 1952 book *Peau noire, masques blancs* (*Black Skin, White Masks*).

Fanon tried to understand and theorize the "violence" occurring in the relationship between the colonized and the colonizer. His studies of violence drew from sociopolitical as well as psychoanalytical observations of the triangular relationship between Africa, Europe, and the Caribbean islands. Several of Fanon's critics have questioned his pervasive use of the term *violence*, suggesting that "by using violence to explain practically everything, violence has come to mean practically nothing" (Perinbam 5). Stemming from political, psychological, sociological, and philosophical domains, Fanon's interpretations reveal, as B. Marie Perinbam explains, a "fully developed concept of violence" (6). In his landmark work *Les damnés de la terre*, Fanon developed a concept of violence in the context of colonialism. He focused mainly on the ambiguities of the nature of violence as they affect and motivate the oppressed (colonized) and the oppressor (colonizer). He identified three main types of violence in the colonial system – physical, structural, and cultural – along with their psychological and cathartic effects. Physical violence refers to the use of military and police power to conquer and "pacify" indigenous peoples and to force them to accept the colonial order. Structural violence is the condition of social injustice and is composed of binary oppositions, one inferior and powerless and the other assumed to be superior and powerful, as in these examples: black-white, colonized-colonizer, poverty-opulence, subordinate-dominant, oppressed-oppressor. Cultural violence consists of the colonial authorities' negation of the culture of the colonized. In *Peau noire, masques blancs*, Fanon expands his explanation of these categories by delineating the psychological impact of the institution of colonialism on the psyche of the colonized. Psychological violence derives from the impact of colonial policy and the ensuing economic exploitation and alienation on the oppressed. It is the result of the combination of physical, structural, and cultural violence. Psychological violence includes brainwashing and threats. It represents the attempt, conscious or unconscious, by the colonizer to create alienated colonized individuals who reject indigenous values and institutions because they are deceived and brainwashed into believing that those values and institutions are inferior to those of the colonizer. The imposition of the colonizer's language (linguistic violence), for instance, falls into this category.

Fanon viewed the colonial world as Manichean, divided between the powerful colonizers and the powerless colonized (*Les damnés* 7; *The Wretched* 38). Violence regiments the relationships between the two worlds. It presides over "l'arrangement du monde colonial" [the arrangement of the colonial world] (9; 40).[2] He wrote, "Leur première confrontation s'est déroulée sous le signe de la violence et leur cohabitation – plus précisément l'exploitation du colonisé par le colon – s'est poursuivie à grand renfort de baïonnettes et de canons [Their first encounter was marked by violence and their existence together – that is to say the exploitation of the native by the settler – was carried on by dint of a great array of bayonets and cannons] (6; 36). Colonial violence dehumanizes the colonized through its main intermediaries, the "gendarme" and the "soldat" (8; 39). With decolonization, the colonized become conscious of what Aimé Césaire called the *mensonge principal* (principal lie) of the colonizer, who attempts to convince them that his values are superior to theirs.[3] In his essay "De la violence" ("Concerning Violence") from *Les damnés*, Fanon predicted that once the consciousness of the colonized is raised, he has to turn to radical action to "seize" the envied position of the colonizer. In view of the Manichaeism that characterizes the colonial world, Fanon postulated perhaps the most controversial notion of violence, that is, the phenomenon of counterviolence: "Cette praxis violente est totalisante, puisque chacun se fait maillon violent de la grande chaîne, du grand organisme violent surgi comme réaction à la violence première du colon. . . . La violence du colonisé, nous l'avons dit, unifie le peuple." [The practice of violence binds them together as a whole, since each individual forms a violent link in the great chain, a part of the great organism of violence which has surged upward in reaction to the settler's violence in the beginning. . . . We have said that the native's violence unifies the people] (51; 93–94).

According to Fanon, violence by the colonized is always counterviolence. On the individual level, he asserted that decolonization could only occur successfully when the colonized not only seized their freedom through a liberation struggle but participated in violent action to expunge the colonial heritage of inferiority and submission: "Au niveau des individus, la violence désintoxique. Elle débarrasse le colonisé de son complexe d'infériorité, de ses attitudes contemplatives ou désespérées. Elle le rend intrépide, le réhabilite à ses propres yeux." [At the level of individuals, violence is a cleansing force. It frees the colonized from his inferiority complex and from his despair and inaction; it makes him fearless and restores his self-respect](*Les damnés* 51–52; *The Wretched* 94). This cathartic violence becomes essential to the process of decolonization. In order to rid itself of the colonial power, the colonized world must resort to violence, a process that is, according to Fanon, a direct consequence of the violent nature of colonial domination. In the colonial world, the colonized learns how to maintain his position of submission. This is why "les rêves de l'indigène sont des rêves musculaires, des rêves d'action, des rêves agressifs" [the dreams of the native are always of muscular prowess; his dreams are of action dreams and of aggression (Fanon, *Les damnés* 18; *The Wretched* 52). Violence becomes a means to dismantle the colonial system and then to replace it with a system built by the colonized themselves. Fanon believed that the colonized could regain their humanity and self-determination by resorting to violence. By emphasizing the cathartic function of violent action, Fanon came to be understood as a controversial advocate of violence. This reputation put him in opposition to pacifists such as Mohandas Gandhi, who upheld nonviolent strategies despite making similar diagnoses of colonial ills that affect the physical and psychological well-being of the colonized.[4]

Fanon's understanding of violence shaped his prediction of postcolonial violence. Violence did not end after decolonization but took new forms. Fanon envisioned the continuation of "tribal" conflicts unless a national consciousness was fostered. He went so far as to suggest that internal violence was the fault of the colonizer because the leader of the colonized learned violence from the masters and would impose this violent urge on his own people (Fanon, *Les damnés* 18). He foresaw, in the case of a non-Marxist revolution, the replication of colonial violence by a new authoritarian elite who had assimilated the colonizer's values. The identification of colonialism as the root of postcolonial violence continues to dictate our interpretation of current forms of violence. As Ato Quayson reminds us, "The postcolony is a place of violence. This violence constituted by the wars and acts of expropriation that undergirded the colonial order becomes endemic in the postcolony and produces a series of persistently violent political and social disjunctures" (192). Fanon's contribution is undoubtedly crucial to the understanding of colonial violence. This book evaluates the validity and the usefulness of Fanon's insights through an examination of writings by African and Caribbean women. Michèle Lacrosil and Ken Bugul offer clear responses to Fanon's theories, especially protesting the place he allocates women in his analyses, while more contemporary writers like Calixthe Beyala and Gisèle Pineau offer examples of the postcolonial violence Fanon discusses in his writings.

In addition to Frantz Fanon's take on violence, my analysis draws its theoretical framework from feminist and postcolonial theories on gendered violence. I adopt postcolonial theory, a field of scholarship originating from the context of the British Commonwealth that puts the colonial experience at the center of the postcolonial individual's identity. As Françoise Lionnet, Anne Donadey, and many other scholars have observed, however, gender has often been a blind spot in postcolonial studies. This book adheres to this criticism but adopts postcolonial theory's useful analysis of the ambivalent nature of colonial experience, specifically regarding concepts of complicity and resistance as well as privileged discourses in women's writings on or of violence. I begin by engaging Frantz Fanon's theories on colonial violence and sexual politics. As stated earlier, Fanon, like his peers, examined the issue of violence in the colonial system, but unlike his peers he extensively if imperfectly considered the position of women in decolonization efforts. Although women writers express views similar to those of their male counterparts, I argue in this work that the originality of female writing, including the selections in this book, lies in their effort to oppose earlier theoretical assumptions about women. I suggest that these novels offer evidence of female writers' attempts to correct and counteract Fanon's contention (and that of his peers) that what happened to the black woman during colonial times was not what colonialism did to her but rather what she let colonialism do to her. I assert that the gendered violence of postcolonial literatures shows that women writers actively oppose the idea that women bring this violence on themselves. Fanon's ambiguities are, of course, symptomatic of the tension between nationalism and feminism and between decolonization and women's emancipation that we find in many other women's literatures.

Current interdisciplinary and feminist scholarship on gendered violence and women's literature, and in particular theories on trauma and literature, invigorates my analysis. In her study on the violence of rhetoric, Teresa de Lauretis regards violence as fundamentally engendered. For her, "representation of violence is inseparable from the notion of gender . . . violence is en-gendered in representation" (240). Basing her arguments on Foucault's study of power and sexuality, de Lauretis identifies his limit as an "unconcern" with what she calls "the technology of gender" — that is, "the techniques and discursive strategies by which gender is constructed and hence, violence in en-gendered" (245). For instance, Foucault's understanding of rape as an act of violence, not a sexual act, is for her problematic (de Lauretis 244). De Lauretis rightly concludes that "violence between intimates" must be seen "in the context of social powers" in which "gender is absolutely central to the family" (241). In addition to adhering to de Lauretis' concise explanation of how discourses of violence are fundamentally gendered, I define gendered violence in the context of feminist resistance to the depoliticization of "private" and "domestic" acts of violence. I understand the concept on a continuum, encompassing acts and sites of violence specific to women, such as domestic abuse and sexual violence, as well as the effect on women of political and historical violence committed within and outside traditional political discourses. I understand gendered violence as a term originating from interdisciplinary studies whose focus is on the physical and psychological impact of violence and conflict on female subjects.

Theories regarding the relationship between psychic trauma and literature have been useful in my understanding of literary representations of traumatic experience. Cathy Caruth has argued that literature and psychoanalysis are bound together by the fact that they both consider "the complex relation between knowing and not knowing" (*Unclaimed Experience* 3). Critics of African and Caribbean literatures have long hesitated to apply psychoanalytic theories that do not account for race to their analyses. Because many of the characters in the texts I examine experience both collective and individual traumas, I find it useful to engage studies on trauma and literature. The writers carefully craft their stories by exploring elements of the ambivalence that characterizes the experience of trauma. In accordance with the conflict between knowing and not knowing cited by Caruth, we find tensions between remembering and forgetting and between silence and witnessing. Even as women's silence punctuates much of the narratives, writers emphasize the characters' paradoxical "imperative to tell" their stories (Laub 63). Kalí Tal defines trauma as an injury to the mind or body that either requires structural repairs or functions as "a life-threatening event that displaces his or her preconceived notions about the world" (15). Narratives of trauma become tools to repair and to heal. Telling one's story is remembering, the opposite of forgetting. Reliving their stories helps victims regain control of life after trauma. I read women's literature about trauma as a form of knowledge production that attempts to denormalize violence against women, to reconstruct intergenerational narratives of female trauma, and to offer, albeit in narrative form, a record of resistance to violence. In addition, I am mindful that, as Caruth reminds us, the story of trauma is not only "the story of the individual in relation to the events of his own past" but also "the story of the way in which one's own trauma is tied up with the trauma of another" (*Unclaimed Experience* 8). Indeed, African and Caribbean women's writings on violence demonstrate a strong correlation between individual and collective trauma.

While I focus on women writers, violence is a significant part of African and Caribbean writing by men as well. Given the context of colonization and slavery, it is not surprising that African and Caribbean writers, male and female, produce an enormous literature on violence. Writers seek to represent the violence that characterizes their history. "If someone had to define, at once, the meta-archipelago's historical novel and its folk narrative, using just two words," writes Antonio Benítez-Rojo, they "would be, unquestionably: *revelar* (to reveal and to re-veil in Spanish) [and] *violencia*" (215). Amadou Koné suggests that "violence" might have been one of the factors in the birth of the African novel (163). The literature of the Négritude movement is commonly considered to be the starting point of written African and Black Caribbean literature in French, though as many critics have pointed out, Africans on the continent and in the diaspora produced literary works prior to the birth of the movement. Cofounded in the 1930s by Aimé Césaire, from Martinique, Léopold Sédar Senghor, from Sénégal, and Léon Gontran Damas, from French Guyana, Négritude was first and foremost a reaction to two forms of colonial violence: acculturation and assimilation. Like their predecessors and collaborators behind the publication of "Légitime défense" and "L'Étudiant noir," the Négritude poets produced a literature of protest. Their writings demonstrate a close relationship between violence in history and violence in literature. Jack Corzani suggests that literature of the Négritude movement and the generations that followed went back to the most violent past, and that these writers focused mostly on the main source of this violence, colonialism. Corzani posits, for instance, that Aimé Césaire's long poem *Le cahier d'un retour au pays natal*, one of the founding pieces of Francophone "Negro-African" literature on the continent and in the diaspora, is indeed "a long meditation on violence in the Caribbean, in an obvious expanded perspective to Africa, to the whole colonial world" (29). Randolph Hezekiah concludes, "The violence of certain images in his poem is an expression of the urgent need to create a new life-force able to transform the poet's decaying world through the cataclysmic forces contained in the volcano, the hurricane, and the earthquake" (381).

Various authors writing after the Négritude era tried to report the experience of violence under colonial rule. In the Caribbean, the list is long as violence and pain are indeed intrinsic to their literature. Most heroes in the Caribbean novel embody victimization by violence. In Francophone African literature, perhaps the most memorable protagonist is Toundi, the hero of Ferdinand Oyono's *Une vie de boy* (1956). Written in the form of a journal, the novel traces the life of a colonizer's houseboy, Toundi, who is killed by violence inflicted upon him for having discovered the white man's "lie" — the so-called superiority of the colonizer's culture. The protagonist embodies colonial violence and its dramatic consequences. Another widely cited example of this literary tradition is Yambo Ouologuem's controversial novel *Le devoir de violence* (1968). Contrary to the views of Fanon and his proponents, who saw the violence of the colonized only in terms of counterviolence against European colonialism and slavery, this novel demonstrates how violence has its origin in Africa as much as Europe. Ahmadou Kourouma's *Les soleils des indépendances* (1970) shows through the character Fama a range of internal and external forms of violence, such as political imprisonment, rape, and murder. Because the main protagonists in these novels are male, scholars have, of course, focused on the male perspective in their study of violence and related issues. In this project, I study similar aspects of violence but add the female perspective, the importance of which has been widely overlooked in African and Caribbean literary criticism, as the following analysis reveals.

Chapter Organization

Violence in Francophone African and Caribbean Women's Literatures is composed of five chapters. Chapter 1 is a close reading of Fanon's writings. I argue that the exclusion of women from his theorization of colonial violence is an assault on women's memory and herstory. While his elaborate theories do not adequately explain the impact of colonialism on the colonized woman, they nevertheless provide us with essential tools for understanding women's colonial and postcolonial experiences of violence.

Chapter 2 primarily addresses Lacrosil's and Bugul's novels but also includes a lengthy examination of Sembène Ousmane's film *La Noire de* . . . I analyze the depiction of women's perspectives on colonial and postcolonial violence, considering central themes like exile, displacement, racism, and the problematics of memory under epistemological violence.

Chapter 3 focuses on domestic or familial violence and female genealogies in Simone Schwarz-Bart's classic *Pluie et vent sur Télumée Miracle* and in the more contemporary novel *Tu t'appelleras Tanga* by Calixthe Beyala. A contrastive critique of different generations of women writers invigorates my analysis as do the current theories on trauma and literature pertaining to victims of domestic and familial violence.

In Chapter 4 I concentrate on language and the female body as sites of violence in women's deterritorialization. In her first novel, Calixthe Beyala privileges the use of violence as a narrative strategy but in doing so ironically exposes the inexpressibility of violence and its ensuing pain. Gisèle Pineau describes "geographies of pain" by skillfully superimposing familial and domestic violence toward a woman's body over a Caribbean landscape that is itself ravaged by hurricanes.

Chapter 5, on war, political violence, and genocide, demonstrates how women's writings about war constitute the quintessential "postcolonial war story." I argue that their work challenges the very concept of war as traditionally written by involving gendered issues like the loss of mates, living under imminent terror, and most of all the tension between forgetting and remembering. My analysis focuses on Bari's autobiographical account of her "war" against Sékou Touré's dictatorship in Guinea, Danticat's fictional account of the 1937 Haitian laborers' massacre in the Dominican Republic under Rafael Trujillo, and Ilboudo's depiction of women and the aftermath of genocide.

1

Exclusion as Violence

Frantz Fanon, Black Women, and Colonial Violence

Critical studies of African and Caribbean women writing remain scarce.[1] The reasons for this absence are twofold. First, at the beginning of the formation of African literary studies in the mid-twentieth century, there were relatively few women writers in Africa and the Caribbean. This was mainly due to the external violence of colonialism, which privileged the schooling of the male. It was also attributable to internal violence originating from precolonial and postcolonial patriarchal conceptions that prevented women in traditional and contemporary societies from expressing themselves or acquiring the same educational level as men. Maryse Condé writes, for example, that "comme dans un premier temps, l'école était réservée aux garçons, elle a introduit plus qu'un fossé entre 'lettrés' et 'illéttrées,' une division radicale des sexes" [Since in the beginning, (European) schools were reserved for boys, it introduced more than a gap between literate men and illiterate women, a radical division between the sexes] (*La Parole* 3).

Second, scholars who preferred to study the growing canon of African and Caribbean literatures ignored the few women writers who existed. Early anthologies of black African literature, such as *Anthologie de la nouvelle poésie nègre et malgache de langue française* (1948) by Léopold Sédar Senghor or *Les écrivains noirs de langue française: naissance d'une littérature* (1965) by Lilyan Kesteloot, hardly include any black African women writers. Carole Boyce Davies and Elaine Savory Fido, coeditors of *Out of the Kumbla, Caribbean Women and Literature*, describe the absence of women writers in Caribbean studies as "voicelessness": "The concept of voicelessness necessarily informs any discussion of Caribbean women and literature. . . . By voicelessness, we mean the historical absence of the woman writer's text: the absence of a specifically female position on major issues such as slavery, colonialism, decolonization, women's rights and more direct social and cultural issues. By voicelessness we also mean silence: the inability to express the position in the language of the 'master' as well as the textual construction of woman as silent. Voicelessness also denotes articulation that goes unheard" (1). This same voicelessness applies even more to African women, who have been historically silenced in various discourses. It is important to point out that Caribbean women such as Mayotte Capécia, Michèle Lacrosil, Maryse Condé, Marie Vieux Chauvet, and Simone Schwarz-Bart were published earlier than Francophone African women writers, though they still did not receive the critical attention that their male counterparts enjoyed.

To understand this voicelessness, I want to go back to Fanon and provide a critical analysis of this major twentieth-century authority, who contributed, perhaps more than any other thinker from Africa and the Caribbean, to the silencing of black women. Despite numerous shortcomings, Fanon best demonstrates the prevalent attitudes toward women's position within the colonial experience. He also provides rare insight into the relationship between black women and men, black or white. Unlike writers of the same period, Fanon wrote about the black woman, but he did so selectively and ambivalently. A study of his position on colonialism and black women is crucial, for he supplies us with useful tools to perceive reactions as well as questions embedded in contemporary literature by women from Africa and the Caribbean.

Over the last few years, there has been an ongoing debate regarding postcolonial conditions. Discussions center around issues related to continuous colonial states in "subaltern" areas such as the third world, in its geographical and ideological senses. These issues, which influence immensely the current discourse on race relations, have dealt mainly with the formation of racial identities as a product of colonial power. However, gender continues to be a problematic question within the postcolonial discourse. The goal of this chapter is to continue the debate over the significance of gender politics by closely examining Frantz Fanons' texts in light of the current postcolonial climate. I attempt to answer the following fundamental questions: What position does Fanon allocate the colonized woman in the decolonizing mission? How does the ambiguous nature of his analyses affect our understanding of the relationship between postcolonialism and feminism?

There is no doubt that Frantz Fanon's writings are by far the most influential sources in the production of today's postcolonial criticism. Critics use Fanon consistently as a basis for discussion on colonizer-colonized relationships and apply his theory to current colonial states. In his article, "Critical Fanonism," Henry Louis Gates Jr. discusses the re-appropriation of Fanon as a "figure of both totem and text" (457). Fanon is what Gates calls "a global theorist" (457), a "collectivized individual" (467), "a composite figure" (459), or "an ethnographic construct" (459), someone who symbolically has come to represent Third World Theory. The postcolonial critic Homi Bhabha has provided what some critics consider to be the reading of Fanon most grounded in post-structuralism (Gates 459). The most famous eulogistic essay on Fanon is undoubtedly Bhabha's "Remembering Fanon," in which the critic defines Fanon's perspective as follows: "He [Fanon] may yearn for the total transformation of Man and Society, but he speaks most effectively from the uncertain interstices of historical change: from the area of ambivalence between race and sexuality" (113). For the purpose of this study, I ask the following questions: What and whose sexuality? Does this affirmation include or exclude the sexuality of colonized women? In another essay entitled "The Other Question," Bhabha discusses the phenomena of stereotypes and discrimination in colonial discourse. He examines the notion of "fixity," which he defines as "the sign of cultural/historical/racial difference in the discourse of colonialism" (66). Nowhere in this category do we see the place of the colonized female. As outstanding and enlightening as Bhabha's readings of Fanon may be, the question of gender is ignored. As we shall see, there is a degree of ambivalence in the way Fanon himself writes the "gender" of the colonized female.

The portrayal of the third-world woman in Western feminism as the ultimate victim has prompted an oppositional discourse by third-world feminists such as Chandra Mohanty. In her article "Under Western Eyes," Mohanty objects to the hegemonic male or female gaze on the "subaltern woman." Her main argument is that "woman" does not correspond to any real woman but simply constitutes an idea in the productive mind of the Western feminist that follows pre-inscribed stereotypes in which the third-world woman is "poor, oppressed and/or deviant" (53).

Although Mohanty's article points an accusing finger at Western feminism for privileging unrealistic images of third-world women, this study demonstrates how Fanon produced and perpetuated this image as well. I identify the kind of stereotypes that were reinforced by Fanon through a hegemonic gaze upon women in the "backward, uncivilized" countries. The mythical status of the figure produced by Fanon's writings and emphasized in numerous interpretations of Fanon's texts most likely intensifies the fixation of these stereotypes.

Many critical studies of Fanon's sexual politics within the colonial experience have emerged in recent years. There are at least two considerable directions in which this criticism evolves. In the first group, critics attempt to uncover Fanon's patriarchal and sexist attitudes toward women in general. Such is the case in articles by Gwen Bergner and Mary Ann Doane. While they provide solid arguments regarding Fanon's unabashed patriarchal and sexist attitudes, these critics, as T. Denean Sharpley-Whiting remarks, unfortunately tend to slip "into a primary discussion of white women, mediated through black female bodies and black men" (156). The second group includes Homi Bhabha, who apologizes for Fanon's blindness to women's position. His own approach, which we will come back to later, is to simply avoid scrutinizing Fanon's treatment of gender.[2] Sharpley-Whiting is another example in this category. She offers a slightly different position than Bhabha's. She cautions against critics' romanticization of Mayotte Capécia's *Je suis martiniquaise*, one of the novels on which Fanon based his criticism of black females in *Peau noire, masques blancs*. Through a reading of Capécia's second novel, *La Négresse blanche*, the critic instead praises Fanon for his "usefulness in revealing Capécia's *blackfemmephobia* and racial *malaise* as an attendant response to the colonial enterprise, and his continued relevance for the colonized in the United States and contemporary black feminist literary and cultural studies" (161–62). While I agree with Sharpley-Whiting that *Je suis martiniquaise* should not be read as a manifesto on black feminism, she quickly dismisses the overtly simplistic statements about black women found in several of Fanon's writings.

Clearly, neither argument captures the often unsettling ambivalence in Fanon's rich discourse concerning his relationship with women of color. I suggest that a close reading of his essays that directly address sexual politics will delineate a complex position that neither overplays nor underplays the visibility of women of color in his texts. Despite the lack of adequate critical feminist readings of Fanon, women are very much present in his writings, whether these originate from Algeria, black Africa, or Europe.[3] *Sociologie d'une révolution* includes the essay "L'Algérie se dévoile," where Fanon examines the position of Algerian women during the processes of colonization and resistance. *Les damnés de la terre* is a collection of essays that makes minimal room for the colonized woman. In *Peau noire, masques blancs*, Fanon mostly treats the subject of "decolonizing the mind," but, unlike the other works, it contains a whole chapter on the black woman. At what point can we say Fanon includes the colonized woman in his theories? An analysis of his writings reveals that the colonized female becomes "absent-present" not only in the eyes of the colonizer but often, as we shall see, in the eyes of the colonized male as well. This absent-present dichotomy points to the ambivalence of the "presence" of women of color in Fanon's writings.

In "L'Algérie se dévoile," his essay concerning the position of the colonized Algerian woman in discourses of colonial penetration and native resistance, Fanon argues that the female body, the one that "hides behind the veil," would become an issue in the battle against colonial invasion:

> Nous allons voir que ce voile, élément parmi d'autres de l'ensemble vestimentaire traditionnel algérien, va devenir l'enjeu d'une bataille grandiose, à l'occasion de laquelle les forces d'occupation mobiliseront leurs ressources les plus puissantes et les plus diverses, et où le colonisé déploiera une force étonnante d'inertie. [We shall see that this veil, one of the elements of the traditional Algerian garb, was to become the bone of contention in a grandiose battle, on account of which the occupation forces were to mobilize their most powerful and most varied resources, and in the course of which the colonized were to display a surprising force of inertia.] ("L'Algérie se dévoile" 18; "Algeria Unveiled" 36–37)

According to Fanon, Europeans followed the famous colonial formula, "Ayons les femmes et le reste suivra" [Let us win over the women and the rest will follow] (18; 37). To accomplish this, they needed to "liberate" the Algerian woman by convincing their society to remove her veil. The metaphor of "uncovering the veiled woman" corresponds to "uncovering Algeria, uncovering her secret, her mystery": "cacher le visage, c'est aussi dissimuler un secret, c'est faire exister un monde du mystère et du caché" [Hiding the face is also disguising a secret; it is also creating a world of mystery, of the hidden] (26; 43). The body of the colonized woman came to represent a national emblem and the land itself. Colonizers were to use penetrating tactics of "saving the Algerian woman" from Algerian males' oppressive and demonizing traditions, represented by the veil.

For the colonized Algerian man, however, the fight took the opposite direction. Fanon writes: "La ténacité de l'occupant dans son entreprise de dévoiler les femmes, d'en faire une alliée dans l'œuvre de destruction culturelle a renforcé les conduites traditionnelles." [The tenacity of the occupier in his endeavor to unveil the women, to make of them an ally in the work of cultural destruction, had the effect of strengthening the traditional patterns of behavior] (31; 49). Thus, the colonized woman becomes entangled in the middle of the battle. Although the "unveiled" woman suffered what Fanon calls "a loss of ease and assurance" in her newly liberated body, she will manage to reinvent herself and play a major role in the war of resistance by using her body as the medium of struggle. When she is asked to play a role in the resistance, the Algerian woman conceals weapons under her veil until the European discovers the ruse. She will then mimic the European dress code and participate in the resistance by hiding her orders in a European purse.[4] She plays the role of both the object and the subject because in this arrangement she serves as a medium of colonial penetration and resistance.[5] The first thing upon which the colonizer lays his eyes is the veil, not the woman herself. Fanon's meticulous observations reveal how the Algerian woman is romanticized, made exotic, and rendered inseparable from the object she was to be rescued from. The Algerian man will also use the power of her veil, which defines her whole world. She in fact becomes the veil itself. She is physically involved in the resistance, yet only her veil makes it into history. For all of Fanon's insights in the matter, the question "what does the Algerian woman want?" never arises. Although Fanon describes the woman's role in the war, it is clear that he places her as a commodity on both sides, between the male colonizer and the male colonized. Her participation in the resistance, however strong, does not provide her with historical visibility.

In *Transfigurations of the Maghreb: Feminism, Decolonization, and Literatures*, Winifred Woodhull asserts that the essay "L'Algérie se dévoile" erases the element of difference between women and men. While Fanon criticizes the incompatibility of Algerian society with Western ideologies including feminism, he wrongly emphasizes the "Algerian woman's harmonious integration into the nationalist movement" (Woodhull 23). By ignoring possible tensions between nationalism and feminism, Fanon repeats the same process of erasing the colonized woman in the decolonizing effort. The colonized man will slowly eliminate her from that history until only the metaphor of the "veil" remains. Woodhull describes the effect of the process by which the colonized male writer, in this case Fanon, writes the colonized female out of her own history: "The unveiling performed by Fanon's text, while clearly intended to enable the Algerian woman to 'relearn her body, reinstall it in a totally revolutionary way,' nonetheless establishes between Western and third-world feminisms a border that today's most productive feminist activity is reopening, both at the level of political action and scholarship" (24).

The example of Algeria demonstrates the dichotomous presence-absence of colonized women in literature and theories of decolonization. This dichotomy is even more pronounced with black women in Fanon's other texts. In *Les damnés de la terre*, the black female is usually absent but appears sometimes almost as an accident. The word *l'homme* (man) appears several times and connotes, according to Bhabha, "a phenomenological quality of humanness, inclusive of man and woman and for that very reason, ignores the question of gender difference" ("Remembering Fanon" 123). Throughout the chapter "Sur la culture nationale" ("On National

Culture"), Fanon refers to the "l'homme de culture" (man of culture), whom we understand as the colonized intellectual attempting to decolonize himself and his country by recovering his culture. Yet at times Fanon writes: "un grand nombre d'hommes et de femmes" [a great number of men and women] (*Les damnés* 54), in which case the author seems to be more inclusive of women in the colonized population.

In her enlightening article on Fanon and gender, Gwen Bergner disagrees with Bhabha's assertion that Fanon uses *l'homme* as a generic term. She argues that "the masculine 'universal' refers not to humankind but to actual men since Fanon describes colonized subjects as studying in Paris, lusting after women, and competing with white men for intellectual recognition" (Bergner 76). Although I agree with Bergner that Fanon is primarily describing a male world, he does, however, refer to women of color studying in France in the essay "La femme de couleur et l'homme blanc" ("The Woman of Color and the White Man"). Fanon writes: "Nous connaissons beaucoup de compatriotes étudiantes en France" [We know a lot of women compatriots in France] (*Peau noire* 38). Fanon chooses not to include these women because he believes that they are trapped in their desire to become assimilated into European culture and have therefore become irretrievable and inadmissible to the colonized community (*Peau noire* 38). This shows not only Fanon's lack of regard for the role of colonized women in decolonization movements but also the mistrust that the black man feels toward the *traîtresse* (traitor) black female, an important theme in Fanon's writings.

In "Mésaventures de la conscience nationale" ("The Pitfalls of National Consciousness") in *Les damnés*, the same image of the colonized woman as "extremely assimilated" emerges. The colonized female constitutes an obstacle to reaching the masses and achieving national consciousness because, as Fanon puts it in one example, she threatens to divorce her husband if he accepts relocation up-country for work.[6] Thus, the woman represents the ultimate embodiment of European assimilation. Fanon offers yet another contradiction regarding the proper position of the woman in decolonization efforts:

> Dans un pays sous-développé, on s'efforcera le plus rapidement possible de mobiliser les hommes et les femmes. Le pays sous-développé doit se garder de perpétuer les traditions féodales qui consacrent la priorité de l'élément masculin sur l'élément féminin. Les femmes recouvreront une place identique aux hommes non dans les articles de la constitution mais dans la vie quotidienne, à l'usine, à l'école, dans les assemblées. [In an underdeveloped country every effort is made to mobilize men and women as quickly as possible; it must guard against the danger of perpetuating the feudal tradition which holds sacred the superiority of the masculine over the feminine. Women will have exactly the same place as men, not in the clauses of the constitution but in the life of everyday: in the factory, at school, and in the parliament.] (*Les damnés* 136; *The Wretched* 202)

Although Fanon in this statement seems to discourage sexism in decolonization projects by inviting full participation of men and women in the cause, the second part of the declaration states that women can work for the liberation of their country but should not expect any constitutional rights. In the presence-absence paradigm, women should be present on the battlefield but absent in the written law.

In her article "The Politics of Admittance: Female Sexual Agency, Miscegenation, and the Formation of Community in Frantz Fanon," Rey Chow emphasizes the role of community in subject formation. She bases her analysis on Fanon's articulation of the notion of community admittance. For Chow, communities form through the "implicit understanding of who is and who is not to be admitted" (6). Admittance signifies not only legitimate entry into the community but also validation of the individual within that community. What does it take for the black woman to be part of the black community? In Fanon's representation, the black woman is inadmissible to the black community because she is potentially "if not always a whore, a sell-out, and hence a traitor to her own community" (Chow 14). To be part of the community, women of color must therefore abide by its rules, which require their sex to stay "put in their traditional position as 'gifts,' as the conduits and vehicles that facilitate social relations and enable group identity" (Chow 20). In this reading Fanon suggests prioritizing the masculine over the feminine.

The question of prioritizing becomes even more important in *Peau noire, masques blancs*. First of all, Fanon describes this collection of essays in his introduction as a search for humanism, coded as the black male's identity: "Vers un nouvel humanisme . . . La compréhension des hommes . . . Nos frères de couleur . . . Je crois en toi, Homme . . . " [Toward a new humanism . . . Understanding among men . . . Our brothers of color . . . I believe in you, Man . . .] (5). It is clear that the person in Fanon's mind is "man." The introduction announces a certain dialogue between the colonized black male and the colonizer white male. The question "Que veut l'homme?" (What does man want?) can be understood as a universal statement, whereas "Que veut l'homme noir?" (What does the black man want?) is specific to black males.

In "Le Nègre et la psychopathologie" ("The Negro and Psychopathology"), Fanon discusses the white woman's psychosexual fear of being raped by a black man. He continues: "Admettant nos conclusions sur la psychosexualité de la femme blanche, on pourrait nous demander celles que nous proposerions pour la femme de couleur. *Nous n'en savons rien*." [Those who grant our conclusions on the psychosexuality of the white woman may ask what we have to say about the woman of color. *I know nothing about her*] (emphasis added; *Peau noire* 145; *Black Skin* 179–80). The famous phrase "Nous n'en savons rien" has been (mis)translated in English as "I know nothing about her." Given that Fanon not only psychoanalyzes the white female and her relationships with the black male but also, as Bergner has concluded, transposes psychoanalytical theories of female subject formation on male racial subject formation, the phrase denotes a lack of sufficient knowledge of how this approach can work for black women. The black colonized woman in *Peau noire, masques blancs* does not have a definable position because the black male takes the position of the feminine, meaning the white female (Bergner 80). The statement "Nous n'en savons rien" has unfortunately been a blind spot for numerous scholars, who have taken it at face value and continue to erase the black woman from Fanon's texts. In fact, while Fanon admits being ignorant of many things about the black woman, he nevertheless devotes a chapter to her. Once again, this indicates that Fanon's stand on the black woman lies in what he says about her as much as it does as in what he does not say. In order to consider Fanon's seemingly ambiguous silence on the black woman, I propose analyzing his study of the relationships between "La femme de couleur et l'homme blanc" (the black woman and the white man) in *Peau noire, masques blancs*. The essay highlights in particular three major instances of ambivalence in Fanon's arguments that cause shifts in the presence-absence paradigm.

The first ambivalence concerns the essay's theme itself. Fanon proclaims that he is going to show how "authentic love" is not possible between the black woman and the white male as long as certain conditions are still present:

> Il s'agit, pour nous, dans ce chapitre consacré aux rapports de la femme de couleur et de l'Européen, de déterminer dans quelle mesure l'amour authentique demeurera impossible tant que ne seront pas expulsés ce sentiment d'infériorité ou cette exaltation adlérienne, cette surcompensation, qui semblent être l'indicatif de la Weltanschauung noire. [In this chapter devoted to the relations between the woman of color and the European, it is our problem to ascertain to what extent authentic love will remain unattainable before one has purged oneself of that feeling of inferiority or that Adlerian exaltation, that overcompensation, which seems to be the indices of the black Weltanschauung.] (*Peau noire* 33–34; *Black Skin* 42)

Fanon's definition of "authentic love" deserves particular attention. In essence, according to the author, "authentic love" is male-oriented, the kind of support that a man receives from a woman in order to sustain his manhood: "Energétiquement, l'être aimé m'épaulera dans l'assomption de ma virilité, tandis que le souci de mériter l'admiration ou l'amour d'autrui tissera tout le long de ma vision du monde une superstructure valorisante." [The person I love will strengthen me by endorsing my assumption of my manhood, while the need to earn the admiration or the love of others will erect a value-making superstructure on my whole vision of the world] (*Peau noire* 33; *Black Skin* 41).

The need implied in words such as *virilité* or *superstructure valorisante* indicates a fundamentally masculinist perspective that valorizes the stereotypical supersexuality of the black male. Indeed, Fanon adopts a universalizing vision of man's "imperative" right to woman's love. Fanon argues that the black woman is not capable of loving the white man because she aims to raise her social and racial status and eliminate his superiority. She is both attracted to his financial status and motivated by a desire to whiten herself. The black female is once again depicted as the ultimate symbol of assimilation and the traitor to the black race. This situation produces a clichéd image seen in Léon Gontran Damas' poem "HOQUET":

> Ma mère voulant d'un fils très bonnes manières à table
> Les mains sur la table
> Le pain ne se coupe pas
> le pain se rompt
> . . . .
> Ma mère voulant d'un fils mémorandum
> Si votre leçon n'est pas sue
> Vous n'irez pas à la messe
> dimanche
> . . . .
> Vous ai-je ou non dit qu'il vous fallait parler français

le français de France
le français du français
le français français

> My mother wanted her son to have good manners at the table / Keep your hands on the table / We don't cut bread / we break it, . . . My mother wanted her son to have the very best marks / If you don't know your history / you won't go to mass / tomorrow, . . . Have I or have I not told you to speak French / the French of France / the French that Frenchmen speak / French French.

In this poem, the black woman represents the Caribbean mother, who perpetuates the colonizing culture by brainwashing the child. Fanon writes:

> Nous sommes avertis, c'est vers la lactification que tend Mayotte. Car enfin il faut blanchir la race; cela, toutes les Martiniquaises le savent, le disent, le répètent. Blanchir la race, sauver la race, mais non dans le sens qu'on pourrait supposer: non pas préserver "l'originalité de la portion du monde au sein duquel elles ont grandi" mais assurer sa blancheur. [We are thus put on notice that what Mayotte wants is a kind of lactification. For, in a word, the race must be whitened; every woman in Martinique knows this, says it, repeats it. Whiten the race, save the race but, not in the sense that one might think: not "preserve the uniqueness of that part of the world in which they grew up," but make sure that it will be white.] (*Peau noire* 38; *Black Skin* 47)

The black woman assumes the role of the colonized mother who thinks that the best thing she can do for her children is to encourage them to adopt the colonizer's culture. By assigning her this stereotypical role, Fanon dismisses the black woman as an irrelevant if not a dangerous element in the survival of the black race. Again, he does not consider the question "What does the colonized woman want?" because she is simply absent as a subject.

Authentic love obtains a negative value because the woman

is incapable of deserving love from a white man. Fanon shifts to another discourse, one between the black man (at least Fanon himself) and the black woman. Fanon's arguments become a sort of black man's complaint about the black female's adoration of the white male. In a vigorous and obviously antagonistic tone, Fanon harshly attacks the black woman and laments her rejection. He rejects the possibility of love between black females and white males and offers a moral lesson addressed to the woman by her country*man*. Fanon uses mockery as a sign of resentment. The following is an example:

> Toutes ces femmes de couleur échevelées, en quête du Blanc, attendent. Et certainement un de ces jours elles se surprendront à ne pas vouloir retourner, elles penseront "à une nuit merveilleuse, à un amant merveilleux, un Blanc." Elles aussi peut-être s'apercevront un jour "que les Blancs n'épousent pas une femme noire." [All these frantic women of color in quest of white men are waiting. And one of these days, surely, they will be surprised to find that they do not want to go back, they will dream of "a wonderful night, a wonderful lover, a white man." Possibly, too they will become aware, one day that "white men do not marry black women."] (*Peau noire* 39; *Black Skin* 49)

In addition to resentment, Fanon exposes his chauvinistic attitude and fear of emasculation. For him, the black woman, the individual who most hides black identity, has internalized hatred of the black male, a feeling that has infiltrated her mind from the white world. To illustrate this hatred, Fanon reconstructs a dialogue between a black man and a black woman using several sources. He cites the following from Michel Cournot: "Toi qui es une négresse – Moi? une négresse? ne vois-tu pas que je suis presque blanche? Je déteste les nègres. Ils puent, les nègres. Ils sont sales, paresseux. Ne me parle jamais de nègres." [You, as a Negress – Me? a Negress? Can't you see I am practically white? I despise Negroes. Niggers stink. They're dirty and lazy. Don't ever mention niggers to me] (*Peau noire* 40; *Black Skin* 50).[7] There is a feeling of rejection that sometimes pushes the black male to retaliate. Fanon's ironic style becomes polemical at times. In order to affirm the black woman's fascination with the white male, Fanon writes as a reminder: "Et quand on lui objecte que des Noirs peuvent lui être supérieurs, elle allègue leur laideur." [And when one points out to her that in this respect some black people may be her superiors, she falls back on their "ugliness"] (47; 58). In this deeply sarcastic statement, the black woman is thus reminded of her inferior place vis-à-vis the black male. In his review of *Nini* by Abdoulaye Sadji, Fanon uses two situations to study black women's reactions. In the first situation, a black man declares his love to Nini, a *mûlatresse* whose foremost desire, as stated by Fanon, is to save her race by erasing from herself all trace of blackness. She rejects the man, and Fanon attributes the rejection to the fact that she is an assimilated colonized individual and has internalized negative stereotypes of black men. In the second situation, Fanon analyzes reactions of people to the following news: "Une nouvelle très agréable . . . M. Darrivey, européen tout blanc et adjoint des Services civils, demande la main de Dédée, mulâtresse de demi-teinte. Pas possible." [Very delightful news . . . M. Darrivey, a completely white European employed in the civil service, has formally requested the hand of Dédée, a mulatto who was only half-Negro. It was unbelievable] (46; 58).

Whereas the reactions to the first situation were negative, the second situation elicits an extremely positive response. Fanon's choice of examples illustrates his disapproval of black women's attitudes. One may wonder, though, why Fanon chose a mûlatresse as the representative black woman in relationships with white men, especially since the setting is Africa. The unanswered question is: Had the woman not been a mûlatresse, would the results have been any different? Through Fanon's contradictory arguments, the reader loses the theme of love, and the woman gradually disappears from the text. When she is present, it is usually in a negative sense. The question of whether love is possible between European men and black women becomes in the process the problem in all relationships between black men and black women.

Fanon's critique of female authors such as Mayotte Capécia is the second instance of ambivalence. It is hard to tell whether Fanon is criticizing the author or her text. As Gwen Bergner notes, Capécia is denied her narrative voice. Fanon bases his arguments on *Je suis martiniquaise*. From the beginning, the reader is confused as to who or what Fanon is referring. We lose the text itself in the process of Fanon's attack on Capécia: "Un jour, une femme du nom de Mayotte Capécia, obéissant à un motif dont nous apercevons mal les tenants, a écrit deux cents deux pages — sa vie — où se multiplient à loisir les propositions les plus absurdes. [One day, a woman named Mayotte Capécia, obeying a motivation whose elements are difficult to detect, sat down to write 202 pages — her life — in which the most ridiculous ideas proliferated at random] (*Peau noire* 34; *Black Skin* 42). While the reader expects to discover why "authentic love" is impossible, the text becomes a polemical exposé by the author, Fanon, who turns quickly to chastise the black woman's conduct. Fanon, as noted earlier, ignores the existence of a fictional narrator in *Je suis martiniquaise*. This dismissal illustrates once again the erasure of the black colonized female, who is reduced to the level of the senseless woman writer. Comparing Fanon's critique of *Je suis martiniquaise* to his review of *Nini*, we are introduced immediately to a double standard. Fanon does not hold the male writer, Abdoulaye Sadji, responsible for his writings but instead sympathizes with him. Indeed, his criticism of *Nini* centers not on the author's intent but on the character Nini, the mûlatresse. Fanon does not question or judge the author and his motives.

The third example of ambivalence involves the total erasure of the black woman from the essay that is named after her. As previously discussed, the authentic love between the black woman and the European man becomes a cause to lament the plight of the black man who is losing the black woman. Perhaps the most compelling example of the disappearance of the black woman occurs in the conclusion of the essay. Fanon goes back to his Manichean paradigm of black man versus white man. Using psychoanalytic terminology, he elaborates on dividing factors such as racism, stereotyping, and the dehumanization of the "negro." Just as the theme of "authentic love" gradually disappears, the woman herself is erased from the text. Fanon's judgment not only dehumanizes her but also erases her presence in the decolonization discourse. Her role is reduced to her counteraction as the ultimate obstacle to the project of decolonization. It is clear that Fanon's arguments do not represent a dialogue between the black man and the black woman but paternalism and chauvinism toward the black female.

The antithetical essay in *Peau noire*, "L'homme de couleur et la femme blanche" ["The Man of Color and the White Woman"], demonstrates further Fanon's position on relationships between men and women in the colonial situation. This time, however, Fanon theorizes the fetishized black man's relationship with the white woman. Important contradictions in Fanon's decolonization theories illuminate the situation of black women. First, in opposition to the bitter and accusing tone of "La femme de couleur et l'homme blanc," Fanon adopts a more understanding and favorable stand. As in the previous essay, the author uses literary texts as evidence to support his theories. He specifically chooses fellow Martinican René Maran's 1947 novel *Un homme pareil aux autres* [A man like others]. In "La femme de couleur et l'homme blanc," race prevails over love as the latter becomes impossible because of racial differences, but in "L'homme de couleur et la femme blanche," hierarchical relationships based on gender replace the race question. The essay reaffirms the notion of man's deserving right to be loved. Indeed, the black man as a man, in the universalized masculine sense, needs to be loved.

Jean Veneuse, the protagonist in *Un homme pareil aux autres*, inquires about the possibility of a relationship with a white woman, Andrée Marielle. His friend informs Veneuse that since he has lived in Bordeaux for a long time, he is indeed qualified to marry a girl from his adopted country, France: "L'Européen n'aimant que l'Européenne, tu ne peux guère épouser qu'une femme du pays où tu as toujours vécu, une fille du bon pays de France, ton vrai, ton seul pays." [Since European men love only European women, you can hardly marry anyone but a woman of the country where you have always lived, a woman of our good old France and only country] (*Peau noire* 55; *Black Skin* 68). This implies that in order to marry a white woman, the black man must deny his origins, indeed his blackness. He must cease to be black and instead become the man, the sexually superior man. He must choose either to be a man or a black individual — not both.

While Fanon does not condone miscegenation, he still shows that black men are capable of deserving white women's love. Unlike the black woman who is foolish to believe a white man can love her, the black man is simply not responsible because he is what Fanon calls an "abandonnique" — that is, an individual with a need that he must constantly try to meet. Fanon justifies Jean Veneuse's behavior in psychoanalytic terms, calling him "un névrosé qui a besoin d'être délivré de ses fantasmes infantiles" [a neurotic who needs to be emancipated from his infantile fantasies] (*Peau noire* 64; *Black Skin* 79). The race aspect disappears as black males' sexual myths are enhanced. Fanon describes the white woman as an object of sexual desire. At the same time, he downplays the importance of power relationships between racial categories. In his conclusion, Fanon discourages the reader from seeing any racial problem in the relationships between the black male and the white woman: "Et nous voudrions avoir découragé toute tentative en vue de ramener les échecs d'un Jean Veneuse à la plus ou moins grande concentration en mélanine de son épiderme." [And I should like to think that I have discouraged any endeavors to connect the defeats of Jean Veneuse with the greater or lesser concentration of melanin in his epidermis] (65–66; 81).

Men face few obstacles to admission to the black community, or at least to the community defined by Fanon. His words here indicate that in terms of admittance, the black man, unlike the black woman, is as Chow states "allowed to go in and out of his society – to mate with white women, for instance, without having his fidelity questioned" (18). According to Mary Ann Doane, "the white mask is most perceptible as a mask in the case of the woman of color who seems more at home in the realm of mimicry" (222). In the following quotation, Fanon apologizes falsely by proposing the possibility of love between the black man and a white woman only to quickly rebuke the black woman: "On s'excusera d'oser proposer un amour noir à une âme blanche. Cela nous le retrouvons chez René Maran: cette crainte, cette timidité, cette humilité du Noir dans ses rapports avec la Blanche, *ou en tout cas avec une plus blanche que lui*." [One must apologize for daring to offer black love to a white soul. This we encounter again in René Maran: the fear, the timorousness, the humility of the black man in his relations with the white woman, *or in any case with a woman whiter than he*.] (emphasis added; *Peau noire* 45; *Black Skin* 56). Fanon creates a certain hierarchy between different oppressions brought on by colonial conditions.

In addition, we cannot ignore Fanon's own implicit presence in his work when he writes of *Peau noire*, "This book, it is hoped, will be a mirror." When we read Fanon, as Gates reminds us, "it's hard to avoid a sort of tableau of narcissism with Fanon himself as the Other that can only reflect and consolidate the critical self" (465). Indeed, Fanon's presence in his text is an important consideration when analyzing his judgments. Some critics, like Gates, have questioned his identity because he writes about different things, situations, and people. For instance, as Gates notes, what position did he have when he wrote "L'Algérie se dévoile" as a psychiatrist in Algeria – that of the colonizer or the colonized? (468). These questions reveal the complexities of Fanon's position as both a writer and a colonized writer.

In this paradigm of presence-absence, the linguistic presence of the colonized woman in Fanons' texts does not guarantee her a corporal presence like that of the black man. In other words, even if the woman is present in Fanon's writings, the author quickly proceeds to erase her, whether by defining her in the negative (she becomes the colonized male's Other), or by simply using her as a medium in colonial discourse. Fanon's essays, especially "L'Algérie se dévoile" and "La femme de couleur et l'homme blanc," illustrate the fact that the woman's presence is blurred by other discussions. These discussions serve to obliterate her while creating an illusion of presence.

Gates proposes that Bhabha's "Remembering Fanon" "can as easily be read as an index to all that Bhabha wants us to forget" (462). What would Fanon like us to forget, or what does he not say that undermines his theories? Fanon never questions what the colonized woman wants and denies this woman a voice. In addition, he takes the colonized woman from specific temporal (decolonizing moment) and spatial (fictive as opposed to real) paradigms, denying her history. He does not write about the colonized woman in terms of what colonization did to her but, instead, in terms of what she let colonization do to her by virtue of her voluntary assimilation and complicity with the oppressor. As demonstrated by his reading of the character Jean Veneuse, Fanon takes an opposite perspective of the colonized man.

In "Carnal Knowledge and Imperial Power, Gender, Race, and Morality in Colonial Asia," Ann Laura Stoler looks at the relationships between gender and race discourses in the colonies, especially what they meant for the wives of colonizers. She suggests that in colonial language, "the very category of 'colonizer' and 'colonized' were secured through forms of sexual control" (52). In other words, sexual control fixed race (55). According to Stoler, some colonial historians have posited that imperial expansion itself was derived from the export of male sexual energy (56). It seems that the tropics provided a site of pornographic fantasies for metropolitan consumption. The first colonial presence was mainly formed with European males, whereas their wives arrived much later. The colonizers lived in *concubinage* with "native women," a system that was later condemned due to the constant threat posed by "mixed children." Despite sexual prohibitions, *concubinage* continued but followed an "asymmetric and gender specific" pattern (85). While sex between white men and native women was permissible and not seriously condemned, it was prohibited rigorously between white women, once they arrived in the colonies, and native men. This asymmetrical paradigm offers the white man more access to both white and native women than the native man. In slavery discourses, the same schema is applicable. In the nineteenth-century American South, a black man suspected of sleeping with a white woman was lynched. Mixed marriages were prohibited in South Africa until a few years ago. It was not until 1967, with the case of *Loving v. Commonwealth of Virginia*, that the U.S. Supreme Court struck down antimiscegenation laws that still existed in some states.[8]

We find the same asymmetrical relations in *Peau noire, masques blancs*. If sexual control fixed race, Fanon controls the sexuality of the colonized in the attempt to reverse the situation. In "Le nègre et la psychopathologie," he attempts to create a "mimicry" of sexual relationships between white women and black men by arguing speciously that white women's fear of rape is nothing more than a manifestation of their sexual desire for the black man. In deconstructing the black man's sexual myth, Fanon creates an interstice that permits unfetishized sex between the black man and the white woman, as in the case of Jean Veneuse. However, in his analysis of Capécias' *Je suis martiniquaise*, Fanon attempts to control black women's sexuality by suggesting that she cannot love or be loved by a white man. According to Rey Chow, the only way the black woman can be admitted to the black community is through sexual limitations imposed on her (17). That is, the black woman has to be sexually available only to the black man in order to fit into black society.

Gates concludes his essay "Critical Fanonism" by writing that "rehistoricizing Fanon, we can hear a lament concerning the limits of liberation" (469). To rehistoricize Fanon also entails questioning his essentializing tendencies with regard to colonized women. Fanon's limits lay in his discourse on issues concerning women, whose existence itself he problematizes. His theories serve to reinforce some stereotypes of "colonized women," such as their status as the ultimate victim and their desire to whiten themselves.

This study is a response to the ongoing third-world antifeminist discourses that often relate women's emancipation movements to a "western idea" and consider these movements as another neocolonial element. This opinion sometimes undermines women's causes in the third world because societies fail to recognize that a woman can desire freedom without Western influences and pressure. Today, the growth of African and Caribbean women's texts is undeniable. In addition to portraying women in colonial and postcolonial contexts, women writers aim primarily to write and right oversights by male writers such as Fanon who have produced written works before them. Indeed, Fanon's presence-absence discourse on colonized women is representative of attitudes of the colonized male elite of his time. In fact, a study of Négritude literature reveals more or less similarly ambivalent relationships between men and women. The male writers either ignored woman's specificity or took her for granted without serious consideration of the colonial impact on her. An extensive analysis of the condition of women in the writings of a major figure like Fanon aims to construct a model and a point of reference from which one can argue the historical motivations of female writers. In fact, one can say that female writers from the 1950s to this day have been trying to remedy their quasi-absence and misrepresentation in anticolonial discourses like Fanon's essays, which show an acute form of what Chow calls "existential violence" (21) — namely Fanon's refusal to acknowledge women in his quest for identification.[9] Fanon's contradictions in his depiction of relationships between black men and black women constitute an excellent example of postcolonial ambivalence.

2

Representing Colonial Violence

Michèle Lacrosil's *Cajou*, Ken Bugul's *Le baobab fou*, and Ousmane Sembène's *La noire de . . .*

In this chapter, I posit that the selected works by Michèle Lacrosil, Ken Bugul, and Ousmane Sembène complicate Fanon's formula for colonial violence by offering a specifically female perspective on the experience and legacy of colonialism's brutality. This chapter discusses these relationships in two different areas. First, I examine the process of epistemological violence — brainwashing through formal and informal education — as a legacy of colonialism. Second, I study the specificity of women's experience within the colonial discourse. This involves a close analysis of Ken Bugul's violent encounter with the West and Lacrosil's depiction of a severe case of colonial neurosis in *Cajou*.

Michèle Lacrosil was born in Guadeloupe. She is known for three novels: *Sapotille ou le serin d'argile* (1960), *Cajou* (1961), and *Demain Jab-Herma* (1967). After the publication of the first novel, Lacrosil moved to Paris, where she taught literature in a high school. According to Robert P. Smith Jr., Lacrosil moved to France because of the harsh reception of her first two books, which she wrote in the form of intimate diaries. In the novels, she engages the reader in a complex discourse on race and gender. Like Mayotte Capécia before her, Lacrosil portrays controversial female characters that identify themselves by the color of their skin. Smith writes that these novels were controversial because "it seems that Miss Lacrosil's books have done much to expose to the world the surprising and shameful hierarchy based on the color of one's skin, which still exists to a certain degree in the societies of the islands of the French Antilles where, because of a tradition not officially sanctioned by metropolitan France herself, whites represent the ruling class, mulattos, the middle class and blacks the subordinate class, socially and economically" (783).[1] Isabelle Gros adds, "Whereas the Caribbean corpus is mainly socio-historical, emphasizing the relationship with the society as a whole, Lacrosil dared to write about the deep self. This would explain why Lacrosil was so criticized, boycotted, and finally reduced to silence after a third novel, *Demain Jab-Herma* (1967), in which she renounces her first writing style, stops doing it in the first person narrative and undoubtedly attempts to enter the canon" (123). With her third book, *Demain Jab-Herma*, Lacrosil subsequently attempted to write a novel less focused on racial hierarchies, but it also failed. Little is known about Lacrosil after this.

While Lacrosil bore the full brunt of the controversy over her books, the Senegalese writer Mariétou Mbaye adopted the pseudonym Ken Bugul on the advice of her publisher in order to shield herself from criticism of her novel *Le baobab fou*. The intensely autobiographical novel's plot clearly reflects the writer's rather traumatic experiences while living in Belgium. Bugul tackles subjects previously untouched by African female authors, using her female protagonist's deep inner thoughts to address matters of sexuality, drug use, and involvement in prostitution. She has since written six other novels: *Cendres et braises* (1994), *Riwan ou le chemin de sable* (1999), *La folie et la mort* (2000), *De l'autre côté du regard* (2003), *Rue Félix Faure* (2005), and *La pièce d'or* (2006). In many ways, these novels are a continuation of Bugul's earlier work as she seeks to understand fully and reintegrate her Senegalese community while portraying current issues in Senegal and elsewhere, particularly those that relate to African women.

Cajou and *Le baobab fou* are written like intimate journals or diaries. *Cajou* tells the story of the title character, alias Monica Kébaire, a highly educated chemist and the self-hating offspring of a white mother and a dead black father, whom she never knew. Cajou suffers from psychological problems due to colonial violence. According to Maryse Condé, Lacrosil's protagonist constitutes "la victime coloniale la plus achevée" [the most completed colonial victim] (*La parole* 31). The story takes place over the course of four evenings, during which time Cajou ponders whether or not she should accept her boss's offer of a promotion. Her suspicion that she was offered the job only because she is a black woman causes her to hesitate. She convinces herself that "ma thèse de doctorat et mes travaux ont fait beaucoup du bruit parce que je suis une fille de couleur, et non en proportion de leur valeur intrinsèque" [my doctoral thesis and my work were noticed because I am a girl of color, and not in relation to their instrinsic value] (Lacrosil 18). The question of "worthiness" provokes several other questions in the novel as well as fragmented memories from childhood. During these four evenings, seated or lying on a couch in her small apartment, alone or with her "Aryan" boyfriend Germain, Cajou goes back to her past and specifically her childhood in order to find out why she suffers from an acute form of inferiority complex. Lacrosil narrates Cajou's story in a fragmented way, revealing piece by piece the nature and source of Cajou's ailment to the reader and the character herself.

The main character in *Le baobab fou* is a young Senegalese woman named Ken who, unlike Cajou, appears self-assured (at least in the beginning) as she roams around Brussels, where she has moved to pursue her studies. Her voyage to Europe becomes a difficult journey of self-discovery as well. After multiple attempts to integrate Europe and cope with its false promises, Ken returns home in order to find answers that could explain her deep identity crisis. Bugul's highly fictionalized but autobiographical novel reveals the complexities involved when the colonized encounters the West. Shocking revelations about Mariétou Mbaye's life in Europe forced her to publish under a pseudonym, as stated earlier. The novel testifies to the impact of colonial violence on an African female subject.

Lacrosil's and Bugul's narratives represent the post-Négritude and postcolonial anxieties of women writing in a world mired in disorder and confusion. In "A New Cry from the 1960s to the 1980s," Marie-Denise Shelton contrasts Négritude literature with the literature that followed the movement. She writes that Négritude was "a period in which the poetics of self-repossession, nationalist and racial affirmation went hand in hand with an emphasis on the themes of virility, potency, verticality, and legitimacy" (Shelton 427). After Négritude, however, "the dominant themes in the literature become illegitimacy, impotence, alienation, and madness." Shelton continues, "The organic sense of territory that the poet of Négritude claimed was replaced by a feeling of utter estrangement and dispossession" (428). Another trend, Shelton notes, was the preoccupation with the inner self and psychology as "determined by the project of Frantz Fanon who, armed with psychiatric knowledge, had undertaken an uncompromising autopsy of the Caribbean mind" (429). Literature by Caribbean women displays these signs of estrangement mixed with deep explorations of the inner-self. As Shelton notes, women's literature belongs to the post-Negriture era because of women writers' preoccupation with themes like the problem of feminine exclusion and dispossession, the enunciation or denial of self, and the engulfment of identity in a web of neuroses and phantasms. In addition, women writers access autobiography in order to express in intimate terms the experience of alienation and self-hatred (Shelton 429).

While Shelton focuses on the trend toward psychologically oriented literature, Maryse Condé proposes a different angle to look at the literary history of the West Indies. She advances the idea that

Caribbean male writers successively or simultaneously established literary orders that other writers have been forced to follow. These models include writers such as Aimé Césaire, Jacques Roumain, Edouard Glissant, Raphaël Confiant, Patrick Chamoiseau, and Jean Bernabé. In contrast to these male writers, women writers bring "disorder" to the literature of the West Indies because, as Condé puts it, "[w]henever women speak out, they displease, shock, or disturb. Their writings imply that before thinking of a political revolution, West Indian society needs a psychological one. What they hope for and desire conflicts with men's ambitions and dreams. Why, they ask, fight against racism in the world when it exists at home, among ourselves?" ("Order, Disorder" 131–32) Lacrosil's *Cajou* belongs to the group of West Indian novels by women that introduce this disorder, a fact that may explain why her work was met with such controversy.

In the African context, establishing literary history is difficult, mostly because written African literature is still relatively younger. Most critics commonly classify literature in two main categories — the Négritude and Post-Négritude eras — and they have attempted to create a more detailed African literary history. In her article "Turning Point in the Francophone/African Novel: The Eighties to the Nineties," Lilyan Kesteloot takes the growing number of links between writing and violence as an indication of the current trends in African literature. She argues that since the 1980s (*Le baobab fou* was published in 1982) African literature has become increasingly violent and unsettling, to the point that it resembles what she calls the "African Absurd." However, Kesteloot concentrates mostly on literature by African men and unjustly posits women's writings as simply novels of manners. With a few exceptions, such as Aminata Sow Fall, African women novelists have indeed concentrated on problems particular to women. Still, some studies, including the article by Kesteloot, simplify the meaning of these novels and therefore miss the complexity of the feminine social world they describe. Bugul's *Le baobab fou* destabilizes such assertions by complicating the so-called women's universe. This novel qualifies as a disorderly novel like Caribbean women's fiction as Bugul breaks with the traditional portrayal of African women's experience by male and female writers such as Mariama Bâ. It should be pointed out that the popular success of Bâ's *Une si longue lettre* coexists with the novel's complex treatment of gender and human relationships — a complexity that continues to generate critical studies.

Cajou and *Le baobab fou* bear striking similarities to each other on a thematic level. Both tell stories about individual female identity crises aggravated by visits to the European countries of the colonizer. Both novels also contain tones of melancholy, self-pity, and pessimism, feelings that escalate dangerously when the female characters approach moments of acute despair. The narratives take the form of personal testimony in their autobiographical nature: the use of *je* (I) implies talking about the self, both physical and mental. Finally, both novels contain a series of lamentations over the loss of the mother as well as losses of identity, history, and memory, following women whose lives end in progressive mental alienation (Bugul) and probable suicide (Cajou). Cajou's and Ken's efforts to remember go beyond the desire to know their personal history; they analyze not only their childhoods but also weigh the effect on their own lives of the trauma endured by their ancestors.

In their works, Lacrosil and Bugul depict various kinds of violence. The writers create female characters that are prone both to self-violence and violence against others. Cajou believes she is inferior to the whites who surround her — her mother, friends, schoolmates, colleagues, neighbors, and boyfriend — and on several occasions feels the urge to cause them physical harm. Throughout the novel, she weighs the decision whether or not to commit suicide (self-violence) or to abort her unborn child. She also endures physical, emotional, and sexual violence from Germain. In *Le baobab fou*, Ken gradually becomes neurotic and suicidal. She also becomes a prostitute and endures physical, mental, and sexual violence at the hands of her male clients and acquaintances in Brussels. In addition, both women suffer daily encounters with racism that constitute acts of violence toward their souls and bodies. The women's journeys toward self-discovery, though mainly mental for Cajou, simply become a road to madness. It is important to note that while Cajou enjoys a certain superiority in the French West Indies because she is a métisse, once she is in Europe her experience of racism equals that of Ken, a dark-skinned Senegalese.

Like their male counterparts living in the West, depicted for instance in the Négritude literature or novels such as Camara Laye's *L'enfant noir* or Cheik Hamidou Kane's *L'aventure ambiguë*, Cajou and Ken exemplify colonial subjects who must engage in an intense identity search. Unlike Laye's *je* in *L'enfant noir*, an individual who seems to enjoy a fruitful memory, Cajou and Ken suffer a great deal of amnesia. This amnesia has numerous causes, the primary one being the epistemological violence that forced Africans and people of African descent to adopt the belief system of the colonizer while simultaneously pushing their own culture into oblivion. This epistemological violence, which involves several driving forces, happens through a process that is well illustrated in *Cajou* and *Le baobab fou*.

The Process of Epistemological Violence

"The French Caribbean is the site of a history characterized by ruptures that began with a brutal dislocation, the slave trade," writes Edouard Glissant in his seminal book *Caribbean Discourse* (61). The dislocation of history along with the inability of people to recall that history result in what Glissant calls a nonhistory. He uses the term *nonhistory* to indicate the absence of memories that would insure the survival of collective and individual histories. The real histories of colonized people have been replaced by a history written and imposed by the West. The power of the new Western history progressively dismisses the histories that existed before the violent ruptures of slavery and colonialism. The traumatic experience of slavery resulted in historical amnesia among the Caribbean people, while colonialism also caused similar effects on both African and Caribbean peoples, particularly on the intellectual élite.

Bugul's Ken and Lacrosil's Cajou engage in a quest for their forgotten historical heritage as a means to resolve their numerous dilemmas and empower themselves for a better future. They undertake the task of unlocking the past in order to understand themselves, make sense of their current lives, and secure their survival. Memory therefore becomes a weapon used not only to revisit the initial trauma but also to change the course of destiny. Different forces contribute to a systematic erasure of memory. With distinctive autobiographical differences, Ken and Cajou each experience serious traumatic events during childhood. Bugul narrates Ken's childhood trauma through a depiction of a seemingly ordinary incident in a child's life. While playing underneath a baobab tree, young Ken finds an amber bead and accidentally pushes it into her ear. This causes her to become permanently deaf, both physically and metaphorically. Her deafness indeed symbolizes memory loss. She says: "Je ne me souvenais pas de la vie à la maison, dans le village depuis la perle d'ambre dans l'oreille." [I did not remember much of life at home, in the village, since the amber bead in my ear] (Bugul, *Le baobab fou* 80; *Abandoned Baobab* 65).[2] Ken's loss of memory did not happen overnight, however. Bugul structures her novel in a way that allows the reader to see how this privileged moment of epistemological violence came about.

The first part of the novel is entitled "Pré-histoire de Ken" (Ken's prehistory). It reads like a legendary story about the birth, destruction, and rebirth of Ndoucoumane, the heroine's Senegalese village. It tells the story of this village where "la journée passa avec des petits instants gais, des instant de somme, des instants de rêve, de travail, de contemplation de l'espace jusqu'à la tombée de la nuit" [the day passed with little moments of pleasure, moments of dozing, moments of dreaming, of working, of contemplating space, until the evening fell] (Bugul, *Le baobab fou* 11–12; *Abandoned Baobab* 5).

The seemingly harmonious life of the village suffers several disruptions, including a tragic fire that destroys everything except a young baobab tree and results in exile for several families. While the "faithful" baobab tree and an ageless "creature" that knew everything about the village suggest the history of the place, disruption arrives when a man comes from the North and settles there with his family. Everything that follows the settlement, whether good or bad, somehow has a link to the baobab tree. The ageless man forewarns the new settlers that "ce baobab est lié à un événement qui va bouleverser une génération entière" [this baobab is linked to an event that will shake an entire generation] (21; 14). The event referred to is the incident involving Ken and the amber bead, which turns out to be part of a broken amber necklace belonging to the wife of the man from the North and mother of his children. The section "Préhistoire de Ken" ends in a "piercing scream" because an unsupervised child has found the amber bead and pushed it deep into its ear (25; 17). The scream has a dual significance. It marks the end of Ken's prehistory and the beginning of her history. In the preface to the second part of the novel, "Histoire de Ken," we learn that it was Ken herself who pushed the amber bead into her ear. Ken becomes part of a generation that will be shattered by the incident. Once again, the event happens under the baobab tree, the eternal accomplice. Ironically, this part begins with the sentence "Ken remembers." What she remembers, of course, is the moment she departed for Europe to finally discover "the land of her ancestors."

Likewise, in *Cajou*, the title character must find her history. Cajou has little knowledge of her slave heritage because of everyone's efforts, including her own, to repress the desire to know. After Cajou becomes disturbed by stories about her father, her mother takes her to a psychiatrist, who suggests that the family avoid talking about the man, her ancestors' migrations, and racial questions (Lacrosil 41). The psychiatrist's recommendations result in a double tragedy. First, they repress Cajou's desire for the black father and replace it with the desire to embrace the white culture, which contributes to the splitting of her subjectivity. This split has a devastating impact because Cajou can never fully identify with the whites, despite the fact that she wants to and lives in an environment apart from people who look like her. Cajou's childhood mission is to "lactify" herself, to adapt Fanon's term, in order to become "beautiful" like her mother.[3] In her adult life, Cajou encounters others like the psychiatrist who tell her to forget about her black ancestors. For instance, Germain, her blond and blue-eyed lover, incessantly encourages her to stop worrying about the past and move on with her life. Cajou never asks others about her past, and she herself dwells on memories of her psychiatric care.

In both novels, after the initial trauma, other agencies and circumstances reinforce the damage done to the women's subjectivities. Among those who contribute to their memory loss are the protagonists' own mothers. As mentioned earlier, Cajou's mother contributed to the burying of her Caribbean roots by taking her to the psychiatrist instead of looking for ways to answer the child's questions about her black heritage. While living in Paris, alone in the white man's land, Cajou's mother dies, and this alienates the daughter even further because she loses her last cultural and biological link to her home (Lacrosil 108). In *Le baobab fou*, Ken strongly resents her mother's abandonment and failure to protect her from injuring her ear with the amber bead, thus allowing memory blockage and widening historical discontinuity. Alluding to the Négritude portrayal of the black woman as well as a traditional perspective toward women, Ken describes the role her mother should have assumed: "La dimension de la femme noire à cette époque était d'assumer le rôle de la source de vie, du symbole de continuité, de zone de refuge . . . Pourquoi la mère était-elle partie?" [The dimension of the Black woman included her assuming the role as the source of life, the symbol of continuity, the realm of refuge . . . Why had the mother left?] (Bugul, *Le baobab fou* 146; *Abandoned Baobab* 126–27).

Ken's and Cajou's relationships with lovers and friends in Belgium and France, respectively, represent both women's desire to be accepted in the West. It is through these encounters in Europe that they learn the extent to which they are "other." For instance, Cajou adopts her name during a conversation with her Parisian neighbor Marjolaine. Marjolaine finds Cajou's original name, Monica, to be inappropriate because it comes from the calendar – the French calendar. Marjolaine remarks: "Je n'aurai pas cru. J'imaginais un nom de fleur. Ou d'oiseau . . . On t'appelait autrement, pas, quand tu étais petite? Pourquoi t'a-t-on affublée des noms de notre calendrier? Quel est ton vrai prénom?" [I would never have thought. I imagined a flower's name. Or a bird's name . . . You were called a different name, no, when you were little? Why would they give you such a name from OUR calendar? What is your real name?] (Lacrosil 118). As it happens, the name *Cajou* has a rather violent origin that reminds the protagonist of her own ambiguity. She narrates: "acajou, ou *cajou*, un fruit curieux, on le dirait double, il symbolise ma propre ambiguïté. Il comporte un pédoncule comestible, 'pomme' odorante à laquelle est suspendu l'essentiel du fruit, une noix dont la coque est vert foncé devient en vieillissant de couleur nègre." [The mahogany, or cajou, a curious fruit, one would say double. It symbolizes my own ambiguity. It has an edible peduncle, a sweet-smelling 'apple' on which the main part of the fruit hangs, a nut whose dark green becomes black when aged] (119).

Cajou is completely cut off from her father's heritage and is constantly asked by friends and co-workers to account for her existence. Although she wishes to stay in isolation for fear of rejection and scrutiny, she cannot avoid meeting people at her apartment building or at work. The people she meets serve merely as replacements in the original triangular relationship between herself, her mother, and the psychiatrist. She has been afraid of rejection ever since her relationship with Stéphanie, a childhood friend, ended because of the intrusion of a third party. Cajou's more recent triangular relationship with Marjolaine ended when Germain entered the picture.[4] These repetitive occurrences make Cajou analyze her past as a strategy to avoid such relationships in the future. She wants to have the same sense of completeness that she sees in her friends. Despite Germain's ill-fated attempts to join her, the journey to discover the origins of her self-hatred is clearly solitary. Many silent moments unfold between Cajou and her white female friends, Stéphanie and Marjolaine, who become increasingly frustrated with her alienation and eventually break away from her. Between Cajou and Germain, there is a "dialogue de sourds" [unproductive dialogue] (Lacrosil 124) whereby Germain is incapable of understanding Cajou's persistent need to journey into the past. Bugul's Ken can glimpse her pre/history and thus draw the conclusion that she belongs neither in the West nor in her family and village. Cajou's problem is even more acute because she has no memory of her race whatsoever, an expected outcome for a Caribbean protagonist who lost, through forced physical dislocation, Africa, the land of origin.

Like Cajou, Ken is also constantly bombarded with false images of herself from former colonialists, Africanists, or philanthropists who think they know Africa and then proceed to tell her who she is. In her identity quest, Ken remembers her family and quickly concludes that colonization is not her only problem. She is also alienated from her family: her mother is absent; her siblings are either much older or scattered all over the country; and, ironically, her father is blind, and since she is metaphorically deaf herself, Ken cannot communicate with him. Ken cannot rely on her family to locate her history because, she writes, there were no "liens vrais qui façonnaient et pouvaient guider les destins" [true bonds that used to shape and could guide destinies] (Bugul, *Le baobab* 129; *Abandoned Baobab* 111). Ken speaks of her isolation:

> J'avais mille choses à raconter, à échanger. L'amour, l'amitié, la tendresse. La violence de la solitude depuis la perle d'ambre dans l'oreille, depuis le départ de la mère, avait développé en moi la notion de l'autre dans des élans généreux. J'étais seule, comme seul un arbre savait l'être.
>
> [There were a thousand things I had to tell, to exchange. Love,

> friendships, tenderness. The violence of loneliness since the amber bead in my ear, since the mother's departure, had developed in me the notion of the other in surges of generosity. I was alone, as only a tree knows how to be alone.] (Bugul, *Le baobab fou* 159; *Abandoned Baobab* 138)

Like Cajou, Ken is isolated and forced to communicate with herself through an interior monologue.

Colonizers employed many weapons to perpetrate violence — not only guns but also religion and school, which brainwashed and encouraged forgetfulness in students. French school serves as the ultimate memory eraser for both Ken and Cajou. After their incidents with the amber bead and the psychiatrist, respectively, the two women have an ambivalent relationship with school. While they excel academically in French school and it offers an opportunity for them to end their solitude, the education they receive completes the erasure of history instigated by the initial trauma. Although always conscious of her alienation, Cajou becomes even more distressed because of her education. Ken, however, uses her own formal education to compensate for her feelings of emptiness, and her education promises her both a new family and a new history, as encapsulated in the phrase "nos ancêtres les Gaulois." She becomes more and more Europeanized in terms of how she perceives her history, and in this way her education defines her identity. As we will see later on, however, Ken eventually discovers "the principal lie," to use Aimé Césaire's phrase, in her schooling, and expresses her disappointment in the education she received about the West.[5] The more confused she gets personally, the more attracted she is to the untold West, with its drugs, prostitution, and sexual freedom. Unable to reconcile her conflicting needs, Ken eventually stops attending classes. As noted by Madeleine Cottenet-Hage and Kevin Meehan, for colonized subjects there is an ambiguous relationship between the desire to acquire knowledge and the knowledge itself, as the latter gradually overwhelms the colonized.[6] In Ken's case, the protagonist realizes that the knowledge she enjoyed acquiring also contributed to the loss of memory and history.

Similarly, Cajou's education gave her a promising career but did not provide her with a resolution to her identity search. She cannot get past the ghosts of her childhood trauma that led to her neurotic behavior. It is also noteworthy that Cajou's career choice defies gender stereotypes like the one held by her mother, who urges her to follow a more feminine career path: Cajou studied chemistry and biology and holds a doctoral degree. On the one hand, I agree with Frederick Ivor Case when he argues that Cajou chooses to study chemistry and biology because "the world of microbes and test tubes, rats and pipettes do not evoke threatening and fundamental questions of the self" (32). In this case, Cajou embodies the cross-cultural image of women's progress in the exclusive world of the white male. On the other hand, it is rather interesting that Lacrosil has her black character specialize in chemistry and biology as these sciences, biology in particular, have been historically used to "prove" racial differences and justify the inferiority of blacks.

Through similar processes, Ken and Cajou are victims of epistemological violence that results in partial or complete memory loss. School, family, and friends contribute to the silencing of their heritage. It is important to keep in mind that colonialism and slavery did not cause historical ruptures of equal intensity. For instance, Ken not only manages to glimpse her "authentic" pre/history but also still has the option to go back to her African village to find her roots. The baobab tree plays a significant role in Ken's memory quest because it was in the village before her birth and thus witnessed her history and prehistory. More importantly, the baobab witnessed the abrupt piercing of Ken's memory: the accidental injury to her ear by the amber bead and her mother's subsequent departure. Finally, the path Ken takes to attend the French school passes underneath the tree, allowing the baobab to witness the process by which Ken yielded her African roots for Western doctrines. Eventually, Ken returns to her village only to find out that the baobab tree has long since died. The death of the tree points to the impossibility of both recovery and Ken's dream of a better future: "Le rêve m'était interdit comme par la suite tout ce qui consistait en la survie de l'irréel, cette illusion qui donnait envie de poursuivre." [Dreaming was forbidden to me, just as later everything that consisted of the survival of the unreal was forbidden to me, that illusion that gave one desire to continue] (Bugul, *Le baobab fou* 181; *Abandoned Baobab* 158). The death of the baobab tree and Ken's failure to go back in time to recapture its testimony symbolize an inability to recover substantial memories from before the deafening incident with the amber bead. Cajou, however, does not have the option of returning to a tangible past. After four nights of an excruciating identity search, she concludes:

> J'étais l'aboutissement d'une série de hasards; mon comportement résultait de mon hérédité, de mon équilibre physiologique (ou de mon déséquilibre!) et des pressions sociales qui s'exerçaient sur moi; tous ces faits, je n'avais pas pu les déterminer dans le passé et ne pourrais les modifier dans l'avenir.
>
> [I was the product of a series of chance events; my behavior resulted from my heredity, from my physiological stability (or lack thereof), and from my social pressures that are imposed upon me; all this, I was not able to identify them in the past and could not modify them in the future.] (Lacrosil 148)

Ultimately, Cajou's childhood psychiatrist allowed the "nonhistory" to occur. Cajou asserts, "One can destroy a portrait but the frame remains" (Lacrosil 26). The experience does not completely erase Cajou's memories. Some traces, the violent ones, remain but in a fragmented state. Cajou as well as other descendants of enslaved people are the victims of consequences of the historical rupture created by the slave trade. Ken's deafness and Cajou's traumatic session at the psychiatrist's office result from the broad trauma of colonialism. In both situations, living conditions favor alienation and historical amnesia, especially when families across generations lack the communication that could create continuity and revival.[7]

Cajou and Ken, like male protagonists in African and Caribbean literature, belong to the generation shattered by traumatic events of colonialism. But how does gender affect Ken's and Cajou's experience of colonial violence? The answer to this question lies in the nature of the impact of colonialism on the two protagonists. While the influence of Fanon on Lacrosil and Bugul cannot be proven or denied at this time, I propose reading *Le boabab fou* and *Cajou* as possible reactions to Fanon's treatment of colonized women. The next two sections examine two consequences of colonial violence: African female's violent encounter with the West and Caribbean female subjects' colonial neurosis.[8]

African Women in the Métropole

Literature provides a privileged insight into social and cultural changes resulting from the contact between different peoples — contacts that may have been caused by politics, economics, or even changes in climate. Francophone African novels and autobiographies, for example, reveal much about the nature of the encounter between the peoples of that continent and colonizers from France and Belgium. But most works, including nearly all criticism of African literature, focus on racial difference and the psychological responses that it generates. For example, the Négritude movement in the 1930s, with its emphasis on race and African culture, constituted one reaction to the French policy of assimilation. Novelists such as Bernard Dadié and Cheikh Hamidou Kane have explored the consequences of travel and study in Europe for young Africans in narratives that reveal much about the impact of the colonial relationship. As examined earlier, Frantz Fanon has analyzed this cultural encounter through the lens of race in his books and essays, especially *Peau noire, masques blancs*. But the racial perspective that marks much of this literature and the criticism it has produced masks a much less understood and little studied dimension of the encounter between Europe and Africa: the role of gender. When women from Africa travel to Europe, is their experience different from that of men? Through a close analysis of the intersection of race and gender consciousness, I locate a preliminary answer to the question of how the experience of traveling and living in the Métropole contributes to the formation of race and gender consciousness for women from Africa.

The evidence for this study comes from two narratives, one by a man and the other by a woman, that convey the traumatic experience of a female who encounters Europe for the first time: Ousmane Sembène's film *La noire de . . .* and Ken Bugul's *Le baobab fou*. I find it useful to involve *La noire de . . .* in this discussion because of its powerful cinematic capacity to depict a black woman's psychological experience in the West. Furthermore, Ousmane Sembène leads the list of African intellectuals, male or female, who have consistently portrayed the unique experiences of women. In addition, the two stories have striking similarities: while the protagonist Diouana in *La noire de . . .* goes to Europe not to study like Ken but rather to serve the French family that had employed her in Senegal, both works feature Senegalese women who migrate to Europe during the immediate postindependence period, and both the film and the novel are rooted in real-life events. *La noire de . . .* is a cinematic adaptation of a short story written by Sembène that was inspired by the actual story of a black maid who committed suicide in the south of France. As noted earlier, *Le baobab fou* is the fictionalized "autobiography" of its author, Ken Bugul. In both cases, the main character suffers considerable trauma owing to her race and her gender.

According to Fanon, the West is a place where the black man is othered and subsequently becomes aware of his "blackness" or his *Négritude*, to use Césaire's term.[9] The othering occurs through the visible signs of the body: skin color, body shapes and manners, eyes, 'white' teeth — all the bodily signs of African "ugliness," a stereotype that developed over centuries from European concepts of the black race. In Fanon's *Peau noire, masques blancs*, the black narrator refers to his encounter with a white child who says to his mother, "Regarde le nègre" [Look at the nigger] (91; *Black Skin* 113). Immediately, the phrase "Look, a Negro" works as "an external stimulus" on the black man. His first reaction is to produce a "tight smile." However, this amusement, signifying his identification and complicity with the white world, quickly turns into the realization that his body has been "étalé, disjoint, rétamé" [sprawled out, distorted, recolored] (91; 113). For Fanon, "le noir n'a plus à être noir, mais à l'être en face du blanc" [the black man must not only be black but he must become black in front of the white man] (*Peau noire* 88). The phrase "Regarde le nègre" generates a profound meaning because it refers to previously established stereotypical images of the animalistic, uncivilized, bad, mean, ugly, and cannibalistic black, quivering with rage (88–93). Within the context of the Métropole, the black man becomes what Fanon terms "sur-déterminé de l'extérieur" [overdetermined from without] (Fanon, *Peau noire* 93; *Black Skin* 116).

Although Fanon's explanation of the consequences of such interracial encounters considerably improves our understanding of the dynamics in the black-white relationship, he once again underplays the experience of gender, particularly in the case of black women in the Métropole. Gender, however, influences the nature of contact between the West and Africa as much as race. One cannot ignore the myth of the "Négresse" in European art and literature that developed over several centuries. In the article "Les romans coloniaux: Enfer ou Paradis," Jacques Chévrier identifies two predominant images of the Négresse in nineteenth-century French literature. The black woman is represented on the one hand as both erotic and exotic (as in Baudelaire's "Les fleurs du mal") and on the other as the principal cause of the European man's decadence (as in Pierre Loti's *Le roman d'un spahi*). Similar images are also present in Négritude poetry but serve entirely different purposes. While the poets sought to represent the Négresse positively, these images ironically served to validate preestablished stereotypes of the black woman.[10] In this analysis, I draw on Fanon's general paradigm of race consciousness but also on the evolution of gender consciousness as exemplified by the experiences of two female protagonists in order to frame the phenomenon in a broader context that includes both race and gender.

The heroines Diouana and Ken are young Senegalese women living in Europe during the 1950s and '60s, when most African countries made the transition from the colonial to the national era. Amid differences in their educational and familial backgrounds, both women idealize the Métropole as a dreamland and a place of tremendous opportunity. Their stays in Europe take a tragic turn as a result of disillusionment and alienation, both physical and psychological. Set around 1958, *La noire de . . .* recounts the tragic life of Diouana, a Senegalese maid who has not been educated in Western-style schools. She eagerly agrees to join her French employers' family in Antibes, France, after the deceitful French woman convinces her how nice it would be in France. Unable to go outside to experience the Métropole because Madame refuses to let her, Diouana uses her time to reassess her idea of the Métropole through flashbacks. Inside the walls of her employer's home, she is being submitted to a West she never envisioned. For the purpose of this study, I will focus on her character portrayal in the film rather than the short story. Françoise Pfaff has detailed the main differences between the story and the script in her book *The Cinema of Ousmane Sembène, a Pioneer of African Film* (1984). One difference is of particular interest. While a third-person narrator recounts the short story, the film shows all events preceding Diouana's death through her own eyes. Because the goal of this analysis is to show the development of the psychological drama in the context of the Métropole, Diouana's perspective is crucial.

Bugul's *Le baobab fou*, as mentioned earlier, is a fictionalized account of the author's experience studying in Belgium. Unlike Diouana, Ken exchanges locations, groups of friends, and lovers in order to find a place to belong. Although Ken is able to move around Brussels in all circles, she, like Diouana, experiences both physical and physiological confinement. Ken finds herself in a vicious cycle from which she cannot escape. Like many colonized subjects, Ken and Diouana at first idealize the Métropole. One sign of their infatuation is that they want to adopt aspects of the Western female body. When her employers ask her to go with them to Antibes, Diouana imagines modeling her corporal appearance on the Western body. She wants to see beautiful stores and pictures as well as buy wigs and silk shirts. Once in the Métropole, however, the French couple does not allow her to go outside and explore France. Nevertheless, Diouana attempts to realize her idea of the West from the inside by using Western objects. During her first days in France, she wears African clothes while cleaning her employers' home, but she then changes into European clothes and wears a wig with straight hair and even high heels to clean the house. Once she realizes that her only experience will be limited to the apartment, Diouana starts wandering among its European symbols. By embracing European beauty standards, Diouana hopes to realize her dream of becoming a member of the desired Western world. She cannot achieve her dream, however, because Madame tightens her control over her maid's body. She orders Diouana to remove the high heels and hands her an apron, a gesture that signals the maid's subordinate social position.

Ken is also preoccupied with the Western body and beauty. On her first day in Europe, in one of her most traumatic experiences, she cannot resist the desire to enter a wig shop. Later on, she alternates between African and European clothing, choosing to "shock" by wearing her exoticized and eroticized African clothes, or to "belong" in her European attire. For both Ken and Diouana, what they wear and how they look are important considerations when trying to integrate the Métropole. Through the corporal experiences of putting on white masks, the women awaken to their racialized female bodies, eventually discovering what Fanon calls "corporeal malediction." This malediction refers to a negative conception of "blackness" as "ugliness" that derives from racist European theories, which early African texts, like Négritude literature, counteracted.

In addition, the protagonists realize that gender plays an important part in their experience of the West. This factor complicates their case considerably. While writers have often represented the black man's experience in Europe as a soldier, worker, or student, Ken Bugul provides an entirely different perspective by writing the story of a black woman. If the only model of Western experience is from a black male's perspective, how will the African woman know what it is to be a "Négresse" in the colonizer's land?

"La noire de . . ." literally means the "black girl of" or "the black girl from." Regarding Diouana, the cineaste Sembène Ousmane explains that "once she left the country, she lost her identity as Diouana. She became someone's black maid. She became an object belonging to a white family — their trophy" (Pfaff 120). Sembène's remarks suggest two things. First, Diouana is marked socially as a maid; as such, her name and identity do not matter. In Dakar, the relationship between whites and blacks appears to be defined mainly in terms of class — as employers and employees. According to Pfaff, "Sembène demonstrates that the social gap he denounces is not so much between blacks and whites but rather between economic classes of people" (117). In *Ousmane Sembène, Cinéaste; première période, 1962–1971* (1972), Paulin Semanou Vieyra echoes the same idea. He wonders whether *La noire de . . .* exposes racism at all (Vieyra 81). While I agree that the employee-employer relationship represents a class inequality, not a racial one, it is important to remember that the French *coopérants* — aid workers sent by the French government — are mere replacements for former colonialists. One may even argue that they are representatives of neocolonialism. Classifying them as part of the Senegalese social structure poses problems because they enjoy certain privileges as members of a perceived superior race whose position is envied and desired by former colonized people regardless of class. The status of French coopérants gives some indication of the extent to which class, race, and gender are intertwined in *La noire de . . .*

Second, Sembène explains that something happens after

Diouana's arrival in the white world: her relationship with her employer changes, and she loses her name and identity to become the white couple's object of display. This idea is similar to Fanon's contention that "le noir n'a plus à être noir, mais à l'être en face du blanc" [the black man must not only be black but he must become Black in front of the White man] (*Peau noire* 88; *Black Skin* 110). Diouana reflects constantly on the transformation in the French couple. Madame in particular is no longer nice to her the way she was in Dakar, where she generously gave the maid her old clothes and shoes. Monsieur and Madame have now become obsessed with the "authenticity" of Senegalese meals and their Senegalese maid. This obsession indicates the colonizer's nostalgia for the old, pre-independence order in Africa. In one conversation, a white man regrets that "since independence, black people have lost their natural predisposition." Ironically, the white man enforces authenticity by making Africans perform their exotic difference and wear masks that correspond to their supposedly "natural predisposition."

In another example from the film of this performance of authenticity, Madame asks Diouana to cook an authentic Senegalese dinner for French guests who apparently have never been to the colonies. Diouana remarks that Madame did not use to eat rice in Dakar. During this "exotic dinner" in which she is the servant, a guest refers to her as an animal that communicates instinctively. The hosts and the guests suggest that her food contains aphrodisiacs, while one male proceeds to "kiss a Négresse" because he has never done so. This scene reveals traditional racial and sexual stereotyping of the black woman as Diouana plays simultaneously the three roles of maid, black, and "Négresse." In light of Diouana's desire to explore the West, her labeling as "the black girl of" or "the black girl from" makes her the other, the person who comes from outside of the white world and belongs elsewhere. Prior to leaving for Europe, Diouana had offered Madame a mask as a sign of trust and appreciation. In her interior monologue, we learn that she expected Madame to provide her with the opportunity to discover the Western world.

Instead, the white couple exhibits her as a Négresse with an "ugly" yet "sexualized" body in front of their white guests.

As Diouana's awareness of race and gender develops, the descent toward self-destruction intensifies, as does the conflict between Diouana and Madame. Diouana starts to show signs of mental withdrawal, but Madame still refuses to let her go outside. She goes as far as to starve Diouana, who, in return, passively resists her bosses' domination by refusing to perform her work. The more Diouana understands her position as a black maid, the more she strips off Western clothes and objects. Eventually, she refuses to eat, and during this hunger strike, she goes back to her African clothes and natural hair. Right before she commits suicide, Diouana takes off all her clothes and puts the wig and European clothes away. "Madame lied to me," she reflects. Diouana's decision to commit the ultimate act of self-destruction signifies a desire to end all her troubles. In her final monologue, she vows to stop Madame's abuse: "Jamais plus Diouana enlève tes chaussures. Diouana, je ne serai esclave.[11] Jamais plus Madame ne me verra." [No more Diouana remove your shoes. Diouana, I will not be a slave. Madame will no longer see me] (*La noire de* . . .). As the story unfolds, Diouana's complex psychological alienation grows to the point of self-erasure.

This progressive psychological drama of denial, objectification, and erasure also plays out in *Le baobab fou*, whose objectified protagonist is Western-educated and more sophisticated than Diouana. In the second work, two events define Ken as a racialized and sexualized body. The first occurs on her very first morning in Brussels. She enters a wig store only to learn that they cannot help her because, Ken interprets, she has no face for white women's "lisse, brune, très longue et très chevelue" [sleek, brown, very long and very hairy wigs] (Bugul, *Le baobab fou* 49; *Abandoned Baobab* 37). Outside the wig shop, Ken looks at the reflection of her face in the mirror. She remarks, "J'étouffais à nouveau parce que ce regard-là, c'était mon regard" [My eyes were bulging, my skin was shiny and black, the face terrifying. I almost choked; that look there was my look] (50;

37). In this traumatic incident, Ken discovers simultaneously her otherness and its associated negative value. The scene is reminiscent of Fanon's encounter with the little boy who equates blackness with ugliness. Ken realizes that she does not "belong."

Ken's second turning point in race and gender consciousness arrives during her search for integration. In her longing to be integrated into the white world, Ken becomes romantically involved with Louis, a Belgian agronomy student. She explains: "Idylle qui me servait à m'expliquer, à m'intégrer, à montrer que j'étais comme eux: qu'il n'y avait aucune différence entre nous, que eux et moi, nous avions les mêmes ancêtres" [The romance served to explain myself, to integrate me, to show that I was like them, that there was no difference whatsoever between us, that they and I had the same ancestors] (Bugul, *Le baobab fou* 54; *Abandoned Baobab* 42). Ken's identification with the white world ends once she becomes pregnant. The experience of bearing a half-European child would have brought her another step closer toward integration, but she decides to have an abortion despite Louis' wishes. At the clinic, the abortion doctor asks her whether her sexual partner was white or black. Ken observes: "Pour la première fois, je me rendais compte qu'une femme pouvait tomber enceinte d'un Noir ou d'un Blanc." [I realized for the first time that a woman could get pregnant by either a Black man or a white man] (59; 46). During the ordeal, she suddenly becomes aware of the overdetermined meanings in Louis' whiteness and her own blackness. The racist white doctor's attitude compels her to detest his white skin and that of her lover. Ken believes that the abortion kills her symbolically, for if the scene at the wig store taught her to hate her black skin, the trip to the clinic taught her to hate white skin. She learns the divisive racial discourse in the context of the Métropole. The symbolic death announces the end of innocence and the end of Ken, who had assimilated misleading images of the West.

Realizing that the Gauls were not her ancestors after all, Ken abandons her studies and begins a life among social outcasts in a world of drugs, alcohol, artists, homosexuality, and prostitution. Even among the outcasts, however, she continues to encounter racism. Although she lives during the era of Western civil rights and feminist movements, Ken rejects them by stating that they still "expose her," thereby amplifying her identity crisis. Like the "overdetermined" black man in *Peau noire, masques blancs*, Ken declares, "Partout, j'étais la seule Noire, certes pas l'ambassadrice du peuple noir, mais à défaut des Pygmées ou de Masaï à moitié nus, celle qui délirait avec eux Blancs, dans une peau noire." [Everywhere I went I was the only black woman, and surely not as ambassador of black people but, as there were not Pygmies or half-naked Masaï, I was the one to carry on with them, the white folks, in my black skin] (Bugul, *Le baobab fou* 101; *Abandoned Baobab* 84). Fanon mentions this tokenism in *Peau noire*, where he writes: "J'étais tout à la fois responsible de mon corps, responsible de ma race, des mes ancêtres" [I was responsible at the same time for my body, for my race, my ancestors] (90; *Black Skin* 112).

Just as it became fashionable during the American civil rights movement for whites to develop friendships with blacks, the "Négresse" became very popular in Belgium and elsewhere after the wave of independence for most Francophone African countries. Like Diouana's employers, Ken's white friends do not miss an opportunity to display her wherever they go. She remarks that at a time when "black womanhood covered the pages of fashion and pornography magazines," Ken feels exposed, stripped, emptied, and displayed by her white friends: "Ils me dépouillaient, me vidaient, m'étalaient." [They were stripping me, emptying me out, displaying me] (Bugul, *Le baobab fou* 102; *Abandoned Baobab* 85). Bugul's words echo Fanon's statement, cited earlier in this chapter, that in front of the whites the black man feels like his body has been "étalé, disjoint, rétamé" ["sprawled out, distorted, recolored] (*Peau noire* 91; *Black Skin* 113). Ken is led to exploit the times by prostituting herself, cashing in on her black womanhood. Someone tells her, "Tu es une noire et tu es belle. Il faut que tu exploites cela." [You are black and you are beautiful. You should exploit that] (Bugul, *Le baobab fou* 120; *Abandoned Baobab* 101). A product of consumption herself, Ken consciously promotes the stereotypical image of the erotic and exotic black woman. For instance, she organizes dinners and exotic games around African themes through which she consciously enacts her race and gender. Like Diouana, Ken is required to play what she calls "le jeu de l'occident" [the Western game] (71; 57), in which she has to display an "authentic" identity as a black woman. This refers to Homi Bhabha's concept of "mimicry," which he explains as "a representation of a difference that is itself a process of disavowal" ("Of Mimicry and Man" 129). Ken's desire to emerge as "authentic" occurs through mimicry that "repeats rather than re-presents" (Bhabha, "Of Mimicry and Man" 128) the required display of false and ironic authenticity.

Their movement in and out of the white world exhausts the two characters both physically and mentally. Although Ken does not commit suicide like Diouana, the end of the novel suggests that she has become seriously mentally alienated from Western society. But can Ken or Diouana return home? To answer this question, let us look at some particularities of the two characters. This study does not contend that the two works are identical. The two female protagonists have significantly divergent experiences of race and gender consciousness. Although Ken and Diouana are attracted by similar "beautiful" images of the Métropole, the backgrounds that inform their experiences are clearly different. Apart from education, they come from distinct family situations. For Ken, colonialism and "becoming a black woman in the Métropole" are not her only problems. In fact, the novel indicates that Ken was already traumatized prior to her trip. In playing the "Western game," she looks for a way to "straighten things out" with her ancestors, the Gauls. Finding these ancestors will help solve her identity problem by giving her a history that her family failed to provide. Her mother abandoned her, and her blind father never gave her any family history. When the West rejects her, Ken's alienation becomes further complicated by the fact that she cannot truly go back. At the end of the story, a severely distraught Ken goes back to her native village in an attempt to recover her history. She had hoped to go to the baobab tree, the novel's metaphor for the heroine's roots. But while she was busy making a "detour" in the Métropole, the baobab tree died, along with her history.

In Diouana's case, her continued physical and mental incarceration and torture — name calling and starvation — add to her alienation and push her over the edge. Some critics have considered the suicide a victory, a conscious act of refusal to become a physical and mental prisoner in the Métropole. At least two scenes at the book's end contradict this interpretation of Diouana's suicide as a victorious act. In the first, her death seems to be particularly unimportant, as people in the Métropole continue to tan on the beach, paying no attention to the news item that announces the suicide of a nameless and homeless young "Négresse." After his sister's death, however, Diouana's brother puts on a mask and starts haunting his sister's French employer. This mask is the same one that Diouana had given to Madame and then, as a sign of mistrust in her employers, eventually took back. This second scene, as Vieyra and Pfaff have noticed, implies not only the white man's guilt but also the lack of resolution and reconciliation between the two parties.

Another major difference between the two protagonists lies in the way in which they respond to the enforced authenticity in the Métropole. Diouana's ultimate act of suicide is also an act of resistance against conforming to the imperialist's idea of an "authentic" African female. The ambiguous ending of *Le baobab fou* can be read as a failure on Ken's part to escape from the "Western game," into which she sometimes finds herself drawn and which she even consciously enacts. Indeed, Ken continues to seek admittance to the West despite continued failures to do so.[12] The differences in the experiences of the two characters are therefore as important to understanding their individual stories as the similarities.

What conclusions can we draw from these examples? Based on

the evidence from these two narratives, gender is clearly a major component in the complex situation that develops when an African woman goes to Europe. The two stories expose the absence of women's experiences in theories of colonialism, decolonization, and neocolonialism. Through Ken and Diouana, the prevalent images of the "Négresse" emerge: she is a black woman who shares stereotypical attributes with black men, as some of the early literature about the Métropole demonstrates. Once in the West, however, the black female protagonist has different kinds of encounters than her male counterparts. The two works directly target the exclusion of gender as a considerable factor in the alienation of the female protagonist. The individual experiences of Diouana and Ken suggest that theories about the encounter between Europe and Africa based on the experience of black males cannot describe sufficiently the experience of displaced female protagonists. Bugul uses Ken to ask, "Pourquoi n'avoir pas prévu la réaction de la femme noire au colonialisme?" [Why hadn't they foreseen the black woman's reaction to neocolonialism?] (*Le baobab fou* 113; *Abandoned Baobab* 96–97). This question summarizes the black woman's frustration over the failure of decolonizing theories to incorporate the impact of colonialism on the black female psyche. Ken and Diouana share their desire for the Western body with the protagonist in Mayotte Capécia's *Je suis martiniquaise*. In his reading of the novel, Fanon dismisses the expression of the black female's experience of colonial traumas as apolitical. An analysis of Ken's and Diouana's experiences reveals that this dismissal is misguided because both the novel and the film contain a strong critique of Western societies and of colonialism, and they examine sexual politics in the larger context of the colonial world. It is also important to point out that this gendered view of the colonial experience does not depend on the author's sex. While Fanon displays ignorance in dismissing the female colonial subject, Sembène Ousmane's depiction of Diouana demonstrates his ability to capture a uniquely female case of colonial trauma.

In fictional portrayals most black female characters are eager to whiten themselves and their offspring. This is especially true of characters in Caribbean settings, as exemplified by Fanon's essays and the poetry of the Négritude movement. The following are a few observations on *Cajou* as a possible literary response to Fanon.

Colonial Neurosis: Lacrosil's Response to Fanon

Reviewing Lacrosil's literary contributions, Frederick Ivor Case asserts that she is often seen as a minor writer, "a writer whose work is so personal that it is of little social importance and a writer who is so steeped in her own psychological complexes that her characters have little chance of rising above their deep suicidal introspection" (30). Case's statement emphasizes how so-called personal writings are often critically defined as being apolitical and therefore of minimal literary value. Lacrosil attempts to undermine this claim by engaging in a discussion with fellow intellectuals and writers like Frantz Fanon. Like Fanon, Lacrosil attempts to dissect the Caribbean psychology, only she does so through the psychological complexity of characters such as Cajou. She is also preoccupied with the Caribbean female mind, but she arrives at very different conclusions than Fanon.

The structure and the language of *Cajou* constitute a strong reference to Fanon's influence, and the novel's atmosphere is reminiscent of his approach. Lacrosil specifically addresses the issue of whether colonial neurosis – a result of the systematic repression of the desires of the colonized – is curable. She makes specific references to psychological life in the novel. While *Le baobab fou* follows a black woman's descent toward madness, *Cajou* describes a black woman's agonizing attempt to get out of this colonial neurosis. Because of the oppressive nature of colonial culture, the colonized are forced to repress any desire to learn about their own culture. The mother and the psychiatrist, for example, contributed to Cajou's neurosis. Implicit in Lacrosil's choice of a psychiatrist as the ultimate repressor-oppressor is the possibility that she was referring to Fanon, who was a psychiatrist. Some artifacts and clichéd scenarios highlight this psychiatric decor. Most of Cajou's reminiscing occurs in her enclosed boarding room, in which we find the stereotypical "divan" [sofa] (79) and "oreillers" [pillows] (80).[13] Germain, Cajou's boyfriend, functions as a psychiatrist who attempts to "cure" her by listening to her with "la tête penchée, les coudes sur les genoux" [his head leaning, his elbows on his knees] while making his own "confession." Cajou sits "au fond du divan-lit" [deep on the sofa], where she can see "un coin de sa joue" [a corner of his cheek] (79). In this role, Germain tries to repair the damage done by the first psychiatrist: he asks Cajou to talk about her father because "il y va de ta santé" [your health depends on it] (213).

It is in this "safe" environment that Cajou revisits her childhood and young adulthood. Unlike Mayotte, who enjoys whiteness in her blood thanks to her white maternal grandmother, Cajou considers her "métissage" a burden. This is the privileged moment in which the heroine enters a world of neurosis, when, as Fanon theorizes, "le nègre esclave de son infériorité, le Blanc esclave de sa supériorité, se comportent tous les deux selon une ligne d'orientation névrotique" [the Negro enslaved by his own inferiority, the white man enslaved by his superiority alike behave in accordance with a neurotic orientation] (*Peau noire* 48; *Black Skin* 60). The psychiatrist diagnoses Cajou with "complexe de frustration" [frustration disorder] and "syndrome dépressif" [depressive syndrome] (Lacrosil 47) as well as "obsession dangereuse" [dangerous obsession] (44). The psychiatrist recommends that the mother avoid talking about her father, the migration of her ancestors, and "questions raciales" [race questions] (41). In addition, he suggests that Cajou seek the company of young children like herself, a prescription that had the following effect:

> A dix ans, ce que je savais ou je me figurais au sujet des problèmes de l'hérédité des êtres, et le sentiment de ma propre laideur, étaient pour moi des obsessions. Un psychiatre a recommandé la fréquentation des fillettes de mon âge. C'est ainsi que Stéphanie Bajères est entrée dans ma vie; j'en ai construit sur elle ma conception de la beauté

> physique et mes rêves; elle n'a pas tardé à me devenir nécessaire. Je désirais la priver de toute autre amitié, l'étouffer et, parfois, la blesser ou l'enlaidir.
>
> [At ten years old, what I knew or what I figured about problems of heredity of beings, and the feeling about my own ugliness, were obsessions for me. A psychiatrist recommended that I associate with little girls of my age. That is how Stephanie Bajeres came into my life; I built my concept of physical beauty and my dreams around her; before long she became indispensable to me. I wanted to deprive her of all other friendships, to smother her and, at times, to hurt or to disfigure her.] (Lacrosil 63–64)

The influence of psychoanalysis on Lacrosil's work is further illustrated in the adult Cajou's repetition of her initial trauma. On several occasions, Cajou recreates the triangular relationship that started between herself, the mother, and the psychiatrist. Following Freud's Oedipus complex, the psychiatrist (as the father) enters the symbiotic relationship between the mother and the child as the disruptive third element of the new triangle. In this context, it is highly suggestive that the white psychiatrist comes to take the place of the dead black father. The other triangular relationship involves Cajou, Stéphanie, and a third schoolmate, Jacqueline. Jacqueline enters the relationship when she invites Stéphanie to a party but fails to do the same for Cajou. This incident terminates the friendship between Stéphanie and Cajou.

As an adult, it is Cajou's triangular relationship with Marjolaine and Germain that leads her to search for answers. Marjolaine and Cajou end their relationship when Germain interferes, first as Marjolaine's love interest and then as Cajou's lover. In addition to playing the role of the psychiatrist, Germain occasionally reminds Cajou of her mother in the way he speaks (204). These roles, combined with the fact that he is her lover, make Germain Cajou's ultimate colonial oppressor. As noted by Isabelle Gros, critics often fail to analyze what she calls "la maladie de Germain" [Germain's malady] (126). This oversight is mostly attributable to the fact that

Cajou believes she deserves Germain's sadistic behavior because she is a descendant of the slaves. Germain repeatedly violates her by forcibly kissing her (155) and raping her (181–83), and he tortures her psychologically about the true nature of her relationship with Marjolaine, among other things. The threat of a possible homosexual relationship between the two women leads Germain to control all facets of Cajou's life, including her workplace, where he manages to find a job.[14] He is indeed "le maître de la situation" [the master of the situation] (164). He comes between the two women by letting Cajou know that she will need his help in order to see Marjolaine again. He tells her: "Il faut que tu sois gentille pour revoir Marjo" [you have got to be nice if you want to see Marjo again] (164).

As noted by Condé, however, "Le couple Germain/Cajou est l'illustration du couple victime/bourreau alors même que ce dernier n'assume qu'imparfaitement son rôle et serait prêt à l'abandonner" [The duo Germain and Cajou illustrates the victim/perpetrator relationship although the former plays his role imperfectly and is ready to abandon it] (*La parole* 32). Indeed, Germain confesses his imperfections to Cajou in an unsuccessful attempt to convince her to marry him. Cajou is never swayed by his effort to bring in the crowd — the white crowd. In fact, the opposite seems true. The more Germain insists that she overstates her problem, the more reluctant Cajou is to enter the white race by way of marriage. She maintains that white society will always reject her.

Perhaps the strongest subtext linking Fanon and Lacrosil is the implicit intertextuality between *Cajou* and Mayotte Capécia's *Je suis martiniquaise*. In his analysis of the text, Fanon bases the discussion on the heroine's concluding remarks: "J'aurais voulu me marier, mais avec un blanc. Seulement une femme de couleur n'est jamais tout à fait respectable aux yeux d'un blanc. Même s'il l'aime, je le savais." [I would have liked to get married, but with a white man. It is only that a woman of color is never respectable in the eyes of the white man. Even if he loves her, I knew that] (Capécia 202). Fanon contends that in such cases the black woman merely seeks to fulfill her natural desire for the white man. In his criticism of the novel, though strong and significant regarding interpersonal relationships between black men and black women, Fanon fails to see beyond the black woman's need to "whiten herself." But the novel offers much more than that. *Je suis martiniquaise* is first and foremost a coming of age story about a character who, like most Antillean blacks, grew up idealizing the white race. A product of a black father and a "métisse," Mayotte is very proud of her white grandmother. She learns the hard way what an older schoolmate had told her as a young girl — that "La vie est difficile pou' une femme, tu ve'as, Mayotte, su'tout pou' une femme de couleu" [Life is difficult for a woman, you will see Mayotte, especially for a woman of color] (Capécia 20). As a young girl, Mayotte idealized a young priest because of his blond hair and blue eyes. As a child, she learns to equate beauty with whiteness and decides that she will love a white man (Capécia 59). She later becomes involved romantically with a white marine officer, André, whom Mayotte thinks is no more handsome than the other men who have courted her such as Horace, the black Martiniquan who took her virginity. Mayotte ends the relationships with Horace because "Le souvenir de mon père me faisait un peu mépriser cet amour physique que mon corps réclamait. En outre, j'étais fière. Je ne voulais plus toucher à ces hommes de couleur qui ne peuvent s'empêcher de courir après toutes les femmes et je savais que les blancs n'épousent pas une femme noire" [The memory of my father made me despise this physical love that my body desired. In addition, I was proud. I no longer wanted to touch these men of color who cannot refrain from going after women and I knew that white men did not marry black women] (Capécia 131).

Mayotte's rejection of black men owes in part to memories of her philandering, irresponsible father.[15] But her aspiration to whiteness is also a result of the colonial legacy. Her choice of a white man produces disappointing results, as Mayotte can never truly expect to stay with André. In addition, family and friends accuse her of betraying the black race (Capécia 191). To her surprise, Mayotte finds herself alone in her belief that white is better, a fantasy she upholds through the son she shares with André. While Fanon criticizes Mayotte the writer for her unwillingness to rid herself of the inferiority complex, he neglects the complexity of interactions between blacks and whites. Lacrosil creates a character whose blackness is only skin-deep, because as Patricia Barber-Williams remarks, Cajou is a "coloured girl with a 'white' state of mind" (11). The author removes all things black from the heroine's environment. The black father is long deceased, and Cajou's mother is forced to abide by "la loi du père" [the law of the father] – that is, the white Father, represented by the psychiatrist. Lacrosil provides us with a different scenario: What happens when, suddenly, the black woman's wish not only to have the white man's child but also to marry him becomes a reality? Is accepting the white man's offer enough to cure a lifelong mental disease that has affected Cajou since childhood?

Cajou consciously questions her involvement with a white man and her unborn child. She ponders whether marrying Germain and having his child will solve her problems. Will the mirrors and the eyes of the Other reflect a satisfying image of herself? Will she be able to marry the two sides of her ambiguity and become a unified self? Finally, the only flight left for her is suicide (205). This outcome is embedded in the nature of black colonial neurosis, defined by Fanon as a "tentative de fuir son individualité, de néantiser son être-là" [an attempt to flee one's individuality, to suppress the self] (*Peau noire* 48; *Black Skin* 60). The normal course for fleeing one's social problems is to leave the island, but Cajou does not have this option because she is already in France. For this reason, the likelihood that she will commit suicide is strong. In fact, the desire for self-annulment informs the entire novel. The protagonist considers suicide as a possible outcome of her introspection. As the novel progresses, she begins to prefer death to repeating the past in the future (188) because she will always be an "outsider" (200).[16] Toward the end of the novel, Cajou's disease worsens. She starts to hear "une phrase musicale" [a musical phrase] that says "DIA-SPO-RA" (199), a word that grows more and more confusing, hammering, and disturbing. The word becomes synonymous with "dispersion," "dissolution," and "destruction" (209).

Some critics have suggested that the scene of Cajou drowning herself in the Seine River symbolizes her attempt to drown the "ugly" image of herself. Her death is therefore a victory because the heroine manages to repossess her body (Paravisini-Gebert 69). However, we do not know whether Cajou actually commits suicide or if her attempt to kill herself will amount to another failure. While *Le baobab fou*'s Ken sinks deeper into madness, Cajou is already afflicted with colonial neurosis because of similar forms of repression. An analysis of *Cajou* reveals a woman who, despite being immersed in white culture to the point of being sick, attempts to secure a satisfying identity for herself. If in the past, scholars focused on race- and gender-specific social and psychological traumas in the context of Métropole-Caribbean relations, the present study demonstrates that female protagonists from Africa experience those types of traumas as well. Cajou, Diouana, and Ken constitute thought-provoking examples of metropolitan encounters during a specific moment in the history of European-African and French-Caribbean relations — namely, the postindependence era. More recent immigration literature testifies to the intricate nature of contemporary African female encounters with the West. During the last few decades, French society has experienced considerable stress as a result of changing attitudes and policies that affect immigrants in France. The problem is too often framed as a series of stark dualities: black-white, Europe-Africa, rich-poor. As the three narratives compared in this study suggest, however, the differences emanating from the encounter between Europe and Africa are more complex than these binaries imply. If they want to grasp fully the impact of that encounter, scholars cannot ignore gender.

3

Writing Familial Violence

Storytelling and Intergenerational Violence in Simone Schwarz-Bart's *Pluie et vent sur Télumée Miracle* and Calixthe Beyala's *Tu t'appelleras Tanga*

In her article "Sheroes and Villains: Conceptualizing Colonial and Contemporary Violence against Women in Africa," Amina Mama locates the source of contemporary African models of patriarchal violence in colonial states. These states not only used the famous colonial formula "Ayons les femmes et le reste suivra" [Let's win over women and the men will follow] ("L'Algérie se dévoile" 18; "Algeria Unveiled" 37) but also adopted European concepts of womanhood such as repressive domestication. Patriarchal violence combines European models of violence against women with models of patriarchal oppression that existed both before and after colonialism. As Mama argues, colonialism "humiliated" African women not simply as "colonial subjects" but specifically as women. According to her findings, "African nationalist discourses have often proclaimed the need to recover the damaged manhood of the African man," relegating the role of salvaging African manhood to the African woman, who was seen as the bearer and the upholder of traditions and customs (Mama 54). I agree with Mama's assertion that "the oppression of women within Europe had a direct bearing on the treatment of women in the colonies" and rendered "African women more vulnerable to the violence emanating from both European and African sources" (Mama 49). But as my analysis of *Cajou* and *Le baobab fou* demonstrates, a discussion of patriarchal violence requires us to look beyond imperial sources. Anticolonial movements did nothing to restore women's dignity or to identify colonialism as a common trauma for both men and women. In this chapter, I continue gauging the specificity of women's narratives by exploring female victimization through socially sanctioned patriarchal violence. Beyond analyzing the nature of private traumas such as domestic violence and abuse, this chapter examines the work of women writers who employ female protagonists to explore how female subjectivities survive through storytelling.

Central to my analysis is the dynamics of female generational relationships, in particular how each female generation survives engendered violence. An examination of Simone Schwarz-Bart's *Pluie et vent sur Télumée Miracle* (published in English as *The Bridge of Beyond*) and Calixthe Beyala's *Tu t'appelleras Tanga* (*Your Name Shall Be Tanga*), reveals how women perceive violence in their lives and empower themselves through the act of storytelling.[1] Both novels recount stories of pain and suffering incurred because of violent and traumatic events in the heroines' lives. Does storytelling constitute a mechanism for healing? Does the medium serve to protect future female generations from violence? In Bugul's *Le baobab fou* and Lacrosil's *Cajou*, female characters are on the verge of madness and suicide. In the previous chapter, I argued that the writers' main characters, Ken and Cajou, blame colonial violence for their plight. The heroines explicitly accuse their mothers of either abandoning them (*Le baobab fou*) or purposefully denying them a part of their black identity (*Cajou*). For Ken, her mixed feelings of hate and desire toward her mother lie in contrast to the feelings generated by the trope of "Mother Africa," in which the African mother embodies continuity in the face of disruptive colonization. Florence Stratton posits that the trope "is deeply entrenched in the male literary tradition" (Stratton 39), starting with Léopold Sédar Senghor. In his poem "Femme noire," for instance, Senghor equates the mother's body with the promised land, a safe place that guarantees continuity for Africans.[2] Female protagonists have reacted differently to the recurrence of the "Mother" trope. In *Le baobab fou*, Ken Bugul imagines a heroine who discovers during her relentless identity quest that her mother does not fit the image suggested by Mother Africa. She is instead an absentee who does not provide her daughter with any sense of continuity. In her text, Bugul describes Ken's trauma as the result of a lack of communication between the character and previous female generations.

Bugul offers a rare examination of the effect of colonial disruption on female generations. According to Odile Cazenave, mother-daughter relationships have not been explored in African literature because "si l'on examine la littérature africaine des années 60 à 80 la mère est toujours présentée comme la mère du fils, jamais de la fille" [if we examine African literature from the '60s to the '80s the mother is always presented as the mother of the son, never of the daughter] (Cazenave 142–43). However, African women writers such as Mariama Bâ allude to the specific difficulties mothers experience when raising daughters. Ramatoulaye, the main character in Bâ's epistolary novel, *Une si longue lettre*, wonders how much freedom to give to her daughters as the generational gap widens. Calixthe Beyala describes conflicts of even greater intensity between mother and daughter as well as how complicity between mother and daughter collapses when the boundaries between "woman-child" and "woman" are not clearly defined. In *Tanga*, for instance, Beyala refers to women in binary terms: "La vieille ma mère," "l'enfant-parent," "l'enfant-pute," "femme-fillette" [The old my mother, the parent child, the child prostitute, the woman-girlchild]. As Juliana Makuchi Nfah-Abbenyi notes, the use of binary terms "is a discursive act that . . . discloses their hyphenated identities as a reflection of the hierarchical society in which they live" (85). The mother, as a figure of authority, becomes the patriarchal messenger sent to enforce the rule of the father. I will add that Beyala's binary terms also complicate the stages of female identity formation between childhood and womanhood. For instance, Beyala sets Tanga, the title character of *Tu t'appelleras Tanga*, as a young daughter who must prostitute herself to provide for her family, finding herself paradoxically in a situation in which she must be the parent to her mother who would lead the family.

In the context of Caribbean literature, the mother has not consistently been the symbol of familial continuity. Like the African mother, she is responsible for raising her children; unlike the African mother, whose role it is to keep the traditions alive across generations, the Caribbean mother has been accused of being the agent of cultural disruption, trying to turn her children into Europeans.[3] In *Pluie et vent sur Télumée Miracle*, Simone Schwarz-Bart makes the mother of the heroine Télumée absent from her daughter's life, but Télumée never longs for her because her grandmother, Toussine, fills the mother's role. Unlike Télumée, Beyala's character Tanga does not benefit from the presence of her own grandmother because the older woman is a victim who later passes on her violent legacy to her own daughter.

In *Pluie et vent* (1979), one of the best-known and most studied novels in Caribbean Francophone literature, Schwarz-Bart follows the lives of the Lougandor women. In the text, the author establishes extensive and powerful links between the protagonist, Télumée, and her grandmother, Toussine Lougandor. Télumée goes through periods of happiness with her grandmother and marital bliss with her husband Elie. She also experiences unhappiness when her marriage crumbles because of severe domestic abuse, amplified by the community's critical gaze. In the end, Télumée manages to live happily after intensive mentoring by Toussine and Man Cia, the sorcerer-healer of the village.

Tanga (1988), Calixthe Beyala's second novel, lacks such female mentors. Applying the same rich and complex narrative strategies that made her first novel, *C'est le soleil qui m'a brûlée* (1987), a success, Beyala depicts a Cameroonian female genealogy in which generations are linked by violence. The protagonist is a seventeen-year-old girl named Tanga who is also called "femme-fillette" (literally "woman-little girl" or "woman-girlchild") because she is forced to grow up fast in a family that can only be characterized as dysfunctional. While dying in a prison cell, Tanga shares her story with a fellow inmate, Anna-Claude, a European woman. In "telling" her story, Tanga filters it through her body to Anna-Claude's, who later "becomes" the young black woman.

Significant temporal and spatial differences characterize the two novels. *Pluie et vent* is set in Guadeloupe around the beginning of the twentieth century, while *Tanga* is set in contemporary Iningué, a Cameroonian shantytown. Yet the texts bear striking parallels. Both writers chose to tell stories set in and around familial and domestic spaces to examine violent acts and their impact on a postcolonial (*Tanga*) and a post-slavery (*Pluie et vent*) family. Both narratives are concerned with the interconnectedness of intergenerational female lives and the influence of past female generations' experience on the intricate nature of women's destiny. In the novels, the writers explore themes of hardship, survival, and empowerment through female solidarity and storytelling. In the next section, I examine different types of violence or violent acts in the two narrative works as a preliminary step to studying the discourse of survival. The analysis addresses the experience of trauma and its violent consequences on the black female psyche.

Stories of Violence

In their novels, Schwarz-Bart and Beyala portray underlying forms of violence particular to each society and era. In *Pluie et vent*, Télumée, like some former slaves and their families, is forced to go back to work for the Desaragnes, a white family composed of descendants of former slave owners that embodies, according to the sorcerer

Man Cia, the status of masters. Man Cia tells Télumée that "si tu veux voir à quoi ressemble un maître, . . . tu n'as qu'à aller à Galba, à l'habitation Belle-feuille, chez les Desaragne. Ce ne sont que leurs descendants mais tu pourras te faire une idée" [if you want to know what a master is like, you've only to go to Galba, to the Desaragnes' house at Belle-Feuille. They're only descendants, but it will give you an idea] (Schwarz-Bart, *Pluie et vent* 60; *Bridge of Beyond* 37). Schwarz-Bart depicts the young woman in a post-slavery environment where the female character Télumée still endures physical, sexual, and psychological violence similar to, if not as severe as, that experienced by her enslaved ancestors. Télumée is continuously subjected to Mme Desaragne's dehumanizing comments about her and black people in general. She reflects: "J'étais maintenant entourée d'yeux métalliques, perçants, lointains sous lesquels je n'existais pas" [I was surrounded now with piercing, steely distant, eyes under whose gaze I didn't exist] (Schwarz-Bart, *Pluie et vent* 91–92: *Bridge of Beyond* 60). In addition, Télumée must endure M. Desaragne's sexual advances, which culminate in an attempt to rape her.

Schwarz-Bart also emphasizes the existence of economic violence in which plantation slavery is replaced by the peonage of the sugarcane fields and factories. Ex-slaves and their descendants live in poverty and must work in unbearable conditions in the Usine Galba factory. The factory possesses not only their miserable dwellings but also the workers themselves (188). The images of sweat and the workers' attempts to escape their miserable life through singing, dancing, and drinking rum reenact the atmosphere of slavery. Amboise, one of Télumée's suitors, states that "les nègres suent tellement que les femmes de blancs en sont fatiguées, rien qu'à voir la sueur" [The Negroes sweat so much that the white men's wives are tired just to see it] (Schwarz-Bart, *Pluie et vent* 205; *Bridge of Beyond* 140). The workers endure slavery-era working conditions and caning from the masters while white people look on. Schwarz-Bart reveals how the Desaragnes maintain their ancestors' negative attitudes and apply them toward children of former slaves.

Finally, Télumée's maroon community experiences violent acts such as murder as well as nature's temper.[4] Télumée loses the two men with whom she had a special bond (her stepfather Angebert and her lover Amboise) to murderous accidents, while a fire disrupts Toussine's happiness by killing one of her children and dispossessing her of her property.

Unlike Schwarz-Bart, Beyala does not make such overt links between contemporary violence and violent events in the past, such as those under colonial rule. By creating Anna-Claude, Beyala attempts to sketch close and positive relationships between African women and women from former colonial powers. She had a similar goal in other works, including *Lettre d'une africaine à ses soeurs occidentales* (1995). In *Tanga*, the writer relates examples of postindependence violence in Africa including political unrest and economic inequality, types of violence that are particularly harsh in the slums of Iningué. Anna-Claude is a teacher who is dissatisfied with her own country and travels to Africa in search of Ousmane, an imaginary ideal man (Beyala, *Tanga* 9; *Your Name* 3). She is arrested while staging a political protest in response to the disappearance of her African students, who vanished after holding a rally against the government. The police labels Anna-Claude an "Elément subversif et incontrôlable" [a subversive and uncontrollable element] (13; 6). In prison, she becomes Tanga's unlikely ally. Whether as its victim or its spectator, Tanga constantly encounters violence. She is arrested, abused, and violated by police. As Beyala conceives of it, Tanga's world is filled with violence at different levels, in and outside of her family. The writer depicts a community that is killing its own children. In one surreal scene, for instance, she shows Tanga lying on a butcher's table, offering her body as the animal for slaughter. In the character's eyes, she is just "une bête de somme" [a beast of burden] (109; 66), alluding to her sexual and economic exploitation. Tanga sees herself persecuted by the community symbolized in the butcher, a community that mistreats its children. In addition to these examples, the discourse on political violence includes incidents of physical and verbal abuse by prison guards. But perhaps the strongest narrative innovation in Beyala's *Tanga* is the rich discourse on familial violence.

Writing Familial Violence

Before Calixthe Beyala, description of African female sexuality was rare. The initial response to her writings was that of shock. Emmanuel Matateyou even wonders if Beyala's portrayal of female sexual scenes is not pornographic, particularly with regard to Ateba, the main character in *C'est le soleil qui m'a brûlée*. As previously noted, Beyala replies that such scenes are part of everyday gendered violence:" "A woman sold or prostituted; a dictator who goes in the street, meets a man and shoots him in the head. They are exactly the same thing" (Matateyou 609). The discourse on violence in most African and Caribbean fiction by male writers has addressed violence within the public arena — an area dominated by anticolonial themes, political and economic violence, and civil or international wars.[5] However, it is important to note that gender violence has been and is still an issue debated by several international organizations. Feminist activists have fought to define gender violence — of which girls and women are disproportionately victims — as a development and human rights issue. In a 1991 report on human rights and women's rights, Charlotte Bunch and Roxanna Carrilo demonstrate that domestic violence is indeed a civil rights issue. Most feminists engage women's and international human rights issues involving child and female prostitution, rape as a weapon of war, and female genital mutilation.

Given this recent interest in gender violence and human rights, literature offers a unique medium in which to debate women's perspectives on violence. Unlike official reports, it provides an excellent means to explore individual traumas and victimized female subjectivities. Through fictional characters, women writers can creatively expose violence that occurs in the private sphere: within the home, among family members, and between husbands and wives. The impulse that Beyala resists, as evidenced by her statement on politics and sex, is to separate the private and the public domains of life. Critics have often dismissed women's works, writing off female concerns as private and therefore apolitical. Beyala's words bluntly tell us that for women writers, writing about private matters means writing about politics. Both *Pluie et vent* and *Tanga* have lifted the silence that usually surrounds private occurrences of violence such as wife and child beating, rape, incest, and forced prostitution. In *Tanga* Calixthe Beyala goes further by creating female characters that enact violence on other women, specifically their own children. Both writers demonstrate the interconnectedness of public and private violence and their effect on social and psychic life.

Social scientists define the parameters of family violence to include a variety of forms of abuse, violence, and aggressiveness between family members. Sociologists also recognize that "awareness of family violence varies between societies, depending on the political, social, economic, and cultural milieu of the country" (Gelles and Cornell 3). In Africa, the Caribbean, and elsewhere, most societies accept or tolerate certain types of family violence. Cultural norms legitimate violent activity within the family that would be considered a violation if it occurred in public situations (Gelles and Cornell 31). Typically, this acceptable "family violence" has particular ramifications for women within the household. The patriarchal hierarchy of most, if not all, modern societies has led to a culturally legitimized marital hierarchy in which wives are subordinate to their husbands. This social structure sanctions violence against women, resulting in humiliation, severe and frequent beating, and possibly even death (Gelles and Cornell 121). In the last decade, women's and children's rights movements have brought family violence into the open, but in many societies, the private nature of domestic violence and child abuse means that most cases are hidden and silenced.

Beyala and Schwarz-Bart include these silenced forms of familial and domestic violence. In their texts, men often commit physical, verbal, sexual, and psychological abuses in the so-called private arena. Schwarz-Bart devotes a large portion of the book to describing domestic violence and its effect on the main character. Télumée endures the "traditional" wife beating, which evolves into the severe, ongoing psychological torment perpetrated by Elie. In *Tanga* Beyala depicts physical and psychological torment and blackmail, utilized both by Tanga's philanderer father and by her unhappy, sexually promiscuous mother. In writing Tanga's story of familial violence, Beyala goes beyond spousal abuse and introduces us to a dysfunctional African family in which the father sexually violates Tanga while her mother keeps quiet, eventually forcing the child into prostitution for economic reasons. In *Pluie et vent*, domestic abuse seems natural to Elie, the perpetrator. He promises to show Télumée what a woman is for: "je te ferai connaître ce que signifie le mot femme sur la terre et tu te rouleras et tu crieras, comme une femme roule et crie quand on la manie bien" [I am going to teach you what the word woman means, and you'll roll on the ground and scream, as a woman does roll and scream when she's handled right] (Schwarz-Bart, *Pluie et vent* 158; *Bridge of Beyond* 108). Some members of the maroon community seem to agree with Elie's attitude, including Laetitia, his lover. She tells Télumée that "la seule place d'une négresse sur la terre est au cimetière" [the only place on earth that belongs to a Negress is in the graveyard] (165; 113). Beverly Ormerod locates "Elie's fall into despair and violence" in "the earlier motif of 'West Indian madness,'" which as she indicates, can also be found in the story of Germain and that of Ange Médard.

Although Schwarz-Bart may seem to naturalize such violence by connecting it to madness caused by climate and the economy, she still paints it as inexcusable.[6] Through Toussine's and Man Cia's voices, we understand Elie's violence as an abomination arising from his spiritual fallout. At the same time, the women see his behavior as merely a temporary occurrence. Armed with Man Cia's supernatural power, the two women at first believe that they can help stop the abuse. When that fails, Toussine eventually advises Télumée to leave her husband. Télumée's community shares an underlying understanding that domestic abuse is one form of human suffering that haunts the former slaves. In fact, fatalism seems to reign over the people as they always anticipate something bad happening. As Mireille Rosello suggests, it seems that their common enemy is none other than life itself, which is always playing bad tricks on them (75). In a way, they all feel "caged" by life at one point or another. When she is asked what a slave looks like, for example, Man Cia responds by telling Télumée to go to the market and look at a caged chicken waiting to die (60; 37). Télumée finds herself caged when she temporally loses her mind to the emotional effects of domestic violence: shame, self-blame, and desolation. Under different circumstances, both Toussine and Télumée lose their sanity: Toussine after losing her child and her possessions in a fire, and Télumée after losing Elie's trust and love. For the Lougandor women, excruciating physical and psychological pain results in temporary madness, which serves the specific purpose of purging the suffering itself. The process ends when the women triumph and come back to reason. During her own period of madness, Télumée ponders the question, what is a woman? (159; 108). Her return to reason is a victory both for herself and for everyone who supported her. In *Pluie et vent*, Schwarz-Bart demonstrates that domestic violence is not simply a private matter between a husband and a wife but has communal ramifications as well. To end it, Télumée must act on her own initiative.

In *Tanga* Beyala attempts to show how the legacy of family violence is passed on from generation to generation. Physical assault in the form of child and wife beating and sexual violence — incest, rape, and child prostitution — dominate the discourse of violence in the novel. Beyala begins the familial history of violence with the story of Princess Kadjaba Dongo, Tanga's grandmother. As a "princess," she enjoys superiority over ordinary people, particularly over men who come to court her and whom she constantly rejects. Finally, a stranger passes through the village and rapes her. As a result of this trauma, Kadjaba Dongo disassociates mentally and physically from the rest of the world and offers her body to several passing men without even looking at them. The superior "princess" has finally been subjugated by men, as if Beyala wanted to show that even a princess is not exempt from male violence. Patriarchy dictates that all women, no matter what their status, must be "handled right."

Recent attempts to explain literary representation of psychic violence help us understand Kadjaba Dongo's disassociative behavior. Critics such as Cathy Caruth, Kali Tal, and Dori Laub have helped interpret literary representations of trauma in light of the increased interest in studies of public and historical traumatic events like natural disasters, crashes, wars, and especially genocide. This interest has been reinforced by a greater understanding of the phenomenon of post-traumatic stress disorder (PTSD), defined as resulting from "a psychological distressing event that is outside the range of usual human experience."[7] In her article "Not Outside the Range: One Feminist Perspective on Psychic Trauma," Laura S. Brown argues that discussions on trauma for the most part focus on public events or collective traumas like those mentioned. Meanwhile, trauma suffered by women and children as a result of a private event, like psychological, physical, and sexual abuse at home, is not accounted for as an "event that is outside the range of usual human experience." This differentiation suggests that familial violence is not a trigger for PTSD because most societies consider it to be a normal occurrence. However, Brown and other scholars question this exclusion of what Diana Russell calls "the secret trauma" of women in her book *The Secret Trauma: Incest in the Lives of Girls and Women*. Brown goes so far as to advocate that "everyday, repetitive, interpersonal events that are so often the sources of psychic pain for women" be considered "traumatic stressors" (108). In fact, women and children who have been sexually, physically, and psychologically abused display the same symptoms observed in soldiers suffering from post-traumatic stress disorders.

One important symptom of trauma is a disorder called dissociation.[8] According to the American Psychiatric Association, victims of this disorder normally experience some of the following symptoms: depression, impairment in personal and professional relationships, sexual dysfunction, anxiety, guilt, shame, self-mutilation, suicidal thoughts, amnesia or fragmented memory of traumatizing events, out-of-body experiences, psychic numbing, and withdrawal. Beyala's female characters, like many female characters in current women's narratives of violence, exhibit similar dissociative behavior. For instance, after the initial rape, Tanga's grandmother's first reaction is to engage in small talk with the rapist: "Il fait chaud aujourd'hui" [It is hot today] (41; 24). The moment she pronounces these trivial words, Kadjaba starts to disconnect from herself, her family, and her community. Because of the repetition and reenactment of the traumatic event — she lets other men penetrate her under the tree after the initial rape — Kadjaba's body and soul become progressively numb. As the narrative evolves, we see how Kadjaba's "illness" produces grave consequences for her children and grandchildren. For Beyala, the consequence of sexual violence is that Tanga's grandmother rejects both motherhood and mothering. Upon giving birth to a daughter, Daba, Kadjaba decides to abandon the child and withdraw completely from the world. This is an unusual choice for an African female protagonist, who, while rejecting the institutional patriarchal burden of motherhood, usually opts for the experience of mothering. Obioma Nnaemeka highlights the difference between motherhood as a patriarchal institution and mothering as an experience, contending that African feminists often refuse to align themselves with Western feminist thought that rejects motherhood. Nnaemeka concludes: "The arguments that are made for motherhood in the African texts are based not on motherhood as a patriarchal institution but motherhood as an experience (mothering) with its pains and rewards" (5).

In the text, Kadjaba's refusal to mother her child, coupled with the desire to withdraw from reality as a result of traumatic experiences, is passed on to her daughter. Yet Daba responds differently to violence. As a product of the sexual violence that took away her mother's love, Daba chooses to "devancer [ait] le malheur" [stay ahead of misfortune] (Beyala, *Tanga* 45; *Your Name* 26). Instead of waiting to suffer violence at the hands of others, she adopts a self-abusive behavior pattern and learns how to commit violence toward herself.[9] She blames herself for what she calls a "détresse accouchée par sa naissance" [sadness, brought forth by her birth] (43; 25). Tanga narrates: "Par rancune envers elle-même, envers ce corps, elle concluait qu'objet maléfique, elle porterait le sien les yeux grands ouverts, pour qu'enfin les peines, les erreurs, les échecs n'encombrent pas son chemin" [Out of spite towards herself, towards her body, she came to the conclusion that she'd bear hers – malevolent object – with eyes wide open so that troubles, mistakes, failures wouldn't encumber her path in the end] (44; 26). As is often the case in novels that depict violence, *Tanga* presents a young girl who resorts to self-violence in order to "free herself" from guilt and future hurt. In a scene mimicking perhaps the original rape of her mother, thirteen-year-old Daba stuffs palm nuts into her own vagina and then proceeds to withdraw them one by one. There is a correlation, at least textual, between self-violence and freedom. Clearly, this is also symptomatic of intergenerational violence.

Tanga punishes herself to preempt what she perceives as an unavoidable future of pain at the hands of others. Daba defines suffering as follows: "Elle disait que la douleur était situation pour oublier le plaisir" [She said that pain was a condition in which to forget about the pleasure] (44; 26). Tanga's mother kills her capacity for pleasure by initiating herself to violence. This transaction provided for her the perfect solution to the threat of victimization. Daba tells herself: "Voilà l'abri, voilà l'abri que ma mère n'a pas su trouver" [There's the shelter, there's the shelter that mother was not able to find] (44; 26). Beyala's novel is narrated by Tanga, who represents the third generation of women in this family marked by violence. In addition to inheriting violence from her mother and grandmother, she suffers repetitive incestuous abuse by her own father that results in a pregnancy and possible infanticide. When her father dies, her mother forces Tanga into prostitution to feed the family, but not before submitting her to female circumcision. After the procedure, Tanga believes that her mother takes perverse pleasure in seeing her daughter suffer, especially when she immediately sends the young girl to sell her body. Beyala describes several scenes in which the mother-daughter relationship is defined by aggression and violence.

By constructing this intergenerational narrative of female trauma, Beyala suggests that passing down violence from one generation to another has severe consequences for society in general and for the female lineage in particular. If violence breeds violence, women who are victims of male violence will themselves begin to impose violence on their children. In the case of *Tanga*, the female children are especially targeted, as the grandmother rejects the mother, who in turn inherits perverted parenting practices. Daba, in fact, resorts to child abuse, or to use Tanga's words, the mother kills childhood: "moi, la femme-fillette soumise aux rites de l'enfant-parent de ses parents puisqu'il convient de commercer la chair pour les nourrir" [I, the girlchild-woman, dutiful in the fulfillment of the rites of child-parent to her parents, since it's fitting that I sell my flesh to feed them] (32; 18). The parallels between Daba and Tanga are striking, particularly how both of them seem to have been doomed from their birth. Tanga in fact uses similar language to reflect on her parents' first meeting as Daba did about hers: "Souvent, j'ai pensé à cette rencontre qui m'avait enfantée, cette rencontre qui m'avait détruite en même temps qu'elle m'accouchait" [I have often thought of that encounter which sired me, that meeting that destroyed me and at the same time gave birth to me] (45; 27). The silence and private nature of domestic abuse also emerges when the mother keeps quiet about the incest and emotionally blackmails Tanga when she expresses the need to stop prostitution. The mother even summons the family elders to remind Tanga of her obligations because the extended family also depends economically on the young woman's prostitution.

Violence committed by the mother has its sources in deeply rooted patriarchal practices that create a hierarchy privileging husbands over wives and parents over children. However, *Tanga* clearly highlights how such patriarchal practices lead females to commit violence toward one another. In Beyala's writings, patriarchal violence or parental violence is carried out by both men and women and results in unusual cruelty toward children, as in this scene from one of Tanga's frequent nightmares:

> Les enfants d'Iningué sont tondus. On leur met un anneau dans le nez. On les parque dans les champs. Ils travaillent sous le fouet d'hommes aux biceps comme des bûches et au crâne de chauve-souris. Une femme cul-de-jatte s'occupe des récalcitrants. On les lui confie, ligotés. Elle les frappe de sa main cornée puis les envoie virevolter. [The children of Iningué are shorn. A ring is put through their noses. They are confined to the fields. They work under the whip of men with biceps as big as logs and skulls like bats. A legless woman takes care of the recalcitrant ones. Bound together, hand and foot, they are entrusted to her. She beats them with her calloused hand, then sends them spinning.] (79; 48)

While Beyala tells stories of male violence, Tanga herself remains focused on how her mother manipulates the patriarchal system to hurt her children. In the quotation above, there are references to concentration camps ("tondus," "anneau dans le nez," "parque") and to slavery ("champs," "ils travaillent sous le fouet"). The male and female guards are either hybrids ("chauve-souris") or mutilated ("cul-de-jatte"), suggesting that these guards have themselves been victims of violence. The legless woman is entrusted with teaching compliance to rebellious children ("récalcitrants"), a role that Daba, Tanga's mother, takes seriously. By inflicting violence on her child, she adopts the role of the patriarchal enforcer. By turning against Tanga, her extended family — and the community itself — sanctions this type of violence, the purpose of which is to reinforce hierarchy.

Daba's violent acts stem from internalized self-hatred that bursts out and which she directs toward her children — a dynamic often found in the case of infanticides. Lacking the ability to exert power over men, women can exercise power over children and other women. Indeed, as Liz Kelly rightly asserts, while male domination has its source in the linkage of power, violence, and sexuality, women's violence originates from their powerless position and resistance to male violence (37). Kelly clarifies, however, that violence by women from a position of powerlessness cannot have the same meaning and foundation as male violence from a position of power (38). Beyala questions how much power men have over children because men and male children are also victims of violence. The novel illustrates that violence inflicted by mothers on their children is just as traumatic and injurious as that enacted by male relatives on mothers and wives. In *Tanga* violence by women has its source in patriarchy, but the originality of Beyala's novel lies in its exploration of women's participation in the problem of domestic abuse. While Kadjaba and Daba are victims of male violence, Tanga's position seems to show, to use Kelly's words, that "being victimized does not remove all responsibility because they have been abused" (40). According to Kelly, violence committed by women has long been surrounded by silence in most feminist theorization of domestic and familial violence. While there are several reasons for this omission, the main one is that most domestic abusers are men. Focusing on the few women abusers might jeopardize the fight against domestic violence, of which women are most often the victims. In the African context, moreover, the question of privileging public over private problems arises: Why focus on individual and domestic issues when the communities are engaged in wars and threatened by hunger and disease?

Beyala's writings have provoked numerous controversies, mainly because of accusations of plagiarism.[10] Underlying this contentious reception of her work is not Beyala's negative portrayal of men (vile, abject, invisible, unnecessary) but rather her portrayal of a women's universe mired in violence. Unlike any other writer, Beyala has exposed the female role in upholding women's oppression. In African literature, woman-to-woman violence has typically involved issues of jealousy between co-spouses in polygamous families. Novels such as *Juletane* by Myriam Warner-Vieyra, *Une si longue lettre* by Mariama Bâ, and several works and films by Sembène Ousmane stage women who perform violence on each other in the context of polygamy. In contrast, in *Tanga*, Beyala creates a woman's voice that goes beyond "mother-blaming." In Tanga's attempts to "denormalize" rape, incest, and the abuse of children, Beyala shows that what women do to one another and to their children is not normal.

In *Tanga*, Beyala questions many accepted ideas about African families. In African literature, sexual violence has represented social, cultural, and political degeneration. In Ahmadou Kourouma's classic novel *Les soleils des independences*, Fama's wife Salimata is raped by a *marabout* who was to oversee the incision. This rape goes hand in hand with the novel's general theme of moral decay and the prevalence of social and political injustices. Rape, then, becomes more than the act in itself; it symbolizes systemic social corruption.[11] Is this the case for *Pluie et vent* and *Tanga*? Schwarz-Bart does not place domestic violence at the center of the story but frames it as part of the narrativization of Télumée's life, which she defines as a series of cyclical ups and downs. Beyala has been more open about her inclusion of violence in her novels. When asked why she paints a grim picture of African youth, Beyala maintained that her fictionalized discourse on the lost generation was inspired by reality (Matateyou 610). Beyala's point of view is consistent with the perspectives in recent novels on contemporary lives in Africa and the Caribbean in which authors seem to avoid metaphoric uses of gendered violence.[12]

Storytelling and Resistance to Violence

> Let me tell you a story. For all I have is a story. Story passed on from generation to generation, named Joy. Told for the joy it gives the storyteller and the listener. Joy inherent in the process of storytelling.
>
> Trinh T. Minh-ha, *Woman, Native, Other* (119)

> Every woman partakes in the chain of guardianship and of transmission. In Africa it is said that every griotte who dies is a whole library that burns down.
>
> Trinh T. Minh-ha, *Woman, Native, Other* (121)

> What is transmitted from one generation to another is not only the stories, but the very power of transmission.
>
> Trinh T. Minh-ha, *Woman, Native, Other* (134)

Schwarz-Bart and Beyala's female characters use storytelling to resist violence in their everyday lives. Indeed, resistance often accompanies violence in women's literature, perhaps as a way to rescue women, at least in narrative form. The female writers rescue Télumée's and Tanga's stories by producing them. They structure the novels around storytelling. Schwarz-Bart has Télumée narrate her own story, while Beyala imagines another character that must tell Tanga's story because the heroine is dying and unable to speak. Both writers choose to put the woman's claim to "herstory" at the center of their narratives. Both texts use storytelling as the ultimate instrument of communication among women while analyzing the dynamics of intergenerational violence. Although both narratives center on women's stories about women, different types of men also appear in the novels. In *Pluie et vent*, men enter women's lives only briefly, even for Toussine, who ends up alone. Good men — those who love and respect women — disappear by death (Jérémie, Angebert, Amboise), as if to say they cannot literally exist or find a place in their community. Bad men such as Elie — the Dominican — and Haut-Colbi beat their wives, leave as soon as they learn of their paternity, or implicitly force women to abandon their children. For them violence against women becomes a sign or logical result of successful manhood. In *Tanga*, Beyala's language and tone suggest the despicable nature of the men Tanga encounters. Tanga's father does not exist as a parent because he transforms her into his "wife" by sexually abusing her and impregnating her. Even Hassan, Tanga's boyfriend, sees her only as a prostitute, "'la femme-plume,' aux pagnes faciles à retrousser," [a free-flying woman, wearing *pagnes* that are easily tucked up] (26; 14).[13] Beyala describes a lineage of females who mimic the father because it is the women's role to implement and reinforce patriarchal rule, especially among their female children. In this manner men are present in the mother's actions.

The physical absence of men in both novels and their first-person narration by women indicate the authors' sense that the stories they write belong to Tanga and Télumée. But they do not belong to the heroines alone. Rather, they take into account the stories of previous female generations. My intention in this analysis is to read *Pluie et vent* as an example of a successful female intergenerational relationship. The novel highlights not only the importance of intergenerational communication but also stresses the act and the process of that communication: "What is transmitted from one generation to another is not only the stories, but the very power of transmission" (Trinh 134). I argue that readers' and critics' fascination with this book owes in part to its powerful narrative medium – storytelling. *Tanga*, as we shall see later, exemplifies a different but no less powerful kind of storytelling.

Télumée Miracle, the Storyteller

"The storyteller, besides being a great mother, a teacher, a poetess, a warrior, a musician, a historian, a fairy, and a witch, is healer and a protectress" (Trinh 140). Trinh's words go right to the heart of women's role as the bearer of history. She adds: "Every griotte who dies is a whole library that burns down" (121). Here, Trihn appropriates a well-known quote by the African historian Amadou Hampaté

Bâ about the male storyteller. Bâ pronounced his original sentence, "Un vieillard qui meurt, c'est comme une bibliothèque qui brûle" [An old man who dies is like a library that burns], while stressing the importance of storytelling and storytellers in Africa during his tenure as ambassador at UNESCO. Whether or not Bâ intended the original statement to apply to female storytellers as well, Trihn's appropriation of the quote puts the often forgotten contribution of women to the art of storytelling at the forefront.

One of the few literary works from the Caribbean read often in Western academic institutions, *Pluie et vent* has been widely criticized, and wrongly so, for being pessimistic, negative, and fatalistic because it does not contain elements of the conventional revolutionary Caribbean novel.[14] According to Maryse Condé, *Pluie et vent* helped shatter the myth of the typical Caribbean protagonist and "place West Indian women where they belong – at the forefront of the daily battle for survival" ("Order, Disorder, Freedom" 163). Mireille Rosello refutes suggestions that the novel is an apology for resignation and that Télumée is an anti-heroine because she does not resist oppression. Rosello argues that the novel contradicts the notion that the oppressed only have two choices: to die heroically or to survive as a coward. She rightly proposes that Télumée's fight to survive is an act of revolt in itself because she has been repeatedly told that, for the oppressed, dying may be preferable to life. In other words, "La survie du Noir n'est pas forcément l'opposé de la révolte, de l'héroïsme" [Black people's survival is not necessarily the opposite of revolt and heroism] (Rosello 79).

As the French title suggests (translated it means "Rain and wind over Télumée Miracle"), Télumée's life consists of a tempestuous series of trials and tribulations. She survives thanks to a remarkable upbringing by her maternal grandmother, Toussine Lougandor. Using lessons learned throughout several generations of the Lougandor female lineage, Toussine provides Télumée Miracle with a desire to live and outlive the suffering she experiences in her surroundings. In *Pluie et vent*, Schwarz-Bart does not focus on violent acts committed by or against the characters. Rather, the novel reads more like a philosophical reflection on the vicissitudes of life. Beyond Télumée's revelations of violent occurrences in her life, the novel also highlights her moments of happiness and suffering. According to Télumée's grandmother Toussine, suffering is part of human life, and the only lesson that future Lougandors can learn is how to stand it – how to conquer it but not necessarily abolish it. This lesson is especially true for those who were enslaved.

Nevertheless, as Ronnie Scharfman states in an article, *Pluie et vent* is a novel that contains a "functioning system" that allows the heroine Télumée to give birth to her autobiography ("Mirroring and Mothering" 88). Indeed, at the beginning of the book, Télumée looks back at her story as someone who has discovered who she is and is undoubtedly comfortable with her identity. She knows how to be content despite life's ruses. The novel begins with her recalling life in Guadeloupe:

> Mais je ne suis pas venue sur terre pour soupeser la tristesse du monde. A cela, je préfère rêver, encore et encore, debout au milieu de mon jardin, comme le font toutes les vieilles de mon âge, jusqu'à ce que la mort me prenne dans mon rêve, avec toute ma joie . . . [But I didn't come into the world to weigh the world's woe. I prefer to dream, on and on, standing in my garden, just like any other old woman of my age, till death comes and takes me as I dream, me and all my joy.] (11; 2)

This image of Télumée standing straight in her garden reappears at the end of the novel: "mais je mourrai là, comme je suis, debout, dans mon petit jardin, quelle joie!" [but I shall die here, where I am, standing in my little garden. What happiness!] (249; 173). As Scharfman suggests, Télumée is aware of her history and is therefore capable of telling her own story, which Schwarz-Bart gives a definite structure in written form. The novel consists of two parts. In the first, entitled "Présentation des miens" [Presenting my people],

Schwarz-Bart shows that Télumée is conscious of the fact that her story begins before her physical birth. The narrator introduces the reader-listener to the four generations of the Lougandor female genealogy beginning with Minerve, her great-grandmother, and proceeding down through Toussine, Victoire, and Télumée. (In addition, Télumée later adopts a girl, Sonore, who disappears from the story after she abandons Télumée.) Minerve is a former slave who found refuge in a maroon community. She adopts a philosophy of life that will have an impact on the generations to come. Télumée describes Minerve as a woman who is determined to confront adversity and survive no matter what obstacles she encounters. Clearly the journey to self-discovery in *Pluie et vent* is primarily symbolic and interior; nothing, including the community's "bad mentality" or nature's bad temper, will stop the Lougandor women from triumphing over life's difficulties.

In the second part of the novel, entitled "Histoire de ma vie" [Story of my life], Schwarz-Bart provides insight into how the narrator's own story parallels that of her female ancestors such as Toussine. "Histoire de ma vie" begins exactly at the moment when Télumée goes to live with her grandmother Toussine at Fond-Zombi. By joining her grandmother, Télumée also encounters another important character: Man Cia, a sorcerer who is feared by most of the community. Through this structuring of the novel, Schwarz-Bart foregrounds female storytelling as biography-history. In their introduction to the essay collection *Out of the Kumbla*, Carol Boyce Davies and Elaine Savory Fido stress the importance of storytelling as a central metaphor in communicating oral history through generations. The autobiographical *I* tells the stories of mothers and grandmothers as its own. In the case of Télumée, "the text becomes a collective story and Télumée's (the granddaughter's) autobiography becomes Toussine's (the grandmother's) biography" (Davies 6). This connection becomes even more apparent when comparing the life stories of Télumée and Toussine. They both experienced strikingly similar problems and joyful moments, each encountering love, loss, betrayal, and madness. They entertained ambivalent relationships with other community members. They have known unimaginable despair, yet their ability to recover from intense hardship is remarkable. Toussine's love for Jéremie transcended even his death: she decides to live near Man Cia, the sorcerer, with the intention of communicating with Jérémie. Similarly, Télumée falls in love with and later marries her childhood friend Elie. During her marriage to Jérémie, Toussine's sense of fulfillment is temporarily suspended during a period of "madness" that follows a destructive fire. But her contentment eventually returns and continues under the critical eyes of the maroon community in spite of the death of her beloved Jérémie and parallel tribulations experienced by her daughters. Télumée herself experiences marital bliss but only at the beginning of her life with Elie. Unlike Toussine, she becomes a victim of domestic abuse. Again, this episode of Télumée's life can only be read as another tribulation that the woman must experience and overcome. In addition to these parallel life experiences, both women receive honorable names from the community. After the fire and the temporary madness, the onlookers name Toussine "Reine Sans Nom" (Queen Without-a-Name), for "[n]ous avons cherché un nom de reine qui te convienne mais en vain, car à la vérité il n'y a pas de nom pour toi . . . nous t'appellerons: Reine-Sans-Nom" [we have tried and tried to think of a name for you, but in vain, for there isn't one that will do . . . , from now on, we shall call you Queen-Without-a-Name] (28; 15). Télumée hears a similar pronouncement: "Nous avons vainement cherché un nom qui te convienne . . . quant à nous, désormais, nous t'appellerons Télumée Miracle" [we have tried in vain to find a suitable name for you, . . . So as for us we shall call you Telumee Miracle (239; 166).

While the two women share similar moments of pain and joy, the key to their successful generational communication is not the reproduction of herstory, especially its painful elements. Rather, the communication from one generation to another focuses on the legacy of survival. Toussine's role is not to prevent trials and tribulations in her granddaughter's life but to provide her with the skills to deal with them. The importance of storytelling resides in the lessons learned by its listeners. By telling her story, Télumée hopes that her fight to live will inspire future generations to do likewise. To ensure the survival of generations of women to come, Toussine Lougandor must fulfill multiple roles. To repeat Trinh T. Minh-ha's words, Toussine must become "a great mother, a teacher, a poetess, a warrior, a musician, a historian, a fairy, and a witch, a healer and a protectress" before she can become an effective storyteller (Trinh 140). After the departure of Victoire, Télumée's biological mother, Télumée moves in with Toussine, who by default becomes the young girl's mother. She offers Télumée a sense of security that the girl feels as soon as she enters her grandmother's house. Télumée describes the almost superhuman nature of the house, which "terminait le monde des humains et semblait adossée à la montagne" [marked the end of the world of human beings and looked as if it were leaning against the mountain] (47; 28).[15] Télumée recalls her first meeting with her grandmother: "Sitôt que j'eus franchi le seuil, je me sentis comme dans une forteresse, à l'abri de toutes choses connues et inconnues, sous la protection de la grande jupe à fronces de grand-mère" [As soon as I crossed the threshold I felt as if I were in a fortress, safe from everything known and unknown, under the protection of my grandmother's full skirt] (47; 28).

The grandmother offers security and protection, as she constantly calls Télumée "mon petit verre en cristal" [my little crystal glass], a fragile and yet valuable woman. In addition, Toussine–Reine Sans Nom plays a crucial role as an educator that prepares Télumée for life. She teaches Télumée about the past, slavery, and her own life experience and how to become an accomplished human being. She whispers songs into Télumée's ears that utilize words of wisdom and metaphors: "Je suis née négresse à chance et je mourrai négresse à chance" [I was born a lucky Negress and shall die one]

(49; 29). Even when responding to specific situations, Toussine puts her advice to Télumée in general terms that can apply beyond the immediate circumstances. Toussine tells Télumée the following about gossip:

> Télumée, mon petit verre en cristal, . . . trois sentiers sont mauvais pour l'homme: voir la beauté du monde, et dire qu'il est laid, se lever de grand matin pour faire ce dont on est incapable, et donner libre cours à ses songes, sans se surveiller, car qui songe devient victime de son propre songe. [Telumee, my little crystal glass . . . there are three paths that are bad for a man to take: to see the beauty of the world and call it ugly, to get up early to do what is impossible, and to let oneself get carried away by dreams – for whoever dreams becomes the victim of his own dream.] (51; 30)

Toussine tells one story about a man and his crazy horse to warn Télumée against the enslavement of everyday problems. A man who is dissatisfied with life decides never to dismount from his horse. As a result, he progressively surrenders his life to the animal until the horse becomes his master. In conclusion, Toussine advises Télumée, "le cheval ne doit pas te conduire, c'est toi qui doit conduire le cheval" [the horse mustn't ride you, you must ride it] (79; 51). Toussine's philosophy is that while life has its ups and downs, each individual must take control of his or her destiny.

The intimate bond between Télumée and Toussine is made of trust, protection, and complicity. Toussine lectures while Télumée listens and asks questions. Télumée remembers her grandmother's words as whispers. As Trihn T. Minh-ha reminds us, "What is transmitted from one generation to another is not only the stories, but the very power of transmission" (134). Télumée recollects not only the words but also how those words were said, invoking the power of transmission embedded in the physical act of storytelling.

Storytellers share the painful and triumphant moments in their own stories in order to provide the next generation with survival skills. The very act of storytelling implies that the storyteller has survived to describe the experience. In her introduction to the essay collection *The Politics of Mothering*, Obioma Nnaemeka emphasizes the link between storytelling and knowledge construction, particularly how gender construction is part of that process. "Gender politics," she argues, "often banish storytelling to the periphery of 'real knowledge'" (6). Male figures have long dominated storytelling itself. Critics have devalued and dismissed women's stories because they concern the so-called women's universe.[16] According to Nnaemeka, this disregard illustrates how knowledge construction is dictated not only by generational differences but also by gender politics. The typical male storyteller, adopting the role of a truly wise old man, will master "issues of history, memory, wisdom and knowledge" (Nnaemeka 8–9). When it comes to "the old woman as storyteller/historian," however, her knowledge becomes gendered: "Because gendered knowledges are also located knowledge, the old woman's interlocutors (the males, in particular) hear not knowledge-in-wisdom in her narrative but the silly and nonsensical sounds of the periphery" (Nnaemeka 9).

In *Pluie et vent*, Man Cia, the sorcerer, is one person who serves as an example of Nnaemeka's hypothesis. Various individuals perceive her as either wise or nonsensical. In the eyes of the inhabitants of Fond-Zombi, Man Cia is not some ridiculous old woman, though people like Abel try to outsmart her. Others take her words and wisdom seriously. Except for Toussine and later Télumée, everyone is afraid of this woman "qui côtoyait les morts plus que les vivants" [who was closer to the dead than to the living] (55; 33), who has the power to transform herself into animals, and who serves as a "healer" and seer of the future. Toussine describes Man Cia as duplicitous: she is "une femme de bien mais il ne faut pas lui chauffer les oreilles" [a good woman but it's best not to get on the wrong side of her] (56; 34). While physically Man Cia is "une quelconque petite vieille de Fond-Zombi" [an ordinary little old woman from Fond-Zombi] (58; 36), what sets her apart from other people, according to Télumée, is her eyes: "Elle avait ces yeux-là . . . immenses, [. . .] de ces yeux dont on dit qu'ils peuvent tout voir, tout supporter, car ils ne se ferment pas même en sommeil" [It was those eyes – huge, . . . the sort of eyes people say can see everything, bear everything, because they never shut, even in sleep] (58; 36). Indeed, Man Cia alone has a specialized knowledge that can be gained only through the actual physical power of her eyes. When she transforms herself into a bird she can see across great distances, and she also sees more than anyone else because she never closes her eyes. Except for Toussine and Télumée, everyone fears Man Cia's knowledge, and the community often sees her as threatening. As noted earlier, Toussine relies on her to keep in touch with the deceased. Upon Toussine's death, Man Cia takes over Télumée's education: "sois une vaillante petite négresse, un vrai tambour à deux faces, laisse la vie frapper, cogner, mais conserve toujours intacte la face du dessous" [Be a fine little Negress, a real drum with two sides. Let life bang and thump, but keep the underside always intact] (62; 39). Man Cia helps Toussine groom Télumée and completes Toussine's instruction by teaching Télumée about the power of sorcery, providing her with knowledge that no one else has. Toussine guides Télumée by teaching her how to acquire the knowledge and wisdom that will enable her to survive being hurt or ridiculed.

How well does Télumée use the knowledge acquired through her grandmother and Man Cia? As mothers, protectors, healers, and sorcerers, Toussine and Man Cia prepare Télumée for life's hardships. Télumée faces episodes in her life that push to the limit her willingness to apply the Lougandor philosophy. Her first important trial arrives when she begins work for the Desaragne family. Because of the constant psychological violence she endures from her masters, Télumée must apply the survival strategies that Toussine taught her. Just like her grandmother, she ignores the verbal abuse and reminds herself to "conduire son cheval" [to lead her horse]

(79). She imagines herself as “une petite pierre” [a small rock] (92), or attempts to “se faufiler à travers ces paroles” [slide in and out of these words] (94), and she resorts to singing in order to lessen her sadness.

When she is not working, Télumée copes with her daily torment by becoming a storyteller herself, turning her experience with the Desaragnes into a story. Télumée’s experience with the art of storytelling re-humanizes her, at least in the eyes of her audience, which reacts positively even when she repeats the same stories. Télumée’s strength comes from her ability to refuse victimization. She did not simply learn “wisdom” as a survival skill but shaped her experience into a story (as Toussine taught her to do) to resist victimization. When M. Desaragne attempts to rape her, Télumée manages to fight back by threatening to kill him, a strategy that works. The heroine, who normally must keep quiet around her employers, is able to resist by talking back. Télumée later reflects on her victory in the following terms: “Le combat avec M. Desaragne était loin, et je n’y avais pas vu ni ma victoire de négresse, ni ma victoire de femme. C’était seulement un des petits courants qui feraient frémir mon eau, avant que je me noie dans l’océan.” [The struggle with Monsieur Desaragne was a thing of the past, and I hadn’t realized the victory I’d won, as a Negress and as a woman. It was just one of the little currents that would ripple my waters before I was drowned in the sea] (112; 73). As Télumée now tells her story, she is aware of how being black and female places her in a kind of double jeopardy. She interprets her victory as personal and not necessarily political, although she understands what her radical gesture means in contemporary race and gender politics. Schwarz-Bart could also be interjecting her own interpretation of the incident in contemporary politics. For the sake of survival, Télumée must simply accept herself as she is:

> Penchée sur mon visage, je songeais que Dieu m’avait mise sur terre sans me demander si je voulais être femme, ni quelle couleur je préférais avoir. Ce n’était pas ma faute s’il m’avait donné une peau

> si noire que bleue, un visage qui ne ruisselait pas de beauté. Et cependant, j'en étais bien contente, et peut-être si l'on me donnait à choisir, maintenant, en cet instant précis, je choisirai cette même peau bleutée, ce même visage sans beauté ruisselante. [Looking at my reflection, I thought how God had put me on earth without asking me if I wanted to be a woman or what color I'd like to be. It wasn't my fault he'd given me a blue-black skin and a face not overflowing with beauty. And yet I was quite content; and perhaps, if I was given the choice, now, at this moment, I'd choose that same bluish skin, that same face not overflowing with beauty.] (116; 76)

Télumée's second trial is her marriage to her childhood friend Elie. Wedded out of love like Toussine, Télumée becomes the object of envy in all Fond-Zombi. In this episode, Télumée plays her role as a happy woman. Feeling apprehensive about the future, she turns once again to her grandmother for guidance, who advises her that according to the Lougandor tradition, she has the duty to rejoice without apprehension because "nous, les Lougandor, ne craignons pas davantage le bonheur que le malheur" [we Lougandors don't fear happiness any more than we fear unhappiness] (137; 92). Télumée's happiness proves short-lived after Elie promises to "handle her right," which means using violence to control her. In a way, his mistreatment of her is an attempt to compensate for his inability "to lead his own horse." Télumée experiences the difficulty of being a woman who not only is blinded by love but also loses control of her life, like her grandmother before her. Because of Elie's physical and verbal abuse, Télumée herself turns into a dehumanized zombie.[17]

Télumée experiences additional hardships after the death of her grandmother. Man Cia takes over as Télumée's mentor and teaches the young Lougandor the art of healing. In the end, Télumée becomes an omniscient figure, a mixture of Toussine and Man Cia in her own eyes and in the eyes of the community that begins to fear her. Although she has gained the knowledge needed to survive,

Télumée is not successful in every facet of her life. Like many other female protagonists in Caribbean literature by women, she is infertile; moreover, she is unable to prevent Sonore, the child she had adopted, from abandoning her. However, Télumée's will to survive lies deep within her, making her capable of focusing on life without selfishness.

Tanga: Breaking from Violent History

Obiama Nnaemeka reminds us that stories affirm the survival of not only the storyteller but also the listeners, who "survive because they have learned from the story" (7). In the context of violence, storytelling derives heavily from what Dori Laub calls "the imperative to tell," especially after a traumatic event. Regarding the survivors of the Holocaust, Laub writes, "The survivors did not only need to survive so that they could tell their stories; they also needed to tell their stories in order to survive" (63). If the main goal of storytelling is to survive, then Beyala redefines the meaning of survival. While Tanga does not save herself through the act of storytelling, she nevertheless preserves her story for future generations. Since Tanga is dying and cannot speak, Beyala must adopt unconventional storytelling, urging readers to suspend their disbelief and see how the heroine's story can be collected, albeit imaginatively.

Beyala cannot structure Tanga's story as clearly as Schwarz-Bart does Télumée's. As noted previously, scholarship on literature and trauma has revealed that amnesia or fragmentation of memory is a normal occurrence for trauma victims. During the moment of trauma, the victim becomes unconscious and thereafter has difficulty describing what happened. The problem of the trauma story is that it cannot be fully captured. Beyala's fragmented style of writing reflects Tanga's fractured and unfocused memory. Unlike Télumée, moreover, Tanga clearly does not have the same knowledge of her family history, which is limited to specific violent events in the lives of Tanga's mother, Daba, and her grandmother, Princess Kadjaba Dongo. And when Tanga refers to her grandmother as the "princess," it is unclear whether this refers to a privileged background or simply her pride.

While Télumée tells her story as a survivor with her head held high, proud of herself, her heritage, and her people, Tanga must obey the patriarchal rule of her father: "N'oublie pas, un enfant doit garder les yeux baissés" [Don't forget, a child must keep its eyes lowered] (Beyala, *Tanga* 18; *Your Name* 9).[18] In this position, Tanga's vision is limited. She can only see legs. As a result, legs become important signifiers in *Tanga*. In all the facets of her life, Tanga can only see legs — her own legs, other prostitutes' legs, her father's legs, her mother's degenerating legs, and the legs of her male clients. It is also noteworthy that the child Tanga chooses to adopt is appropriately named "Pieds-Gâtés" (Rotten-feet). Forced by previous generations into a limited and distorted view of the world, Tanga does not learn how to survive human suffering. She lacks the skills that would help her overcome the legacy of violence. Like her mother and grandmother, she must abide patriarchal expectations of a girl by keeping "les yeux baissés." Unlike Télumée, who has been groomed to survive, Tanga has been trained to suffer in silence, looking down at legs.

Tanga's lack of knowledge is deeply rooted in the female lineage's legacy of violence and subsequent silence. After the rape of Tanga's grandmother, Kadjaba Dongo, and the resulting birth of Tanga's mother, Daba, her grandmother tells her descendants that she cannot hear or see, effectively stating that no one should count on her. Similarly, Daba refuses to transfer any knowledge to her daughter Tanga and confesses that she lacks interest in acquiring knowledge.[19] Daba goes so far as to suggest that their roles be reversed — that Tanga become the working parent who must reconstruct familial knowledge. Tanga remembers her mother's words: "Cette rencontre qui plus tard me dira: puisque tu es là, puisque tu es vivante, assieds- toi sur l'éboulis des siècles, nourris-nous de ton corps. *Nous ne savons pas, tu sauras pour nous*." [That encounter which was to say to me later: since you're here, since you're alive, have a seat on the debris of the ages; feed us with your body. *We no longer know, you'll know for us*] (emphasis added; 45; 27).

This silence, transmitted from one generation to the next, explains Tanga's desire to "tuer le vide du silence" [kill the emptiness of silence] (Beyala, *Tanga* 15; *Your Name* 7). Tanga decides to stop the cycle of violence and ignorance, which she does in two ways. First, she severs ties with her mother: "J'ai décidé de vivre, je n'ai plus rien à voir avec la vieille la mere." [I've decided to live, I've nothing to do with mother old one any longer] (59; 35). In rejecting her mother, Tanga aspires to become "a normal person," dreaming of an ideal French bourgeois life away from Iningué: "J'aurai ma maison, le jardin, le chien, la pie au bout du pré, des enfants . . . Des enfants, des vrais, pas cette enfance d'Iningué où l'enfant n'a pas d'existence, pas d'identité." [I will have my house, the garden, the dog, the magpie at the end of the meadow . . . Children, real ones, not this childhood of Iningué where the child does not exist, has no identity] (76; 46).[20] This dream leads Tanga to her second decision: to adopt a child. Tanga states: "A Iningué, la femme a oublié l'enfant, le geste qui donne l'amour, pour devenir une pondeuse. Elle dit: 'L'enfant, c'est la sécurité vieillesse.' D'ailleurs, le gouverneur en personne médaille les bonnes pondeuses. Service rendu à la patrie." [In Iningué, the woman has forgotten the child, the gesture that brings love – she's just an egg-laying hen. She says: "A child is the security of old age." Besides, the governor himself hands out medals to women who have large families. For service rendered to the fatherland] (94; 57). The quotation suggests nationalism based on patriarchy, encouraging women to reproduce. Tanga's tries to reconstruct motherhood by giving a chance to used and neglected children. She carefully and methodically mothers Pieds-Gâtés, also called Mala, an abandoned and exploited child. Tanga wants to give love and security to the child. In most of her novels, Beyala depicts a childhood that has been damaged, sometimes beyond repair. Mala exemplifies that image in *Tanga*. He is accustomed to roughness and proves to be difficult to approach. He initially rejects Tanga because he is weary of her intentions, even considering her "dingue" [crazy], and "habitée par le diable" [inhabited by the devil] (92). Beyala illustrates the dire future of children in her imaginary city through Tanga's failure to tame Mala before she dies. Tanga's only hope of saving the future generation lies in her story, which she is able to impart only after encountering the idealistic Anna-Claude in prison. For Beyala, the sharing of history not only assures Tanga's survival but also becomes a possible solution to women's victimization. In prison, Anna-Claude persuades Tanga to tell "herstory" so that it can survive after her death. Because Tanga is unable to speak, the women must become creative and find nontraditional means of transmitting oral history. Tanga suggests that they hold hands so that Tanga's story may pass into her cellmate's body. In order to receive Tanga's legacy, Anna-Claude, an educated white European woman, must become a young black African woman. Tanga will ironically survive in a white woman's body.

The relationship between Tanga and Anna-Claude fulfills multiple needs for both women and is quite unusual. This is best illustrated in the following passage: "Leurs corps s'enlacent. Anna-Claude pleure. Tanga trace sur son cou et son flanc des sillons de tendresse. Elle lui dit de ne pas pleurer. . . . Elle lui dit qu'elles frotteront leur désespoir et que d'elles jaillira le plus maternel des amours." [Their bodies intertwine. Anna-Claude weeps. Tanga traces grooves of tenderness on her neck and her loins. She tells her not to cry. . . . She tells her that they will stroke their despair and that the most maternal of all love will gush forth from them] (74; 45). In this quotation, the women simultaneously become lovers and mothers for each other as they symbolically reconstruct and attempt to repair their ill-fated mother-daughter relationships. Tanga acts like a mother toward Anna-Claude by calming her when she becomes agitated. Anna-Claude's desire throughout the novel is to mother all children. In prison, Tanga gives her an opportunity to do so. In their respective studies of *Tanga*, Juliana Makuchi Nfah-Abbenyi and Rangira Béatrice Gallimore liken Tanga and Anna-Claude's relationship to what Adrienne Rich calls "the lesbian continuum," or what Alice Walker terms "womanism," in which women develop close and intimate relationships that may include but are not limited to sexual relations. Such intimate relationships represent attempts to fill the lack of love, sexual or otherwise, which both women have experienced. While in *Tanga* the mixing of maternal and sensual love may come dangerously close to incest, the novel depicts protagonists who must play multiple roles to fulfill what is missing in their lives. I may also add that the fact that the two women are both powerless facilitates their alliance without the risk of either participant abusing the other.

Like Schwarz-Bart, Beyala emphasizes the process of transmission as much of the story itself. She creatively utilizes the physicality of storytelling to stop gendered limitations of knowledge production. Telling "herstory" becomes an important tool for passing knowledge to others, which will in turn stop the cycle of violence from previous female generations. Through her heroines, Beyala depicts an exploited and traumatized *femme-fillette* (woman-girlchild) who desires to control her own story and, like Schwarz-Bart's Télumée, is able to produce her story. The act of telling her story transforms Tanga from a mere objectified being to the subject of her own history. She counteracts her mother's disinterest in self-knowledge. Tanga tells Anna-Claude: "Mon histoire sera le pain à pétrir pour survivre. Laisse-moi la libérer pour construire le futur." [My story will be the bread dough that must be kneaded in order to survive. Let me free it up so as to build the future] (38; 22).

Through Anna-Claude, the novel calls for a true internationalization of women's solidarity, a theme that Beyala explores further in her later novels. To authenticate this solidarity, the European woman must not only listen to and tell the story of the dying Tanga but also channel her story by entering her body. This is reminiscent of psychoanalytic transference, wherein the psychoanalyst takes over the role of the victimizer(s) to help the patient recall certain portions of her life, and which requires that patients transfer feelings they have for important figures in their lives onto the analyst. In Anna-Claude's case, however, this analogy is not exact. On the contrary, Anna-Claude aims to embody the victim herself not to cure the dying Tanga but to remedy whole societies through the story. In order to stop violence against children and deliver Tanga's story truthfully, Anna-Claude must absorb the raw story through a bodily transfer. While the relationship between Schwarz-Bart's characters is characterized by complete trust, Beyala, as noted earlier, tells Tanga's story in fragments partly because of the uneasy relationship between the storyteller and the listener – Tanga and Anna-Claude, respectively. Tanga must constantly interrupt the process of storytelling when she detects lack of trust on the part of Anna-Claude. Since the story is literally being poured into Anna-Claude's body, the assumption is that there should be no judgment or editorializing on the part of Anna-Claude. The story must be retold as given by Tanga. Once internalized by Anna-Claude, Tanga's private suffering becomes politicized. A woman who is passionate about decrying political abuses, especially those involving violence against children, will tell Tanga's story to the world. However, Anna-Claude's usefulness in carrying on Tanga's story is suspect for two reasons. First, those in Europe and in the imaginary Iningué, where the story is set, see her as insane, a fact that may discredit her storytelling. Indeed, she risks becoming the nonsensical one that Nnaemeka warns against in the context of knowledge construction and storytelling. Second, Tanga and Anna-Claude's differences have the potential to make the listener incredulous. Tanga is black, uneducated, colonized, and oppressed. Anna-Claude is white and educated, and she originates from the country of former colonizers and oppressors. These differences must be bypassed if Tanga's story is to survive, but can Anna-Claude's internalization of this story be believable to her listeners or the novel's readers?

Both *Pluie et vent* and *Tanga* urge us to recognize women's storytelling as a powerful means of transmitting history, and in turn they offer resources for women's survival. In both novels, surviving on a daily basis requires different types of skills. For instance, at the Desaragne household, Télumée learns how to tune out the abusive words by becoming like "une petite pierre" (a small stone) and by turning a deaf ear to Mme Desaragne's verbal abuse. Tanga resists her mother's torment by passively and actively disobeying the latter's orders – refusing to prostitute herself for the family, for example. Through words and looks, Tanga and her mother constantly scrutinize each other, watch each other's movements, and prepare for their next confrontation. But the most remarkable and paradoxical mode of resistance is the use of silence, as evidenced in the way Tanga passes on her story to Anna-Claude. Silence, or a lack of valuable communication within the female lineage, is arguably at the center of Tanga's problems, and yet by approaching it creatively, Beyala shows that women can also find solutions in silence. As in other novels analyzed in this book, silence is a major theme in the context of gendered violence. It is, however, seldom understood as a tool for resistance to violence.

4

Sites of Violence

Language, the Body, and Women's Deterritorialization in Gisèle Pineau's *L'espérance-macadam* and Calixthe Beyala's *C'est le soleil qui m'a brûlée*

Calixthe Beyala and Gisèle Pineau explore further the concept of "geographies of pain" by depicting intimate space, language, and the body as sites of pain, exile, and resistance to violence.[1] In the tradition of women's literature, the two writers turn their attention to internal sources of violence and, through their characters, condemn those who still focus solely on the external factors of violence. They ask questions such as: How can women successfully re-territorialize their violated bodies within the intimate spaces from which they have been exiled? How can they overcome linguistic limitations in expressing pain? Beyala sees linguistic violence as a means to liberate women, whereas Pineau chooses to rely on metaphors. For both authors, however, language obtains a healing role because writing itself functions as an act of resistance to pain and an exercise of freedom.

Space, Violence, and Knowledge in Gisèle Pineau's L'espérance-macadam

The concepts of space and location have always been vital to understanding Caribbean literature. Négritude, Antillanité, and Créolité — the three major literary and theoretical movements associated with this body of work — seek to define Caribbean identities by highlighting the meanings of space in which these identities have been deterritorialized. Because identity in general and Caribbean identity in particular is constantly shifting, it must be redefined accordingly. In postindependence, postslavery, and postcolonial contexts, exploration of space plays a crucial role in negotiating transitional identities. As Randolph Hezekiah puts it, "at the root of such an exploration lies the feeling of spatiotemporal dislocation experienced by people transplanted from a vast and distant continent to the confinement of a small island and subjected to an alien culture" (382). "Une population transbordée" (a transshipped population), to use Edouard Glissant's term, that is deterritorialized, dispossessed of its culture, and detached from its African territory through the slave trade attempts to re-territorialize itself "ailleurs" [elsewhere] (Glissant, *Le discours antillais* 100).[2] While Négritude claims Mother Africa, the Antillanité and Créolité movements both seek, at varying degrees, an understanding of Caribbean identity within its complex, ambiguous, fragmented, and hybrid physical and human geography. Space implies a reassessment of values associated with it. As illustrated in many writings by Caribbean male and female authors, gender discourses require a considerable reevaluation of Caribbean space.

In this section, I analyze Gisèle Pineau's complex portrayal of Caribbean space in her novel *L'espérance-macadam*. I argue that for the female generations represented in the work, knowing one's intimate geography despite its instability is crucial to acquiring freedom from "geographies of pain." In order to truly be liberated and empowered, the novel's main narrator, Eliette Florentine, must not only acquire what Trinh T. Minh-ha terms "territorialized knowledge" but also exercise her liberty. In *L'espérance-macadam*, Pineau depicts the link between the Caribbean environment's unpredictable and often violent temperament and its inhabitants. In the novel, natural disasters such as hurricanes destabilize both physical and human geographies. My examination focuses on how the novel depicts the intersection of physical and human geographies in the domestic space.

In September 1928 a hurricane of unparalleled force destroyed Guadeloupe, killing over five thousand people and leaving thousands more wounded by the experience. This hurricane, known as the Cyclone of '28, has since become an important part of Caribbean history and cultural myths. Pineau weaves together the story of this natural catastrophe with those of her female characters. The cyclone and Hurricane Hugo of 1989 frame the events told by the different narrators in *L'espérance-macadam*. Pineau makes references to hurricanes within stories of domestic and sexual violence. Eliette attempts to reclaim her life after a lasting experience of pain and trauma. Her recollections and subsequent inferences constitute the story. Set in Savane Mulet, an isolated village in Guadeloupe, the story begins when a powerful hurricane passes through the village and destroys everything in its path. As a consequence, Eliette, at eight years old, loses her memory and her voice. She also endures extensive emotional and physical harm. Eliette's mother subsequently goes mad. Throughout the remainder of her life, the mother will obsessively retell the story of the fateful night, particularly emphasizing how "la poutre," the supporting beam of their house, literally pierced Eliette and caused her daughter's sterility. Eliette will later confirm her suspicions that this was not the real reason for her demise. It was not the cyclone that destroyed her but her father, who savagely raped her during that ill-fated night. The novel recounts how another case of incest involving a young neighbor forces Eliette to piece together this painful past, which for sixty years has paralyzed her verbally and socially. Eliette eventually overcomes her paralyzing fear of "cyclones" and "men." Through a meticulous study of the quintessential intimate space, *la case*, she is subsequently able to utilize her newly found freedom to save female children from "les yeux mauvais" [evil eyes] of the hurricane (Pineau, *L'espérance-macadam* 160).

La case is synonymous with several terms in French, including *hutte* and *cabane*. Most dictionaries define this typical dwelling in undeveloped tropical areas according to its physical characteristics, such as a "[h]abitation en paille, en branches d'arbres etc., dans les pays tropicaux" (*Le grand Larousse*). These definitions neglect the word's connotation in the history of slavery as mostly unstable yet permanent housing. The *Oxford English Dictionary* makes the subtle distinction between *huts*, *cabin*, and other terms in the same semantic field. The dictionary, for instance, is more precise regarding the historical connotation of *cabin* as "[a] permanent human habitation of rude construction. Applied esp. to the mud or turf-built hovels of slaves or impoverished peasantry, as distinguished from the more comfortable 'cottage' of working men, or from the 'hut' of the savage, or temporary 'hut' of travelers, explorers, etc" (*Oxford English Dictionary Online*). Based on works set in the Caribbean and the Americas, like the French translation of Harriet Beecher Stowe's *Uncle Tom's Cabin* — *La case de L'Oncle Tom* — or Joseph Zobel's *La Rue cases-nègres*, *la case* would indeed correspond to *cabin*.

La case constitutes a crucial locus in *L'espérance-macadam*. The narrative directs the reader's attention not only toward the usual sources of trauma that affect the community, such as natural and historical violence, but also and perhaps more importantly toward sources of trauma that are more hidden within much more limited intimate spaces. In the novel, the Cyclone of '28 becomes more than a cosmic disaster when other equally and perhaps even more devastating events, like acts of domestic violence, occur simultaneously with it. *L'espérance-macadam* stresses the importance of exploring one's intimate space. I interpret this as part of the Créolité project to turn inward and consider the Caribbean landscape as a permanent living space, not as a mystified transition toward the Métropole, Mother Africa, or another imaginary "promised land." While this cyclone and others are well recorded in people's memories and in history and geography books, Pineau seeks to document the fateful night on a microspatial level by telling the story of a girl who is destroyed by her own father in a limited geographical area – that surrounding the hearth. A novel about "cyclones" thus transforms itself into a study of domestic space. It recounts how this space is a site of harrowing events that deeply affect women and children, whose personal safety is threatened within it by enraged "elements." Renélien, one of Eliette's husbands, summarizes the link between physical and human geography as follows:

> Comme la terre pouvait être secouée de tremblements, les cyclones chavirer les montagnes, la mer emporter la vie, il savait qu'en deçà des façades, belles figures et douces paroles, il y avait des éléments enragés, endormis, prêts à se soulever [Since any tremors could start shaking the earth, cyclones could tumble mountains to the ground and the ocean whisk one's life away, he knew that beyond appearances, pretty faces, and sweet words, raging elements lay dormant, ready to be unleashed]. (110–11; 106)

Emilia Ippolito notes that "intimate narratives remain firmly within the broader postcolonial framework in that they prove to be as much explorations of national and political, as of personal concerns" (9). Clearly, in this novel, as is often the case in women's literature, personal and public spaces interplay to produce a multifaceted imagery of Caribbean geography. With the violence of history as a backdrop, images of violated and traumatized Caribbean geographies overlay equally ravaged images of human bodies in their homes. The overlapping discourses of violence highlight tensions between the personal and the political and between the individual and the community. These interpositions constitute the novel's main narrative strategy. The language borrowed from historic and natural violence accounts for the mixture of individual experiences of violence within collective trauma.

When Eliette's mother recounts the event, she refers to it as "la passage de La Bête" [the passage of the Beast] (95). This phrase undoubtedly echoes "le passage du milieu" (the Middle Passage), a clear reference to the voyage of African slaves that produced their deterritorialization. In her madness, Eliette's mother repeatedly tells the story of the Cyclone of '28 to her daughter, insisting that Eliette was a victim of the storm. When Eliette reviews her mother's version, she realizes the true identity of "La Bête." Natural and *unnatural* sexual-domestic forms of violence coincide in one moment and become inseparable and damaging. Pineau superimposes images of Caribbean landscapes that have been threatened and destroyed repeatedly by history and frequent hurricanes over revelations of intimate violence. Throughout her work she has considered the ambivalent relationship between the temperamental island of Guadeloupe and its people. *Le papillon dans la cité* (1992) concerns the fragility of Pineau's native butterfly-like Guadeloupe. In 1998, she also published an illustrated book for children, *Le cyclone Marilyn*, on the hurricane of the same name. Other Francophone Caribbean writers have borrowed often from descriptions of the island's unstable geography to articulate feelings of physical, spiritual, and psychological deterritorialization. They have also sought to use the exploding energy of the island in their own process of de-alienation. For instance, Aimé Césaire, in *Cahier d'un retour au pays natal*, confronted "cette plus fragile épaisseur de terre" to explore the possibility of *enracinement* "au bout du petit matin" [at the end of daybreak] (8). Portraying the lives of three female generations, Simone Schwarz-Bart's *Pluie et vent sur Télumée Miracle* demonstrates the specificity of women's spatial position within the "île à volcan, cyclones et moustiques, à mauvaise mentalité" [volcanic, hurricane-swept, mosquito-ridden, nasty-minded island] (11; 2).

L'espérance-macadam reinstates, in a much more contemporary setting, themes found in *Pluie et vent sur Télumée Miracle*. The two novels both highlight the relationships between women and space and more specifically the ways in which women achieve self-realization within such an ambiguous site, a place where deterritorialized and transplanted people attempt to "se change[r] en autre chose" [to transform themselves into something else] (Glissant 40).[3] As noted in the previous chapter, Ronnie Scharfman reads *Pluie et vent* as a novel that contains a "functioning system" (88). Télumée's story represents a successful identity quest of a female character that knows who she is and is comfortable with her identity. Her success materializes more definitely in the appropriation of her *case* and her garden. Indeed, the images of Télumée standing in *her* garden, seen at the beginning and at the end of the novel, illustrate a woman who has conquered a small part of Caribbean space. The power of Télumée's voice comes from the fact that she not only owns her space but has also claimed it: as she states, "Je mourrai là, comme je suis. Debout dans mon petit jardin, quelle joie" [I shall die here, where I am, standing in my little garden. What happiness] (Schwarz-Bart, *Pluie et vent* 249; *Bridge of Beyond* 173). Marie-Denise Shelton argues that Télumée's successful recovery from all her pain owes to the fact that she "draws her energy from the language and culture of the island, which mediates her entrance into the world of identity, presence and continuity. Télumée is not extradited outside of her body. . . . *She feels right at home in the island*" (emphasis added; 432).

Like Schwarz-Bart, Pineau emphasizes women's need to appropriate Caribbean space. In *L'espérance-macadam*, the author expands the discourse of appropriation by describing complicated factors involved in women's deterritorialization within microscopic intimate spaces. One such complication is the issue of domestic and sexual violence. Although Schwarz-Bart's Télumée enjoys the security of her grandmother's *case*, she herself was a victim of Elie's violent outbursts in the home they shared. Her grandmother and others around her interpret his behavior as a manifestation of the so-called Caribbean madness, which is rooted in historical violence. Eliette's observations throughout *L'espérance-macadam* seem to support the idea that the psychological impact of slavery causes men to commit violence. Eliette states, "A Ti-Ghetto, quand le Cylone a traversé, les jeunes frères de Moïse couraient déjà après des soleils d'artifice." [When Cyclone came through Ti-Ghetto, Moses' young brothers were already running after false suns](13; 7–8). Her statement suggests that individuals were victims of trauma before contemporary manifestations of violence. In foregrounding the issue of intimate violence, Pineau posits that badly conceived Creole patriarchal culture causes additional damage to women. The author does not evidently want to equate or supplant the metaphoric rape symbolized in the Middle Passage with the rape of Eliette. Rather, she emphasizes the multilayered pain and suffering women must often endure because of the double legacy of historical and patriarchal rape within an unstable physical environment. If Guadeloupe is geographically situated in the "eye of hurricane," it is the woman or the female child that is at the center of the perverted eye of the father, "La Bête," within domestic and intimate space.

Eliette's mother explains that her daughter was destroyed internally when the house's central beam collapsed and penetrated her. "La Poutre," which can be translated as "the beam" or "the pillar," constitutes the main support for the house. When it crashes, the whole house follows. Likewise, the beam represents the father, who causes the home to collapse when he violates his daughter. Savane Mulet has no shortage of collapsing homes. Far from being a "Baudelairian paradise," as Jack Corzani calls Caribbean geography in general, Savane is a land "of cyclones, earthquakes, tidal waves, volcanic eruptions," and "genocides" (Corzani 15). Natural and historical disasters converge to create tragic human geographies. Founded by Eliette's stepfather, Joab, a man of good intentions, Savane Mulet gradually becomes the chosen locus of souls in transition. Its deterritorialized people, dubbed "zombis des temps nouveaux" [zombies of the new age] (24; 19), attempt to escape everyday violence by smoking Zeb, which supposedly saves their souls (130–31; 125–26).[4] People from different backgrounds – migrants looking for places to rebuild after hurricanes and volcanoes, Rastafarians attempting to reverse the course of the Middle Passage – pass through this community on their way to the "promised land." Pineau describes Savane Mulet as follows:

> Ici-là, les roches n'étaient pas rondes et lisses comme ailleurs dans la Guadeloupe, mais longues et semblables à bras et jambes. Ma Manman murmurait que c'était sûrement les corps fracassées-démembrés-pétrifiés des anges rebelles, du temps où le Bon Dieu avait fait un grand ménage dans le ciel, précipitant sur la terre les suppôts de Satan [There, the rocks weren't round and smooth like elsewhere in Guadeloupe, but long, like arms and legs. My mama mumbled that they were probably the broken-dismembered-petrified bodies of apostate angels, from back when the Good Lord had done his spring-cleaning in heaven and cast the followers of Satan down to earth]. (23; 18)

Savane Mulet's treacherous nature and temperament contribute to the postcolonial *déchirement* of Caribbean people: "les roches acérées, la mer et ses requins se chargeait de déchirer les corps" [the jagged rocks, the sea, and the voracious sharks would tear the bodies apart in no time] (22; 17). The physical geography testifies to cyclical occurrences of violence in this enclosed community that is set "dans la chambre même du diable" [in the devil's own bedroom] (25; 19). Originally built in the tradition of *marronnage* as a site of resistance and renewal, the place becomes more and more a site of evil and inaction.

Eliette recalls that the community had been the scene of three major crimes: a husband who murders his wife, a woman and a jealous lover who murder her fiancé, and a case of infanticide. Each of these crimes occurs in an intimate space to which the community turns a blind eye. Like her neighbors, Eliette remained largely indifferent to these crimes. Things change when a fourth crime is suspected in the house next door. The incident starts when police arrest Rosan after his daughter Angela accuses him of incest. When Eliette sees Rosan sitting in the police car, she wonders with fear what crime he might have committed in his house. Eliette's fearful reaction indicates that there is a connection between the arrest and her own story of trauma. Her voice becomes more fragmented, switching from the first-person narrative *je* to the third-person *elle*, while her symptoms of aphasia and social phobia intensify.

After Rosan's arrest, Angela's mother Rosette predictably accuses her daughter of lying. She continues to doubt the story even after her husband confesses to the crime. In the last part of the novel, Rosette attempts to overcome her denial by reexamining her house to see if she missed any clues. She locates the crime scene in Angela's room. Rosan had built it as an extension to their bedroom after a hurricane partially destroyed the original house. Rosette is baffled by her ignorance of what went on in her home. By all accounts she leads a perfect life, with a husband who loves and provides for her and children who seem happy. Yet her daughter had been violated under her nose since Rosan had yet to install a door to separate the two rooms. Like Savane, Angela's room had slowly become "la chambre du diable." How could she have missed it? This is a question that Rosette never manages to answer. Pineau's careful depiction of Caribbean space on both macrocosmic and microcosmic levels provides insights to understanding the cause of Rosette's blindness.

Eliette remembers Rosette as a typical Savane woman who "flottait dans cette espérance" [was floating in that dream] (76; 71). The narrator paints a grim portrait of Savane women, who were, she says, "égarées, tournée-virées par le roulis de la vie, elles étaient brisées sans le savoir" [bobbed-bounced in life's roll, they were broken without even knowing it] (14; 8). Though lost and beaten by life repeatedly, these women continue to hope for a better future. Like other lost souls in Savane, Rosette considers herself in transition as she waits for a better life and a better *case*. Eliette describes her as having two faces, one that detests the world around her and another that only sees the good to the point of blindness (27). On the one hand, she spends her time in the house complaining about her situation. On the other, she is easily seduced into believing that deceitful paths lead to happiness. Of Savane, Rosette states, "ce pays qu'on dénommait Savane, respect! C'était un dernier coin de maudition . . ." [this place they called Savane – respect! – was the last bastion of accursement] (178; 173). To survive, she devises plans to escape her unhappiness. She listens and dances to Bob Marley's revolutionary songs, particularly "No Woman, No Cry," whose lyrics encourage the black woman not to mourn her condition. When dancing, Rosette floats into a world of endless hope, her feet removed literally from the floor, from the territory she believes she has demarcated.

In her search for liberation, Rosette joins "La Tribu d'Israël," a group of Rastafarians who are moving through Savane on their way to a mythical promised land. Caribbean people based their early identity quests on their ties with Africa. For instance, Marcus Garvey's "Come Back Africa" movement relied heavily on this traditional imaginative geography of Africa for self-affirmation. Decentering African identity is at the basis of the Créolité and Antillanité movements, as they both seek to recenter identity within the Caribbean space. Like the Rastafarians, Rosette indulges in Zeb and explores the possibility of liberation from Savane. However, her hope of finding a permanent space is short-lived. Among the Rastafarians, she especially admires Sister Beloved, a woman who to her symbolizes strength and exemplary female determination. However, Rosette soon discovers that this woman, who seemingly enjoys unusual power in her community, is also a battered woman. From then on, Rosette starts demystifying the group, whose members' behavior contradicts their ideals. In Pineau's novel, the Rastafarian movement offers tired discourses of liberation and bewitching promises of a Biblical paradise. Rosette later concludes that "ce paradis-là dont ils avaient soi-disant hérité n'était pas du côté de Savane" [the paradise they had presumably inherited was nowhere near Savane] (137; 132). In the end, La Tribu d'Israël perishes in a storm while singing their revolutionary songs.

Instead of drawing strength from what should have been an eye-opening encounter with La Tribu d'Israël, Rosette enters farther into a state of acute blindness and despair over her situation and that of Savane inhabitants. She resorts to inventing dreadful tales about the quasi-unavoidable fate of "wretched" Caribbean people, which she dictates to Angela. In one story, she explains how Pain came to rule the world by plotting to kill Hope. Rosette is reminiscent of Séraphine, Eliette's mother, who, after losing her *case*, fully embraces a fatalistic vision of life. Believing that nature can strike at any moment and transform hope into despair, Séraphine states, "Tu peux connaître des matins de plume sans souffrance, et tu chantes Gloire à Dieu! Mais, quand vient le serein, un cyclone bien enragé peut décider de charroyer *ta case* et ravager l'espérance de ton jardin." [You might know featherlight mornings when you sing out Glory be to God! But when the evening dampness falls, a right angry cyclone might decide to cart off *your cabin* and wreak havoc in the garden of your dreams] (emphasis added; 10; 4).

In her article "Cotton and Iron," Trinh T. Minh-ha stresses the need for women to acquire what she calls "territorialized knowledge." Knowing the place, the land, and the space where one lives, Trinh writes, "secures . . . a position of mastery: I am in the midst of a knowing, acquiring, deploying world – I appropriate, own and demarcate my sovereign territory" (327). Lost in a false hope of the promised land and blinded by Zeb and fruitless myths, Rosette becomes exiled from her own space, which has now become a place of evil. She realizes now that by failing to "master" her own space, she has contributed to her own deterritorialization from a domestic space fashioned by a man: "La malheureuse avait seulement péché par son aveuglement. Rien vu. Rien entendu que les voix sur ses disques de Reggae." [The miserable woman had only sinned out of blindness. Seen nothing. Heard nothing but the voices on the reggae albums] (196; 191). Pineau shows that the home, which women are supposed to dominate but from which they find themselves exiled, has always been a site of conflict, as Ippolito notes (38). Although domesticated women spend much of their time in the home and presumably demarcate the space better than anyone else, the *case* in *L'espérance-macadam* is depicted as a site of pain, violence, exile, and crime. Women are disenfranchised within it, and as "manmans aveugles, muettes et sourdes" [mamas . . . deaf, dumb, and blind], they are oblivious to this space (15; 9).

Unlike Rosette and other women in Savane, Eliette appears to have created and appropriated her *case*. She repeatedly affirms her happiness in delineating her space, her retreat. Yet it is clear from the beginning of the novel that Eliette has her own story of deterritorialization. In fact, her *case* resembles a prison rather than a true refuge, because she remains in it solely to isolate herself from the community. The causes of her social phobia can be traced to her trauma during the Cyclone of '28. In the aftermath of storms, people are able to rebuild houses, roads, and other pieces of infrastructure. Rosan's sole worry while in prison is that Rosette might not be able to prepare adequately for Hurricane Hugo. Victims of metaphorically collapsed homes cannot rebuild them so easily. For Angela, as Rosan puts it, "Il pouvait rien y faire" [There was nothing he could do about it] (190; 185).

In cases of violent victimization, as Laura E. Tanner writes, "the fragmentation of the victim's physical form is accompanied by an assault on subjectivity that leads to a radical alteration of world view" (3–4). Ever since the Cyclone of '28, Eliette has never recovered from the sexual trauma and has remained constantly afraid of men and cyclones, hiding behind carefully chosen marriages.

Although she eventually recovers from her aphasia — she can now speak to people — her inability to adapt and talk without fear with her neighbors indicates that she remains aphasic at least metaphorically. Her voice is stifled. She is known as "cuisses serrées" [legs closed tight] and the "Négresse cent pour cent aristocrate" [one hundred percent negress] (105; 100), references to her frigidity, a reputation acquired after she was caught attempting to hide her face from men behind a newspaper.

Despite her voluntary seclusion, she cannot prevent "les bruits du dehors" [outside noises] from forcibly entering her house (28). She takes in the totality of Savane's pain (27). Like other community members, she passively witnesses crimes and other evil in Savane: "Elle était toujours à l'abri dans la paix de sa case, complice de tous les complots, témoin sans paroles, comptant les coups de sabre, les coups de conque-lambi tocotoc tocotoc, les coups de poing, de fusil, et aussi mesurant les souffles drus des corps en grand combat" [She'd always remained safe within the peace of her cabin, consenting to all the conspiracies, wordless witness, counting the stabs of the cutlass, the blows of the conch shell clonk clonk clonk, the punches, rifle chots, and also sounding out the heavy breathing of bodies in close combat] (92; 87). In this enclosed community, in which inhabitants believe that they are brothers and sisters, uncles and aunts, nieces and nephews, people see but refuse to acknowledge that they know, that "Tout le monde savait" [Everyone knew](168). Evidence of domestic violence can be heard during the night: "La nuit se réveillait toujours percée des cris de femmes battues ruant folles au-devant d'esprits mauvais" [Night always came to life shot with the cries of women being beaten, cavorting crazily, fleeing before evil spirits] (119; 114). Eliette often reacts to these incidents with statements such as "Je me mêlais de rien" [I didn't get mixed up in any of it] (26; 21). While she does not act against violence, Eliette has what she terms a "maladie de la pensée" [the malady of thought] (16), a reference to her obsessive concern with what happens in her community.

Eliette is forced to confront her own story of trauma when

Angela's accusations surface. The protagonist can relate to Angela's story and the tragic convergence between natural (Hurricane Hugo) and unnatural (Rosan's crime) violence. She finds herself reliving the night of the Cyclone of '28, whose full story is confirmed by an aunt. Eliette finally admits to herself what really happened. For Eliette this confrontation is liberating. She expresses her freedom through a song that tells the passing cyclone, "Personne ne te craint plus" [Nobody is afraid of you anymore] (195). As the story evolves, hurricanes obtain new meanings. The two cyclones that frame the story begin to serve different ends. While the Cyclone of '28 destroyed Eliette, Hugo plays a therapeutic role for her. As she regards Hugo's "passage," she remarks: "Le cyclone avait tout écrasé et piétiné. Y avait rien de bon à ramasser. Rien qui mérite un rapiéçage. Fallait pelleter tout ça et avec, dans le même ballant, les secrets, la honte, la mauvaiseté de Savane." [Cyclone had smashed and trampled everything. Nothing worth patching up. Nothing good enough to salvage. Would just have to plow it all under, that and the secrets, the shame, the sinfulness of Savane in one fell swoop. Just had to make a clean sweep and bury it all] (7–8; 1–2). Angela, for her part, invites Hugo to cleanse and reconstruct her, to "nettoyer son corps au plus profond, de la remettre toute entière comme avant, au temps de l'innocence" [thoroughly cleanse her body, put it all back together again just like before, back in the days of innocence] (207; 203).

What can Eliette and Rosette do after demystifying the home, denouncing fruitless and mythical forms of liberation such as Rastafarianism, or confronting a phobia? How do they reconceptualize their freedom after acquiring it? This question goes beyond seeking territorialized knowledge or mastering space. In an interview entitled "Space, Power and Knowledge," Michel Foucault offers a possible visualization of the relationship between space, knowledge, and freedom. On the subject of liberation, Foucault states, "I do not think that there is anything that is functionally — by its very nature — absolutely liberating. Liberty is a practice. . . . The liberty of men is never assured by the institutions and laws that are intended to guarantee them . . . 'liberty' is what must be exercised" (245). Later he adds, "If one were to find a place, and perhaps there are some, where liberty is effectively exercised, one would find that this is not owing to the order of objects, but, once again, owing to the practice of liberty" (246). If no spatial identification can guarantee absolute liberation, then practicing liberty may be a crucial action in the process of acquiring freedom. Télumée's act of telling her story is certainly an exercise in freedom and is possible only because she is a survivor who "territorialized" her space. As Shelton argues, Schwarz-Bart "asserts the urgency and necessity of collective liberation" (432). Télumée reaches to the collectivity by suggesting that her story may be liberating to future generations. However, the possibility of liberation exists on a symbolic level because the collectivity is supposed to learn from Télumée's personal experience. Pineau pushes the practice of liberty further in *L'espérance-macadam* by transforming Eliette into an active practitioner of liberty.

Eliette ends her indifference to social crimes and rescues Angela from her collapsed home. Coincidentally, Angela turns out to be Eliette's niece, as predicted by a Haitian fortune-teller who had promised Eliette that one day she would mother a niece. Her father, who disappeared after the Cyclone of '28, had had a son, Rosan, with another woman, a fact that remained unknown to Eliette, who assumed she was an only child. Eliette wonders if Rosan's sexual violence was naturally inherited from his father. By offering a safe space for Angela, Eliette contributes to the denaturalization of intimate violence. Similarly, by writing *L'espérance-macadam*, a novel in which domestic violence takes center stage, Gisèle Pineau provides a medium through which to discuss uneasy contemporary topics like sexual exploitation of children in Guadeloupe and elsewhere.

No longer afraid of "men" and "cyclones," Eliette works to rebuild her frigid body as Hurricane Hugo approaches at the end of the novel. When she hears Bob Marley's song "No Woman, No

Cry," she decides to open up her body to the music around her. She asserts that "elle avait le droit de laisser entrer la musique dans son corps. Puisqu'elle était de chair" [she had the right to let the music into her body. Because she was made of flesh and blood] (194; 190). Dancing to the same song that had served as Rosette's misdirected escape signifies triumph over a lifelong resistance to knowledge. The novel ends on a note of hope: "il faudra reconstruire sans doute" [we would probably have to rebuild] (219). But this time the term *reconstruire* applies to *la case* in both its human and physical senses.

Recasting enclosed Caribbean space, Pineau reevaluates the relationship between Caribbean people and the space in which they live and have been deterritorialized. Home should be one's permanent space, mastered and then reclaimed as a site of empowerment. By closely examining intimate space, Eliette's story of liberation transforms geographies of pain into geographies of resistance. Similarly, Calixthe Beyala's character Ateba desires freedom from everyday violence not only for herself but also for women in her community whom she encourages to seek knowledge. In her first novel, *C'est le soleil qui m'a brûlée*, Beyala seeks to represent deterritorialized African women whose goal should be to recover their lost voice and freedom. Like Pineau, she explores the connections between the problems of freedom and the violated female body. Pineau successfully utilizes language and imagery from the temperamental Caribbean environment to examine the possibility of women's resistance to violence. Beyala creates a female character that attempts to find language to denounce female victimization but is confronted with linguistic resistance to pain, anger, and frustration.

Linguistic and Corporal Violence in Calixthe Beyala's C'est le soleil qui m'a brûlée

C'est le soleil qui m'a brûlée concerns the struggles of Ateba Léocadie, a nineteen-year-old woman who lives in a slum known as Quartier General, or QG. Ateba becomes conscious of herself, her body, and her surroundings. From her observations of women's lives in the QG, Ateba, like Tanga in Beyala's *Tu t'appelleras Tanga*, is determined to break the miserable chain of violence that links her life to that of her mother, grandmother, and great-grandmother. Ateba's mother, Betty, a prostitute, abandoned her when she was nine years old. An aunt, Ada, raised Ateba but brought the child her share of abusive fathers. While Tanga's and Anna-Claude's objective is to save children, Ateba wants to save women and get them "back to the stars." According to her woman-centered creation myth, women lived among the stars before descending to earth and subsequently falling under male subjugation.

Like Pineau's character Eliette, Ateba is a woman concerned about the condition and the future of women in her family and community. While Pineau stresses the impact of violence on women's ability to speak, Beyala considers the capacity of the violated body to tell the story of violence when words fail. If Pineau fruitfully represents the broken body by drawing a parallel with the broken house and geography, Beyala emphasizes the difficulty of representing the broken body through the use of broken language. Beyala also uses spatial language to describe women and men's lives. For her heroine Ateba, gazing upon the miserable QG and its reigning apathy is something that she experiences physically. The woman's body reflects the space she inhabits. The unhappiness she senses "survient toujours dans son corps et lui donne des frisson" [emerges inside her body and causes her to shiver] (35; 17). The female body is presented as slowly and continuously degenerating, an image juxtaposed with the dying QG: "Les façades des maisons ressemblent à de vieilles dames ridées et les vieilles dames ressemblent à de vieux bidons rouillés, les uns comme les autres rongés par la vie, momifiés par l'attente de la vie." [The fronts of the houses resemble wrinkled old ladies and the old ladies look like old, rusty tin cans, all of them gnawed at by life, mummified in their endless wait for a life] (18; 5). Throughout the novel, Beyala focuses on the female body not only as a space to decipher the language of violence and pain but also as a means to liberate women's voices that heretofore have been condemned to silence.

The novel's narrative voice is doubled because the female subject is physically and mentally split. In a public presentation, Beyala explained this split and the need for women to reunite their body and soul in *C'est le soleil*:

> Ce Je dont je vous parle, est celui de *C'est le soleil*. Il est une chose qui pense, qui écrit, qui se fait tantôt première personne, tantôt troisième. Il tente d'assembler les morceaux de moi-même, les bras, les jambes. La tête, les pieds, les émotions, les rires, les pleurs, pour en faire un corps humain, une pensée humaine. [This *I* that I am talking about, is the one in *C'est le soleil qui m'a brûlée*. It is something that thinks, writes, that is sometimes in the first-person and sometimes in the third-person. It attempts to put together scattered pieces of myself, arms, legs. The head, feet, emotions, laughter, tears, in order to make one human body, one human thought.] (Quoted in Gallimore 23)

According to Pius Ngandu Nkashama, the description of the physical body in African texts "n'est pas seulement un cadre du décor, elle procède même de la thématique essentielle par laquelle se fonde la construction du roman" [does not only serve as decor but also constitutes the essential thematic that forms the basis of the novel] (Nkashama 107). In *C'est le soleil*, the discourse on the female body refers to the woman's desire to reappropriate a body that has been somehow disassembled. Beyala's words describe a nonunified subjectivity whose foremost desire is the reunification of its mind and physical body. Her narrative explores extreme and painful connections between the violated female body and the search for a female subjective voice. Cultural taboos deny women a voice, a prohibition that leads most female protagonists to madness and silence.[5] Those who speak up or write violate more than the code of silence because "to write honestly may thus mean transgressing, violating the literary boundaries of the expected and accepted" (Lashgari 2).

In fact, *C'est le soleil* textually infringes upon several literary and linguistic boundaries. Whereas Pineau uses the language of history and geography to correlate geographical and female violation, Beyala takes recourse to linguistic violence. Chantal Zabus notes that textual or linguistic violence is normally understood "as violation (cf. Fr.: violent/violant) as in 'to violate,'" — that is, "to disregard, fail to comply with, act against the dictates or requirements of the European prose narrative" (122). In the general introduction, I discuss Frantz Fanon's contention that, in the context of theorization of colonialism, "violence is a cleansing force. It frees the colonized from his inferiority complex and from his despair and inaction; it makes him fearless and restores his self-respect" (*Wretched* 94). Critics have reevaluated this Fanonian cathartic use of violence and challenged its usefulness in rehabilitating the colonized. For instance, Elisabeth Mudimbe-Boyi contends that Fanon's model of cathartic violence allowed the colonized neither to eliminate the inferiority complex nor to remove the colonizer from his superior position (103). Mudimbe-Boyi suggests that writers found an alternative therapeutic tool in depicting violence in literature. They transcended their desire to commit actual violence by violating the language of the colonizer. In doing so, the writer regains freedom and counteracts the effect of colonial violence and the ensuing corrupted postcolonial condition. Mudimbe-Boyi rightly affirms that, unlike the real violence used in autocratic and manipulative systems, violence in writing can provide "a space for freedom in which the writer can insert political and esthetic demands" (117).

Beyala's language carries traces of thematic violence. Themes of rape, murder, verbal, and imagined violence require the use of appropriately violent language. To do so, the writer breaks with the standard usage of the French language. She must adapt this colonial language to a specific socioeconomic milieu to express the propensity of violence in the QG. In the interview, Beyala geographically located her language in contemporary Africa and specifically in shantytowns like New Bell, where she grew up. She declares that "le français de New Bell, c'est le français de demain. Ce ne sera pas cette langue de Baudelaire, figée et morte quelque part" [the French of New Bell, is tomorrow's French. It will not be the language of Baudelaire, rigid and dead somehow] (Matateyou 606). The lexicon Beyala uses to describe life and pervasive violence in the inner city perhaps best captures linguistic violence in the novel. The narrative begins as Jean Zepp, Ateba's neighbor, attempts to find a taxicab that will take him from his factory back to the QG. When he finally finds one, he quickly realizes why no one was willing to give him a ride. The air is hypnotizing, the humidity is nauseating, and the misery is murderous. It is a world dominated by fluids (sweat, filth, spit, semen, vomit) that ooze out of the bodies of its inhabitants. Even solid things decay and liquefy, like the melting road tar that sticks to Jean's plastic shoes. People and things are slowly but continuously dying. The suffocating heat counters the seemingly cold gazes of passive dwellers.

Verbal violence, which includes insults, scolding, and name calling, characterizes interpersonal relationships between Ateba and other characters. Violence of this kind is not only linguistically "injurious," to use Judith Butler's term, but also reaches the victim's soul and therefore constitutes emotional violence. Ateba constantly falls victim to the scolding of her aunt and Jean, who call her a tramp or slut. When given the opportunity, Ateba retaliates against them linguistically. In conversations with other characters, she uses aphorisms, abstracting sentences and concepts in order to irritate her interlocutors. Beyala's choices of words and phrases underscore Ateba's verbal resistance to men's domination. The heroine uses minimalist sentences that say a lot in a few, carefully chosen words. She aims to disconcert her interlocutors, something that seems to secure her superiority over men. Here is an example of a conversation between her and Jean Zepp:

> Je veux te parler, lui dit Jean d'une voix sourde. — Je t'écoute. — Je veux que tu cesses de tuer l'amour. — Je ne le tue pas, je l'accouche. — T'es une conne. Accoucher l'amour? Laisse-moi rire. Tu

> ne sais même pas faire ses gestes. — Je sais. Je sais que je sais. La femme doit se protéger. C'est à elle qu'il faut donner les gestes. — Tu es complètement folle. [I want to talk to you, Jean tells her in a toneless voice. — I am listening. — I want you to stop killing love. — I am not killing it. I am giving birth to it. — You're a damn fool. Giving birth to love? Don't make me laugh. You don't even know how to make the gestures. — I do know. I know that I know. Woman must protect herself. The gestures must be made to her. — You're totally insane.] (Belaya, *C'est le soleil* 124; *Sun Hath Looked* 83)

Ateba's verbal interactions with women are no less violent. When Irène, her best friend, tries to find a way out of an unplanned pregnancy, she considers naming any man among her sexual partners as the father. Ateba quickly reacts: "Je me demandais si tu choisirais un Blanc ou un Noir." [I was wondering whether you'd choose a white man or a black one] (130; 88). These words cause Irène to cry, a reaction that sadistically pleases Ateba. Her statement passes judgment on her friend, who serves both black and white clients as a prostitute. If Ateba levels linguistic violence against men as a way of venting her anger toward them, she does the same to women in order to awaken their consciousness.

Many critics have rightly characterized Beyala's style as "carrefour où se croisent et s'entrecroisent divers types de caractéristiques formelles; elle soumet tous les aspects du roman traditionnel africain à un polymorphisme constant et opère une sorte d'osmose entre l'oralité africaine et le nouveau roman français" [a crossroad of different types of forms; she submits all the aspects of the traditional African novel to a constant polymorphism and operates an osmosis between African oral literature and the French New Novel] (Gallimore 145). The use of multiple voices and fragmented narration, together with the mixing of registers (formal and informal, standard and colloquial, written and spoken) and genres (poetry, prose, songs), punctuate linguistic violence in *C'est le soleil*. Beyala constructs a nonlinear narrative through the lack of chronology, the use of flashbacks in the story, and several "histoires à tiroir" (stories within stories). The fragmented narrative is perhaps more confounding to the reader when the author does not offer transition words to distinguish between present and past events or explain the limits between real and imagined violent events. In one scene, we see Ateba being raped by a policeman during a raid. It is not clear to the reader whether the rape or even the raid is real or imagined, or whether Ateba is the victim at all.

On the relationship between violence and language, Paul Ricoeur reminds us that "[v]iolence that speaks is already a violence trying to do right, and begins to negate itself as violence" (qtd. in Whitmer 119). In many ways, Beyala's recourse to writing violence and writing with violence serves as an alternative to committing actual violence. The result of this exercise is "une langue violée, violentée, demystifiée et démythifiée" [a language violated, desecrated, demystified and demythified] (Gallimore 181). Linguistic violence becomes a tool to break the silence and express anger while practicing liberating subversion. But Beyala's aesthetics of violence go beyond a simple alienation of the colonizer's language. Nkashama observes in his study of contemporary African literature that whereas one is tempted to say that textual violence is caused by the traditional refusal to adopt classic French, "il faudrait dépasser ce stade élémentaire, et envisager une théorie plus efficiente, qui intègrerait d'autres éléments de la psychologie des auteurs, en rapport avec la violence à travers l'écriture littéraire" [one needs to go beyond this elementary stage and look for a more efficient theory that will integrate the authors' state of mind in relation to violence through literary writing] (Nkashama 110).

In *C'est le soleil*, Ateba's state of mind is of interest because the heroine is herself a writer who struggles to put this violence on paper and thereby "tuer le vide du silence" [destroy the emptiness of silence] (*Tanga* 15; *Your Name* 7). Ateba writes to suppress silence, express anger, and call for radical female consciousness. In her essay "Le rire de la Méduse," Hélène Cixous discusses what she calls the "universal" woman, "la femme en sa lutte inévitable avec l'homme classique, [. . .] une femme-sujet universelle, qui doit advenir les femmes à leur(s) sens et leur histoire" [the woman in her inevitable fight against the classic man, . . . a universal woman-subject who must bring women to their senses and their history] (39). Cixous vigorously denounces the deplorable situation of the woman in many cultures, a condition she relates to her past. In this women-denigrating past, whose consequences resonate in the present, the woman is considered to be inferior, powerless, and subordinate to men's will. Ateba adopts a similar notion of womanhood, and her mission is to "liberate the woman from her past" (Cixous 41). Like Cixous, Beyala uses writing to recover the bodies of women – in her case, those of Ateba and others in the story who are prevented from speaking. Ateba understands that writing the woman's body will not only liberate her but will also expose men's crimes against humanity by inscribing them in written texts.

From the beginning of the novel, we sense that Ateba makes the decision to unseal her lips and express her outrage over the past, present, and future conditions of women when she declares:

> Aujourd'hui, j'en ai marre! Ras le bol! J'ai envie de parler . . . J'ai terriblement envie de parler de cette aube triste, de ces heures qui ont couru avant l'arrivée de l'homme. Je puis dire sans attenter à la vérité que c'est sa faute . . . Tout est sa faute . . . [Today, I'm fed up! Totally fed up! I feel like talking . . . I have a terrible urge to talk about that sad dawn, about those hours that fled by before the arrival of man . . . Without doing violence to the truth, I can say that it is his fault . . . Everything is his fault . . .](13; 2)]

Ateba tries to find her voice and a creative force to vent her anger through writing. Despite her intense desire to unseal her lips and denounce men's violence against women, the young protagonist finds herself in the same situation as Eliette in Pineau's novel. She is unable to act upon her wishes. Ateba never effectively communicates with the women she is writing for, and she painfully watches them fall into inevitable tragedy. Her work is ineffectual mainly because it is difficult to lift silence on social taboos. Writers like Ateba must confront how the limits of the language they use to write violence make it difficult for them to destroy the silence that surrounds women's lives.

While Eliette and Ateba both use their rooms as sanctuaries, Ateba, unlike Eliette, does not try to isolate herself out of fear but utilizes the space as a place of revolution. In the room, away from the noises of QG, she writes to expose men's crimes against women. In a place where "the past is no longer," she feels calm and closer to the women for whom she writes. She is therefore able to "make[s] them her witnesses" (Beyala, *C'est le soleil* 57; *Sun Hath Looked* 33). The object of her quest is to write women's fragmented past and present in order to recover womanhood. In a fragmented slogan-like language rich in metaphors, she explains her writing goals: "Briser le mur du passé. Déchirer la mémoire . . . Tressaillir à la vue d'un papier. Retrouver les indices. Retracer les chapitres d'une vie. Retrouver Betty. [. . .] Cataloguer la femme pour se retrouver." [To crack the wall of the past. To shred the memory . . . To thrill at the sight of a piece of paper . . . To find the signs again. To retrace the chapters of a life. To find Betty again. [. . .] To catalogue the woman so as to find herself] (88; 56). Ateba wants to counteract the horrific images of the QG "parce que les horreurs qui déferlaient sans cesse à mes yeux m'avaient appris l'art de voir sans voir, et de ne voir que ce que j'ordonnais à mes yeux de prendre" [because the horrors that ceaselessly surged up before my eyes had taught me the art of seeing without seeing, and of seeing only that which I ordered my eyes to take in" (11; 1). But can Ateba successfully write to women about the pain she witnesses?

In *The Body in Pain* (1985), Elaine Scarry identified the limitation of language to express pain. One important aspect of pain is its ability to destroy language, the power of verbal objectification and perception. Unless accompanied by physical damage, pain resists objectification, or language. Borrowing from psychoanalytic terminology, Scarry asserts that "physical pain does not simply resist language but actively destroys it, bringing about an immediate reversion to a state anterior to language, to the sounds and cries a human being makes before language is learned" (Scarry 4). Similarly, in her writing endeavors, Ateba realizes that she is incapable of transcribing physical pain endured by women in her life. While recognizing that what she has to say is important, she notes that the effect of patriarchal cruelty cannot be expressed on paper. After spending an entire night writing, she tears up the letter "page par page, mot par mot" [page by page, word by word] (48; 26–27) in a methodical act of violence. She experiences a sense of failure, as shown in this quote: "Le lendemain matin, elle a plusieurs dizaines de pages. Elle les relit. Elle les trouve bêtes. Elle pleure. Dieu a certainement râté sa vie pour avoir créé de telles imbécillités." [The following morning she has dozens and dozens of pages. She rereads them. She thinks they are silly. She cries. Surely God has made a mess of his life for having created such idiocies] (48; 26).

If narrating pain and suffering is impossible, Ateba must conjure up an alternative. She becomes the woman activist who uses quasi-political slogans as a medium to raise women's consciousness. Much in the tradition of *littérature engagée*, African women writers have considered writing an indispensable tool for questioning patriarchy. Mariama Bâ, for instance, regards books as powerful weapons, "a peaceful weapon perhaps, but they are weapons" (qtd. in D'Alméida 6). Beyala creates a character whose political writing requires political language. Ateba makes a checklist of rules and duties she must follow. In this listing her priority is clear:

> REGLE NO 1 RETROUVER LA FEMME REGLE NO 2 RETROUVER LA FEMME REGLE NO 3 RETROUVER LA FEMME ET ANEANTIR LE CHAOS
>
> [Rule no. 1 find woman again. Rule no. 2 find woman again. Rule no. 3 find woman again and annihilate chaos (102; 67)]

Ateba's repetition of "retrouver la femme" is perhaps an expression of her yearning for Betty, the mother who abandoned her. It also connects her with all women lost because of abuse, such as Irène and Ekassi, and women who are still being violated, like Ateba's aunt Ada. Stripped of unnecessary details, political language allows the concretization and politicization of the fight against violence, which has proved difficult to translate in literary fashion. As the story progresses, Ateba's desire to raise political awareness among women becomes more and more intense, to the point that "rien d'autre ne l'intéressait plus que de rassembler les femmes et de leur dire de se tenir prêtes, de ne pas râter les étoiles" [nothing else interested her – only gathering the women, telling them to be prepared, not to miss the arrival of the stars] (123; 83). She is confident in the future of women, affirming that "one day the country will belong to them" (132; 89). But Ateba is a lone activist who, like Eliette, "practices her freedom" in the confinement of her room and is therefore unable to communicate with other women. She spends much of her time wishing she could speak, but her words remain stuck in her throat: "elle aurait aimé . . . mais elle n'a rien dit à cause des mots qui restaient collés à ses lèvres" [she would have liked . . . But she said nothing because the words remained glued to her lips] (115; 76). In addition to these aphasic attacks, her frequently abstract imagination clouds some elements of her political agenda. For instance, other points on Ateba's checklist are to "revendiquer la lumière, retrouver la femme et abandonner l'homme aux incuries humaines" [lay claim to the light, find woman again, abandon man to human carelessness] (118; 79).

Ateba's creativity does not limit itself to phantasmic visions of violence but also allows her to dream of the reconstruction of womanhood. Scarry establishes a correlation between pain and imagination. Because it is difficult to explain pain, people often invent a way to describe some aspect of it: "the story of *physical pain* becomes as well a story about the expansive nature of human *sentience*, the felt-fact of aliveness that is often sheerly happy, just as the story of *expressing* physical pain eventually opens into the wider frame of *invention*. The elemental 'as if' of the person in pain ('It feels as if . . .,' 'It feels as though . . .') will lead out into an array of counterfactual revisions entailed in making the world" (Scarry 22). Scarry suggests that if violence and its ensuing pain unmake or destroy the world and language, imagination can reconstruct the world. Writing allows Ateba, or for that matter Beyala herself, to use her imagination and reconstruct her story and womanhood. Ateba uses her imagination perhaps most powerfully when she revises women's history and invents a new myth of genesis in which women play a central role. According to this myth, once upon a time, the woman was a star. When she could no longer stand to see man's suffering down on earth, she came down to help him heal. She brought with her containers of light and gave him abundant love. When she considered her mission finished, the woman wanted to go back and regain her position among the stars, but she quickly realized that the man had robbed her of her containers of light and built a barbed wire fence to prevent her from leaving. Since this original betrayal by man, women have never stopped suffering (166–67; 114). Clearly, Ateba subverts the traditional myth of creation and origin in her culture in which the woman, like Eve, is usually the guilty party who brings down the man, Adam, as well as African creation myths in which the "woman has often been relegated to a secondary role," as Mineke Schipper explains (24).

Ateba wants to secure the long overdue return of the woman to her place in the sky and recover the containers of light withheld from her. But her efforts to eliminate violence by denouncing and purging it through writing as well as her attempt to raise women's consciousness seem a lost cause because she is unable to reach women through her writings. Once again, she has to turn to something else. That something else appears at the end of the novel, when she commits murder. Ateba wanders the streets and scours bars in search of men whom she considers responsible for her best friend Irène's death.

In the end, she lures a man and kills him to avenge Irène. This ultimate act of violence, correctly characterized as symbolic by Richard Bjornson in *The African Quest for Freedom and Identity: Cameroonian Writing and the National Experience*, becomes a sign of her failure to resolve peacefully her conflict with men. Confirming Fanon's belief in the notion of counterviolence, the act of violence appears to be her last chance at liberation because writing, her weapon of choice, ends in failure. However, the end of the novel suggests that Ateba and her spirit remain separated. Nothing meaningful is therefore accomplished in the act of counterviolence.

If Ateba, the character, fails to communicate with other women, Beyala successfully conveys to the reader the seriousness of the topic of violence and women by writing about the violated female body. The female body as the bearer of women's pain becomes the main narrative focus of *C'est le soleil*. In this work, linguistic violence is interconnected with the language of the body, as it is in *Tanga* and *L'espérance macadam*, which tie the representation of the female body to generational or familial violence and the Caribbean space, respectively. Beyala named her novel *C'est le soleil* after a biblical verse that constitutes the preface:

> Je suis noire et pourtant belle, filles de Jérusalem [. . . .] Ne prenez pas garde à mon teint basané: C'est le soleil qui m'a brûlée. Les fils de ma mère se sont emportés contre moi, Ils m'ont mise à garder les vignes. Ma vigne à moi, je ne l'avais pas gardée! [I am black but comely, O ye daughters of Jerusalem [. . . .] Look not upon me, because I am black, because the sun hath Looked upon me: my mother's children were angry with me; They made me the keeper of the vineyards; but mine own vineyard have I not kept.] (qtd. in *C'est le soleil*; *Sun Hath Looked*)

As Gallimore notes, the verse implies that the narrator's skin was not always black but became so because she stayed in the sun too long in order to accomplish her patriarchal duties. In my assessment, what is interesting in Beyala's work is not particularly the race issue, however, because the geographical setting of the novel implies that the stories concern inhabitants of the QG, who are most likely of the same race. Rather, it is the fact that violence inscribes and leaves markings on the victimized female body. The author writes the female body as a physical bearer of men's injustices, and it becomes both testimony and language. In the novel, Beyala presents a familiar social discourse on the female body. The character Jean Zepp distinguishes between two categories of women. In the first category, we have "les épousables" (the marriageable), those who use their bodies to follow traditional patriarchal expectations, like procreation. The second category consists of women appropriately called "les autres" (the others), including subversive women in provocative clothing who are considered prostitutes whether they are or not (72; 45). In the novel, the term *prostitute* extends to women who are shamelessly outspoken and who refuse to abide by traditional expectations of womanhood.[6] During her first meeting with Jean Zepp, he refers to her as "la pute," "la garce," and "la salope" [whore, tramp, slut] (Beyala, *C'est le soleil* 23) because Ateba dared to offer her opinion. From the moment she speaks her mind, the young woman ceases to be "une fille bien" [a good girl] who could have become his wife (23).

In *C'est le soleil*, Beyala describes how women are trapped between two different societal expectations. On the one hand, a woman has to remain a virgin in order to be respectable, and on the other, men constantly seek sexual favors from her. As an example, Ateba's body is controlled by Ada, her aunt, who at some point submits the young woman to a humiliating and public test of virginity after she suspects that Ateba has been sexually active.[7] Jean Zepp and others often gaze upon Ateba's body, which they constantly want to possess sexually. Throughout the novel, women themselves do not control their own bodies. This is particularly true for characters that are prostitutes, like Irène, Ateba's best friend. From the moment he pays Irène for sex, the man believes her body belongs to him. During that time, the female body is present only in the eyes of the proprietor, or the man. The man's gaze on the female body robs the woman of her own body.

Because of conflicting social rules, women are torn between societal expectations and their true desires, and the consequences are sometimes physically and psychologically damaging to the female subject. As demonstrated in Beyala's *Tanga*, her heroines often exhibit dissociative symptoms in order to cope with trauma. Similarly, in *C'est le soleil*, women consciously or unconsciously separate the body from the mind in order to cope with traumatic situations, motivated by the "besoin de se fabriquer un double" [need to construct one's double] (30). The result of this coping method is a split subjectivity, which Beyala illustrates through double narration. The story is told both in first- and third-person narratives. The first-person *Je* (I) plays the role of the disembodied consciousness that gazes upon the *Elle*, or Ateba, the representative of the physical body as it moves and acts in the society (11–13; 1–2). Beyala bases the novel's premise on the constant conflict between the young woman and her conscience, a tension that is never resolved. Although the invisible spirit *Je* understands Ateba's unhappiness, it can do nothing about Ateba's double life. During the day, Ateba performs the duties expected of a woman. But her nights are filled with her true desire, to reunite her body and mind. In fact, it is during the night that Ateba kills a man in order to avenge Irène and all victimized women. When she wakes up in the morning, "elle reprend sa vie de femme" [she goes back to her life as a woman] (*C'est le soleil* 30).

Because they are almost always separated, the two entities are not at ease in the presence of each other. The revolutionary thoughts inhabiting Ateba's spirit are hardly coordinated with the actions of the physical body. The spirit is not aware of every action performed by the body, and Ateba frequently avoids listening to her inner self. The two are barely ever unified as one person because when that almost happens, "Elle [Ateba] sursaute quand elle me [l'esprit] sent dans son temps." [She gets startled when she becomes conscious of my (the spirit) presence in her mind] (118). Beyala's discourse on the body also juxtaposes its two opposite physical experiences, namely pain and pleasure. In order to establish women's self-sufficiency, Ateba first sets out to experiment on her own body by masturbating and discovers that it can be a source of pleasure. Of Ateba's transgressive act, which she accomplishes at night, Eloise Brière writes:

> La vision du corps que propose Beyala dérangera nécessairement, car elle prend le trait physiologique distinctif de la sexualité féminine, et l'affirme non comme source de mal (. . .), mais comme source d'auto-appropriation, comme marque de l'identité féminine. De cette façon, l'écriture du corps est le reflet de la reconstruction de l'identité féminine moderne. [The concept of the body that Beyala proposes will certainly disturb, because it looks at the distinctive physiological aspect of female sexuality and affirms it not as a source of evil (. . .), but as a source of self-appropriation, as a mark of female identity. In this way, the writing of the body reflects the reconstruction of the modern female identity.] (Brière 135)

Ateba visualizes women's destiny in the reappropriation of their own bodies. She attempts to prove that when reappropriated, the female body can empower women. But Ateba, determined to free women and herself, is the only one to actively seek that pleasure. In fact, the epitome of the discursive body in *C'est le soleil* is the female body in pain.

The novel represents pain in its narration of rape. In her analysis of *Le devoir de violence* and *La vie et demie*, Eileen Julien observes that the representation of sexual violence in these novels is not the central issue but "rather a measure of the sickness of social and political relations."[8] In other words, "sexual violence and rape become near transparent signs of something else" (Julien 160–61). Julien concludes that rape is never treated as an aberration or a sick act but rather as a symbol of power (161). In *C'est le soleil*, rape is pervasive and is a major part of the QG's ills and perversions. In the protagonist's eyes it is both a sign of male power over women and an aberrant act. Its symbolic representation is neither an abstracted image nor a gratuitous instance of violence, as it appears in *Le devoir de violence* and *La vie et demie*. Rape represents what it is: an act of sexual violation and a social disease. Unlike most women in the inner city, Ateba is a virgin. As mentioned earlier, her body is tightly controlled by her aunt. While her virginity remains intact until the end of the novel, Ateba's imagination provides her with a perspective on the experience of rape. In fact most instances of rape in the novel are products of Ateba's imagination. Sometimes she imagines violence suddenly, with no provocation, while other times she does so as a result of seeing other women whom she considers victims. For instance, when she discovers Jean with a girl, Ateba is so horrified that she has visions of her own body being raped. The narrator-spirit explains Ateba's panic: "Le temps pour Ateba n'existe plus . . . Puisque la femme écartelée est elle, elle doit s'écarter, courir ailleurs, castrer la douleur." [Time no longer exists for Ateba . . . Since she herself is the woman who is ripped apart, she must withdraw, run elsewhere, castrate the pain] (39; 20). The power of her imagination is so extreme that she sometimes loses her physical body as it dissipates into those of other women. In one moment, Ateba wakes up in a panicked state thinking that her body has left her. She wonders, "Et si durant la nuit un esprit m'a emprunté mon corps . . ." [And what if a spirit borrowed my body from me during the night . . .] (79; 50). This out-of-body experience is symptomatic of rape trauma and is similar to what *Tanga*'s Kadjaba Dongo undergoes. After several such experiences, Ateba becomes more acutely repulsed by every sexual act between a man and a woman, whether or not the encounter constitutes rape.

In their introduction to *Rape and Representation*, Lynn A. Higgins and Brenda R. Silver emphasize another view of rape that we find in Ateba. The story of rape often has two conflicting sides that usually make the act of rape disappear. In courts, rape cases frequently pit a woman who experienced the event as rape against a man who did not perceive it as such (Higgins 2). Higgins and Silver's theory applies to one example in Ateba's story. Despite her distaste for men, Ateba at one point gathers up her courage and decides to lose her virginity to a man. But as soon as the man starts to approach her, she is overcome with feelings of panic and nausea, as if she is going to be raped. She endures the act but fights him to the end. She considers herself violated, while the man swears that the sexual encounter was a moment of love (150–51; 102–3). Beyala constructs other female characters in the same way. They not only display abhorrence for the male kind but also resemble Ateba in their effort to separate the body from the soul. Women in *C'est le soleil* purposefully keep their own bodies in the void, especially Ekassi, a secondary character who enters prostitution to earn enough money to free her husband from prison. Upon his release, the husband abandons her because of what she did to bail him out. Begging him to stay, she tells her husband that with her clients, she was not all there, and that it was just her body: "Rien que du corps" [It was only a body] (63; 38).

Additionally, women in Beyala's novels attempt to protect themselves by rejecting everything male in their bodies. In *C'est le soleil*, the ubiquitous practice of abortion is primarily a rejection of motherhood. Indeed, women refuse to play their social role as procreators. It is also a symbolic gesture to cast off men. After her husband abandons her, Ekassi continues prostitution and, as an act of resistance, never bears any children. The novel does not state whether Ekassi has abortions or whether she simply cannot have any children. The narrator only describes Ekassi's childlessness as follows: "Son ventre s'offrait, accueillait leur sexe imbécile puis, rejetait dans le vide où elle s'était retirée leur sève inutile. Elle se soumettait à tous les désirs mais tenait son ventre dans l'absence." [Her womb would offer itself up, welcome their idiotic sexual organs, then reject their useless sap into the void where she had withdrawn.

She submitted to all their desires but kept her inner core away from them] (62; 37). Abortion becomes a cleansing tool to eliminate traces of male invasion from a woman's body. The novel contains several references to the fact that men have soiled women and that these women then need purification. Ateba constantly washes herself after each sexual incident, real and imagined, in order to eliminate the presence of men not only in her body but also in the bodies of other women. Crying becomes one cleansing phenomenon: "Elle pleure, elle demande aux larmes de venir, de venir, de transformer sa vie en un gigantesque lac et de la purifier, de sanctifier sa vie. Puisque l'homme l'a obscurcie avec ses calomnies, puisqu'il l'a souillée avec ses mains." [She weeps, she asks her tears to come, to keep coming, to transform her life into one gigantic lake and to purify it, to sanctify her life. Since man has darkened her with slander, as he has sullied her with his hands] (24; 9). Ateba remembers washing her mother after the latter returned home from nights with clients. At times, the young woman would get the urge to enter her mother's body and purify each vein and artery of "mauvais sang, leur sang qu'ils déversaient en elle" [that bad blood, that blood of theirs they poured into her] (104–5; 69).

The desire to purify her mother often leads Ateba to express violent inclinations. Speaking of male victimizers, Ateba is overcome with violent feelings: "Elle aurait voulu les battre, les broyer, les mordre, les mutiler" [She would have liked to beat them, crush them, bite them, mutilate them] (105; 69). This desire will become reality when Ateba commits murder to avenge Irène's death. In *C'est le soleil* the male body is reduced to its mere insatiable sexual appetite. Ateba experiences sadistic pleasure in witnessing a circumcision ceremony. Her imagination becomes even more vivid and violent. She entertains a desire to inflict violence on the boys' bodies. She states, "Je chante et dans mon fort intérieur j'imagine un paysage fait de prépuces encore palpitants, épinglés artistiquement sur un tableau de liège comme des papillons" [I am singing and deep inside me I imagine a landscape made of still-quivering foreskins, pinned artistically on to a cork board like butterflies]" (40; 21). Ateba is, however, aware that the practice of male circumcision may be the source of women's suffering. She reflects that "il fera désormais partie de la corporation et, comme les autres, il transmettra la souffrance" [he'll be part of the corporation from now on, and he will pass the suffering on like the others] (40; 20–21). Eileen Julien remarks that women often represent "the abject" in narratives of violence (179). *C'est le soleil*, however, also puts men in the abject position. Beyala presents the female body as being constantly in pain. Ateba learns to recognize signs of pain, such as the bulimia and anorexia that her mother develops to keep an attractive body for her male clients. Over time, these markings serve as a reference code for Ateba that signifies women's physical and mental pain.

Dying or dead female bodies are prevalent in *C'est le soleil*. During her childhood, Ateba witnessed the degeneration of her mother's body. Throughout the novel, the reader follows a gradual destruction of Irène's body that culminates in her death. For women, pain attains its logical end in death. Death is, of course, essentially a total lack of feeling in one's body. The violated female body ceases to exist after having slowly lost its capacity to feel because of repetitive trauma. When Ekassi dies, the narrator describes her body by contrasting it with other forms of life: "Ekassi est allongée sur un grand lit. Morte. Les cierges autour d'elle le disent assez . . . Autour d'elle, des mouches volettent, nombreuses et grasses." [Ekassi is stretched out on a wide bed. Dead. The candles around tell the story . . . Flies buzz around her, many of them, fat ones] (50; 28). Because death destroys pain, the dead female body obtains positive qualities. Such is the case with Irène's body, which, in death, attains purity at last: "le visage a acquis cette pureté que seule la mort ou l'enfance sont à même de donner" [her face has acquired that purity which only death or childhood are able to offer] (165–66; 113) The juxtaposition of death and childhood is significant. Childhood ideally symbolizes the absence of life's sufferings and misgivings. But since one cannot return to childhood, death becomes an attractive option. Ateba herself eventually considers suicide as a way of escaping her female destiny.

By studying the female body in her society, Ateba concludes that women's bodies are only partially autonomous, and that they are in an intense state of suffering because they are soiled and exploited by patriarchal traditions. She is determined to tell other women that "tu es pour toi, ton corps est à toi, prends-le" [you are for you, your body is yours, take it] (Cixous 40). The novel's dedication reads: "Pour Asseze S., toi la femme dont le silence a su si bien me parler" [For Asseze S., you, the woman whose silence knew so well how to speak to me]. The body in *C'est le soleil* seems to speak when women's voices have been silenced. The novels of both Pineau and Beyala argue that to "liberate" themselves, women must act to recover and reappropriate their bodies and by the same token recover their language.

5

War and Political Violence

Nadine Bari's, Edwidge Danticat's, and Monique Ilboudo's Literary Responses to Gender and Conflict

In this chapter, I examine how women writers redefine war in their writing about political violence. The term *war* normally refers to a "hostile contention by means of armed forces, carried on between nations, states, or rulers, or between parties in the same nation or state; the employment of armed forces against a foreign power, or against an opposing party in the state" (*Oxford English Dictionary Online*). This definition needs to be expanded to include several consequences of war with a disproportionate impact upon women, such as sexual violence; the destruction of family and the loss of husbands, sons, and daughters; the dispossession of homes; and starvation.

In the last few years, much has been written about the effects of war and political violence on women and children. Research in the social sciences has demonstrated that women do not experience wars, whether internal or external, in the same way that men do. As part of the noncombatant population, however, they constitute the majority of refugees and other displaced populations and have come to be known as the faces of war. Books about rape as a weapon of war and child soldiers have demonstrated that women and other members of society's most vulnerable classes, while they do not generally participate in physical battles, constitute the community that suffers from them the most.

Because of these issues, which testify to the specificity of women's experiences of political conflicts, I align myself with scholars who redefine the term *war* as something more than simply "conflict" and include these other aspects that affect the larger communities. In this chapter, I examine gendered aspects of the women's "postcolonial war story" in texts by three female writers: the Franco-Malian Nadine Bari on Sékou Touré's dictatorship, the Haitian-American Edwidge Danticat on the ongoing state of terror in Haiti, and the Burkinabé Monique Ilboudo on women and the aftermath of the 1994 genocide of Rwandan Tutsi.

Women and the War Story

In his article "La Guerre chez les romancières," (War in women's novels), Jean-Marie Volet offers a literary survey of African women's writings on war.[1] He remarks that though women writers from Francophone Africa have made significant contributions to the literature on war, critical attention has focused mostly on what are traditionally considered to be women's discourses — family, birth, the education of children, women's sexuality, and the pitfalls of polygamy. However, women's treatment of "nontraditional" topics, like war and other forms of political conflict, has been neglected. The fact that critics do not discuss war should not come as a surprise: African women write rarely about war, at least war in a conventional sense, because they have no authority to do so. As Miriam Cooke explains: "More than most human activities, war has been considered the literary purview of those few who have experienced combat. Those who had not been at the front had not authority to speak of the dead and the dying. Women, therefore, clearly had no right to speak" (3). In order to discuss war in women's literature, the very definition of war needs to be reviewed and broadened to contain women's experience in it. I am interested in recent feminist efforts to study various discourses that may help re-envisioning the concept of war. Addressing the question of "what constitutes war," Cooke proposes what she terms the "postcolonial war story" as an alternative to master war narratives. She suggests that in the context of war, "there is no one history, no one story about war, that has greater claim to truth but that history is made up of multiple stories, many of them herstories, which emanate from and then reconstructs events." She adds that "each story told by someone who experienced a war, or by someone who saw someone experience a war, or by someone who read about someone who saw someone who experienced a war, becomes part of a mosaic the many colors and shapes of which make up the totality of that war" (Cooke 4). Applied to women's literature, the concept of the postcolonial war story challenges the very category of war. The master war narrative, which recounts an event known as war, relies heavily on conventional dichotomies like war and peace, beginnings and endings, and victories and defeats. The postcolonial war story and the question of gender blur these dichotomies.

Chris Cuomo is another critic who questions the scope of the war story. In "War Is Not Just an Event: Reflections on the Significance of Everyday Violence," Cuomo disputes the idea that "war is a realm of human activity vastly removed from normal life, or a sort of happening that is appropriately conceived apart from everyday events in peaceful times" (30). She adds that "most discussions of the political and ethical dimension of war discuss war solely as an *event* — an occurrence, or collection of occurrences, having clear beginnings and endings that are typically marked by formal, institutional declarations" (Cuomo 30). Cuomo looks at war in the broad context of state-sponsored violence. Her take on war exemplifies current feminist preoccupations that testify to the need to include, in war discussions, issues of sexual violence, family annihilation, and environmental destruction. This inclusion establishes a definition of war that takes into consideration possibilities of resistance even for those who do not participate in combat but are directly or indirectly affected by it. Furthermore, if war is not just an event but a phenomenon, as Cuomo asserts, it is not limited to a specific time period or to particular forms of aggression. For Cuomo, "peacetime" or everyday military violence, though it occurs outside the boundaries of declared wars, plays a major role in feminist criticism of war.

Dictatorship is perhaps the most visible form of government that uses violence as a way of controlling people during so-called peacetime. Often referred to as "dirty war," state-sponsored violence constitutes an undeclared war that has no clear beginning or end, yet the effect on women as wives and mothers is limitless. In recent decades, genocide has become part of internal war discourses, particularly within authoritarian governments in which people are killed for who they are as a result of dictatorial incitements. I interpret Bari's and Danticat's writings on war in this broadened context of the postcolonial war story.

In 1984, Ahmed Sékou Touré, one of the most visible leaders in postcolonial Africa, was pronounced dead in an American hospital. As one critic put it, Guinean people reacted with both disbelief and apprehension. On the one hand, they could not believe that this good news could be true; on the other, they were afraid that it was just another one of Sékou Touré's ploys. As Charles E. Sorry notes, Sékou Touré's death "mettait providentiellement un terme à l'ère la plus cruelle de mémoire de Guinéen" [providentially put to end the cruelest era of this Guinéan's memory] (145). Early in his career Sékou Touré had been the quintessential symbol of African revolutionary movements alongside prominent figures such as Nkwame Nkrumah, having led Guinea to become the first French sub-Saharan African colony to respond with a resounding "NON" to Charles de Gaulle's politics of assimilation. As president of Guinea, however, he became the embodiment of dictatorship. While Sékou Touré's contradictory image as both "le héros et le tyran" (the hero and the tyrant), to use Ibrahima Baba Kake's term, defined the essence of his twenty-six-year reign, biographers such as Sorry have demonstrated that almost immediately upon taking power in Guinea, the dictator began eliminating everyone suspected of plotting against his regime. Many intellectuals, writers, military officers, and politicians were forced into exile, imprisoned, and even executed. Several of those who survived Sékou Touré's gulags have documented their experiences in memoirs.[2]

The Franco-Guinean author and political activist Nadine Bari has written extensively about Sékou Touré's regime. Often described as the first Guinean female writer, Bari was married to one of Sékou Touré's victims, Abdoulaye Djibril Bari. Her first three books chronicle the twenty-year search for her husband after he disappeared in 1972 while attempting to join his family in France, where they had sought refuge from Sékou Touré's unstable and unpredictable persecution of *comploteurs* (plotters). Published in 1983, the first book, *Grain de sable: les combats d'une femme de disparu* (Grain of sand: the struggles of a disappeared person's wife), follows her initial search, which as the title indicates proves to be fruitless. Written like a diary, the text is heavily documented with extensive footnotes and copies of her correspondence with several concerned parties. From 1986, the second book, *Noces d'absence (Nuptials in absentia)*, is a highly fictionalized long letter to her missing husband Djibril. Bari copes with her realization that even after the death of Sékou Touré she will not find Djibril. The third text, *Chronique de Guinée* (Guinea chronicles), was written close to twenty years later, in 1994, and describes the end of her search, when she discovers what could be Djibril's grave. Besides the trilogy, Bari has produced two other books: *Guinée: les cailloux de la mémoire* (Guinea: Stones of Memories) in 2003, a biographical essay about a missing close friend; and, in 2005, the novel *L'oeil du heron* (The eye of the heron), set in contemporary Guinea. Bari's testimonials locate the war story between fiction and reality, as the writer-narrator must imaginatively reconstruct memory to repair her torn personal life. Yet like Primo Levi — who in *Survival at Auschwitz* finds it important to reiterate, though unnecessarily, that "none of the facts are invented" (6) — Nadine Bari prefaces *Guinée: les cailloux de la mémoire* with a similar reminder: "L'auteur regrette de devoir préciser que, malheureusement ces personnages ont tous existé et que les faits sont tristement exacts. Car la réalité de la Révolution dépasse le fruit de l'imagination." [The author regrets having to specify that all these characters existed and that the facts are sadly exact. Because the reality of Revolution goes beyond the fruit of imagination].

While war is not officially declared in Guinea, Madame Bari finds herself in a long fight against not only Sékou Touré's regime but also his international allies, including France, her mother country. The disappearance of her husband provokes a deep identity crisis in a woman torn between two national identities as well as remembering and forgetting. Bari's position in this search is complicated by her "postcolonial identity." Married to a Guinean man, she is herself a French white woman who follows Djibril to his country to build together a family while he participates in building the economy of the newly independent Guinea. Throughout her writings, the author's struggle with this double identity is apparent. As a French woman, she is placed on the side of the colonizer, but by marriage and love, she is expected to embrace her husband's culture. Bari's postcolonial war story begins when she learns that her husband has been arrested. Unsurprisingly, she tries to find the truth concerning his whereabouts, even attempting to enlist the help of religious authorities in the Vatican, because she is Catholic, and in Mecca, because her husband was Muslim. She retraces his footsteps following rumors and testimonials of people she encounters in her search, yet at every step, obstacles to reconstructing Djibril's story accumulate. By the end of her search, she has contacted, worked, or fought with both Amnesty International and the French government of Giscard D'Estaing. She has also founded an association of French women in her situation in Strasbourg called L'Association des familles françaises de prisonniers guinéens (Association of French families of Guinean prisoners)].

In the tradition of testimonial and autobiographical literature, Bari's trilogy serves multiple purposes. First, the texts serve to denounce state-sponsored abuses. Second, they commemorate the memory of the disappeared. Third, writing allows Bari to do what Adrienne Rich calls "resisting amnesia." Last and perhaps more importantly, the act of writing is part of the process of self-healing after the pain and torture of "vivre dans l'ignorance" (living in ignorance) of what happened to the loved one. As noted by several scholars, autobiography is the quintessential "post-colonial genre of resistance and counter-discourse" (Ippolito 3). To write about one's experience of violence is to denounce and therefore resist and counteract the intended effect of Sékou Touré's dictatorship. Dubbed "le meilleur policier de Guinée" [Guinea's best policeman-woman] by Lansana Conté, Sékou Touré's successor, Bari uses writing to engage in political activism (*Noces d'absence* 96). Autobiography as activism offers alternative stories to official versions filled with silences and lies. In her article "Between Amnesia and Anamnesis: Re-Membering the Fractures of Colonial History," Anne Donadey describes the tensions between omissions in official history and the reconstitution of personal histories as part of the dialectic of amnesia and anamnesis. She suggests that anamnesis, which in the postcolonial context involves "piecing together of a collective history," becomes "a way of resisting the occlusions created by official history, or recovering the traces of another submerged history in order to create a counter-memory" (111–12). Bari aims to close the disconnect between the official story put out by the government and the evidence showing that her husband was a victim of Sékou Touré's killing machine.

Victimized by a regime that insists on silencing her in the name of national unity, Bari writes to lift the silence over the human rights abuses rampant in Guinea. Her writings form counter-memories that offset violence committed by the state, and her work becomes an act of resistance against the silencing of official history. Sékou Touré is not the only target of her revelations. Bari also exposes religious organizations that refused to help families in need on the grounds that they would not involve themselves in political issues. In her accounts the French government seems to privilege collective interests at the expense of the individual. While Bari actively attempts to raise awareness about Guinea's disappeared, France is more interested in reestablishing Franco-Guinean relations, which had ended after the 1959 referendum awarded Guinea independence. For the French government, "leurs maris sont devenus de grains de sable qui agacent à peine les dents de l'engrenage financier des relations franco-guinéennes" [their husbands have become like a needle in the haystack that hardly bother the workings of the Franco-Guinean financial apparatus] (*Grains de sable* 124). Both Guinea and France make empty promises and continue to silence Bari and the other families of the victims. Even after Sékou Touré's death, she finds herself confronting the silence of the official record. When she asks why the new government has not found the missing, she is told that it is for "des raisons de droit et d'équilibre national" [questions of rights and national stability] (*Noces d'absence* 20).

In her article "The State, the Writer and the Politics of Memory," Elisabeth Mudimbe-Boyi argues that in official history "silence might be legitimated as a morally justifiable State action and it is deemed in the interest of building a national identity" (114). In the interest of nation building, governments allow themselves to "confiscate memory" or put "history under surveillance" (157). The writer, however, can effectively counteract the official story by turning to metafiction. Borrowing from Adrienne Rich, Donadey states that in relationship to amnesia, anamnesis becomes "a particular way of 'resisting amnesia'" (111). In addition to denouncing state-sponsored violence, Bari's autobiographical writings serve to resist both collective and individual amnesia. On the collective level, for Bari, "une société sans mémoire est une société suicidaire" [a society without memory is a suicidal society] (*Noces d'absence* 82). On a personal level, the writer often expresses her fear of forgetting her husband. For instance, his corporeality begins to fade in her memory. Upon her return to Guinea after Sékou Touré's death, Nadine realizes that her memory of Djibril has become fragmented and disembodied, and she finds herself desperately observing pedestrians in the hope of finding Djibril. Yet all she can recognize are body parts — hands on one person, teeth on another — that resemble those of her husband. She can no longer visualize him in full. The project of reconstructing his story helps satisfy her need to revive Djibril's body. In the letter to her missing husband that constitutes the majority of her epistolary novel *Noces d'absence*, Bari writes: "Je m'acharne à t'exhumer de l'oubli où tu t'enfonces malgré moi." [I persist in exhuming you from oblivion where you sink deep despite my efforts] (15–16). Her repetitive use of words such as "faire revivre" and "exhumer" indicates that the act of writing somehow contributes to memorializing, commemorating, and even resurrecting Djibril. The use of "exhumer" is particularly interesting because it refers to the literal exhuming of anonymous graves in the hope of finding her husband's body or of digging through clues to recover his story. More importantly, the act of exhumation is a necessity under a dictatorial government. As Bari gradually finds out, the very existence of the traitors, the "ennemis de la revolution," is put into question.

Bari's situation illustrates why the definition of war writings must be extended. She never experiences war in the strictest sense. The government arrests and executes her husband in secret, away from the public eye, and officially denies that such an event ever occurred. Nadine Bari, like other widows of war, suffers the loss of her husband but with a *différence*. In Guinea, there are no institutions and language in place to express the situation. The missing become neither prisoners of war nor heroes. In addition, Sékou Touré refuses to acknowledge their disappearance or even their execution. It therefore becomes impossible for these women and their children to claim such a loss without a physical body or death certificate. By refusing to recognize formally their disappearance, the government denies the existence of these individuals. For instance, Sékou Touré's regime decides to annul the marriages of the condemned. He also suggests that the wives and children of the condemned may be guilty by association and that in order to rid themselves of this *tare* (defect; stain) they must remarry within six months and therefore change their names and those of their children. As he put it, "il est clair que continuer à porter le nom d'un traître constitue une sérieuse atteinte à la Révolution" [it is clear that to continue to bear the traitor's name constitutes a serious attempt at the Revolution] (*Grains de sable* 75). When he voids these marriages, he also eliminates entire families by refusing to give offspring a Guinean birth certificate. Women and children are forced to give up their names. Sékou Touré manages to suppress the existence of his opponents by erasing them completely from their descendants' lives. For Bari, then, writing becomes not only an act of commemoration of loved ones but also proof of life for entire families.

From Love of Husband to Love of the Land

Bari's preoccupation with truthfulness is evident in her narrative strategies in the trilogy. While her writing flows easily, Bari composes her books with academic rigor, documenting her sources thoroughly. At the bottom of the page, the reader often finds reference notes and additional explanations. She cross-lists her books, sending the reader to a particular text whenever necessary. As "le meilleur policier de Guinée," she pays attention to details and questions every contradiction. It often seems like the narrator and the reader discover clues regarding Djibril's mysterious disappearance simultaneously. Like a detective chasing a story, one about war in this case, mental calculations are required. The reader follows the narrator's additions, subtractions, deductions, and conclusions with each new lead. New clues are followed, new deductions made. It becomes a game of logic, plausibility, and possibilities. Perhaps Bari's most effective "detective" technique is her inclusion of correspondence and pictures of people and places involved in the whole affair.

Naming is another investigative tool. Exposing names becomes a way to discover and publicize the story but also a method of denouncing and pressuring the states and organizations involved. Bari's use of multiple narrative styles reveals a woman mindful of uncovering the truth. Her style shows rigor, but at the same time it is reflective and confessional. The diary-like style of writing allows Bari to convey to her readers the sense that her ordeal is real. The three books in the trilogy contain various forms and genres. In fact, Bari labels the first and last volumes "témoignages" (testimonials), whereas the second volume, *Noces d'absence*, the long letter to her husband, reads like a novel. *Noces d'absence* is perhaps the most personal, an emotional outpouring addressed to her husband, whom she must resign herself to "marry" in his absence.

Despite the thoroughness with which she focuses and describes her search, Nadine Bari never recovers "la vérité objective" that she has been seeking. As Mudimbe-Boyi observes, the project of reconstituting a story that counteracts the official version often results in failure because it is dangerous. To be somewhat successful, writers resort to metafiction. Bari's use of metafiction in *Grain de sable* consists of the constant interpellation of her husband, as she draws him into the process of discovery while recounting her frustrating search and declaring her love and hopes for the future. Bari's narratives interweave biographies of the loved one with histories of Sékou Touré's regime. Her writings are also highly autobiographical, focusing on her own attempt at self-healing. The underlying quest in the trilogy largely involves the identity search of a Franco-Guinean woman who is attempting to recover the love story of her life. Because she fails to recover her husband, she is forced to seek an alternative story for the sake of mourning and self-healing. Bari eventually transfers the love she felt for her husband to Guinea, the land she believes he left her as a legacy through a dream. She is essentially forced to produce an autobiography in order to rearrange her life and belong to a world without Djibril.

Bari is mindful of issues raised by her problematic identity. In

Grain de sable, she becomes a de facto outsider to her native France and her adoptive country Guinea, and her victimhood is put in doubt. Bari is, however, able to use her double identity to her advantage in *Noces d'absence*. She is able to infiltrate Guinean society with the help of her in-laws. At the same time, because she is French and a foreigner, authorities are willing to receive her in their offices. But it is undoubtedly her investigative skills and her identity that ultimately enable her work. *Chroniques de Guinée* describes what appears to be the last leg of her journey. In the book, Bari finally discovers Djibril's grave after realizing that Guinea is her husband's legacy and that his community fully embraces her. Bari's final epiphany is that she must bury him so she can transfer the love she has for him to Guinea. This love is especially apparent in *Noces d'absence* when she compares her husband to his country. In the book's dedication, she writes of Guinea, "j'aime comme on aime son compagnon de vie, avec ses qualités et ses défauts" [I love like one loves one's life companion with their qualities and limitations].

Danticat's Poetics of War

In *Ecrire en Pays assiégé-Haiti-Writing Under Siege*, Agnès Sourieau and Kathleen M. Balutansky consider the Haitian writer in the context of war. The writer is under siege because he or she is writing under "military attack, resistance, blockade and loss of freedom" (25). Haitian writers have always found imaginative ways to expose recurring reigns of terror and tyranny "from the first slave rebellions to the latest dictatorships" (Sourieau and Balutansky 29). Like most Haitians who write "in blood," Edwidge Danticat explores both external and internal sources of violence.[3] In *The Farming of Bones*, she studies a woman caught in the war against Haitians in the neighboring Dominican Republic. In *Breath, Eyes, Memory* and *The Dew Breaker*, Danticat explores life during the terror of dictatorships and the period following them, which, as Joan Dayan reminds us, "is far more serious in its effects than Duvalier's dictatorship" (286). Like Nadine Bari, Danticat sets out to "piece together" the officially silenced history of her native Haiti. Through fictional female characters, the writer reconstitutes the real-life 1937 massacre of Haitians in the Dominican Republic and the impact of militarization on women. The result is an alternative war story that consists of elements similar to those found in Bari's work. In these three novels, there are no wars officially declared, yet people die or disappear, and women are victims of endless militarized violence. In Danticat's novels, tragic fate clearly weighs down on characters whose solutions for freedom seem geared toward violent self-destruction. However, Danticat's work reveals how writing about war serves as an act of resistance to destruction because it documents the past. As Myriam Chancy reminds us, under Duvalier's dictatorship amnesia was "the surest means to survival for most Haitians" (305). By writing forgotten histories, Danticat expresses the desire of most Haitians for "regaining memory" and "halting the process of amnesia (Chancy 305).

Journey to the Painful Place

Edwidge Danticat was born in Haiti and immigrated to the United States at age twelve. She revisits Haiti's long history of war from exile, more precisely from what Elaine Savory terms "ex/isle conditions." Savory writes that exile is "the condition of separation from the country of birth" (170), while ex/isle is "a creative, if not painful space in which woman's writing become a means to construct images of progressively developing subjectivities" (176). Although ex/isle describes the separation of an identity "based complexly in first self-definitions in terms of ethnicity, class, gender, nationality, generation," Savory emphasizes the writers' ability to create within that condition (170).

Danticat belongs to a long tradition of female Haitian writers, such as Marie Vieux Chauvet and Jan J. Dominique, who have written about Haiti from that painful space in their attempt to document, albeit in fictional form, women's experiences of war and political violence. Scholars have focused for the most part on

Chauvet's 1968 novel *Amour, colère et folie*, a fictional account of the horrors of Haiti's François Duvalier, known as "Papa Doc." Duvalier was president of Haiti from 1957 until his death in 1971. In 1961, he declared himself president for life. His son Claude, alias "Baby Doc," took over after his death and continued his father's legacy of violence. Papa Doc's regime as well as a militia under his control known as the Tontons Macoutes are the subjects of Chauvet's novel, which goes "from Love to Madness, by passing through Rage" (Scharfman, "Theorizing Terror" 231). Chauvet's complex narrative treats the effects of economic, racial, and internal wars on three sisters. Critical work regarding the book initially focused on violence against women as part of a masculinist nationalistic discourse in which the woman's body represents the land that has been violated by external assailants. Chancy, however, reads Chauvet's text as a refusal "to collapse the female character's violations with metaphoric 'rapes' of the nations." Chancy contends that in doing so Chauvet "gave voice to a suppressed reality of gendered violence and documented unrecoverable historical occurrences." Reading the text solely as a mythical representation "demonstrate[s] the extent to which women's lives in Haiti remain invisible" (Chancy 309). In the autobiographical novel *Mémoire d'une amnésique*, Jan J. (Gigi) Dominique explores childhood events and traumatic experiences generated by both the first American occupation of Haiti and dictatorships, and she testifies to a woman's desire to free herself from a history of violence that marked her both personally and as part of her society. Irline François states that Dominique "offers an indictment of the Duvalier regime which she views as characterized . . . by widespread repression and by its unprecedented violence directed against women" (287).

In her writings, Danticat also tries to reconstitute female subjectivities that have been lost because of ongoing violence in and outside Haiti. Danticat's particular contribution to the fictionalized study of gendered violence in Haiti is that she covers these stories from the perspective of a female generation that, like Danticat herself, barely lived these events first-hand. Danticat's stories are told from the point of view of young female characters that, like her, live in exile. Amabelle Désir (*The Farming of Bones*) lives in the Dominican Republic, while Sophie (*Breath, Eyes, Memory*) and Kâ (*The Dew Breaker*) live in the United States. Unlike many other exiled Haitians, many of these women did not flee as a result of being direct victims of Haiti's political violence. Kâ was born in exile, while young Sophie, like Danticat, joined parents who had already fled to the United States. Amabelle is cared for by a Dominican family that finds her at the Massacre River after her parents' accidental drowning. With the possible exception of Amabelle, these young women appear to live stories of war and violence primarily through the experiences of previous generations. However, Danticat's texts demonstrate that her generation nevertheless has a strong connection to militarized violence. Her characters are effectively "bastards" of the dictatorship. They are either products of rape (Sophie and to a certain extent Kâ), orphaned (Amabelle), or are abandoned and deceived by Haiti and its history of violence. Though these women live away from the center of dictatorial chaos, the remnants of violence forcibly accompany them in exile. Danticat's protagonists typically encounter madness as a result of violence. In *The Dew Breaker*, a seamstress is convinced that her Macoute torturer follows her everywhere she moves in New York City. A young nurse isolates herself with her eyes fixated on the psychiatric ward of the hospital, symbolizing her madness. Anne, Kâ's mother, attempts to survive by hiding alongside her ex-Macoute husband and taking her religious beliefs to the extreme. Others maintain isolated lives, incapable of forming relationships with family and friends. The many exiled women who struggle to forget their traumatic past obviously bear the remnants of war. In *Breath, Eyes, Memory*, Martine, Sophie's mother, seeks solace in silence in order to forget, while her daughter desperately works to destroy that wall of silence in her own identity quest.

Like most products of exile, Danticat's main characters have a natural need to understand their complex identity, particularly the Haitian history from which they are disconnected. Danticat's meticulous writing methods involved several research trips to Haiti to collect both oral and written testimony. Her fictionalized accounts of Haitian women's lives combine imaginative work with careful research into the historical eras of her characters, as evident in the acknowledgements sections of the books. Through these characters and their stories, Danticat is able to journey farther into Haiti, creating a trajectory of memory that reveals her heritage.[4] Similarly, her heroines tirelessly re/search their origins. They are, as Kâ in *The Dew Breaker* explains, women "with a single subject" (4). Kâ is an artist who several times attempts to capture and represent her father by sculpting his elusive, scarred face. Her father turns out to be a former prison guard who worked for the dictator. *Breath, Eyes, Memory*'s Sophie returns to Haiti to re/search the sites and sources of her multigenerational pain because her mother refuses to share the stories with her. In *The Farming of Bones*, it is her decision to return to the Dominican Republic to revisit the sites of her pain that finally ends Amabelle's suspended life in Haiti, where she had spent decades waiting in vain for loved ones. In writing and seeing the past through characters of her own making, Danticat produces a narrative through visiting that "painful space." She revisits the painful space of genocide against Haitians by Trujillo's government and of personal history as the daughter of dictatorship. These women go from innocence to discovery of their painful stories. As we shall see, Danticat presents stories of violence and resistance to it on a continuum, from political to familial violence and vice-versa. Sophie discovers that her mother was raped by a Macoute taking advantage of his position of authority over her and that she is the product of that violent encounter with Duvalier's political representative. Kâ's journey ends with her father's confession that he was not the prey but the hunter, making her the daughter of a Macoute. Sophie and Kâ become the faces of dictatorship both literally and figuratively. Upon revisiting the sites of her pain, Amabelle discovers that the intimacy she shared with her adoptive Dominican family was indeed false because of her Haitian heritage.

Danticat's novels continue this tradition of giving voice to women's experience of historical violence, and the novels exemplify another attempt by women writers to inscribe women's experience of war. By focusing on a female character's point of view, her novels restore women's history. As several scholars have shown, Danticat provides a literary space to collect women's history through textual testimony. I read Danticat's texts as narratives of the postcolonial woman's war story, resulting from women's experience with dictatorship and militarization. Danticat explores the theme of war through women's effort at resisting amnesia (*The Farming of Bones*), through a study of the impact of militarized violence on women (*The Dew Breaker*, *Breath, Eyes, Memory*), and, finally, through a discourse of gendered violence on a continuum that goes back and forth between the private and the public.

Resisting Amnesia in The Farming of Bones

The Farming of Bones is a tragic love story involving Amabelle Désir and Sebastien Oneus. Both are Haitians who live and work in the neighboring Dominican Republic, she as a domestic and adoptee of a Dominican family, he as a migrant worker in the cane fields. They become separated in 1937, the year when *antihaitianismo*, a term used to describe racial prejudice against Haitians who lived in the Dominican Republic, culminated in the massacres of Haitians. Amabelle manages to reach Haiti, but Sebastian, most likely killed during the massacres, never returns. Though Amabelle is a fictional character, her story echoes Nadine Bari's postcolonial war story in many ways. They both lose their mates to dictatorships. Both women carry out their lives with a single mission: to find the truth behind their mates' unexplained disappearances. The construction of one's identity is tied to the recovery of the story of the missing loved one. Amabelle spends a lifetime waiting and searching for Sebastien. *The Farming of Bones* is a first-person narrative in which she seeks to remember and tell her story as a survivor of and witness to the massacre of Haitians.

The problematic of remembering and forgetting is at the center of Danticat's poetics of war. If amnesia was "the surest means to survive dictatorship," as Myriam Chancy reminds us, the writer creates a female character who goes against the grain and establishes that remembering is surviving. Amabelle's lifelong mission is to fight amnesia and not to forget Sebastien and others who disappeared during that chapter of Haitian history. Her resolve opposes the disinterest of Yves, a fellow survivor whose family welcomes her in their home in Haiti. Yves is not interested in telling his story because, as he states, "you tell the story and then it is related as they wish" (Danticat, *The Farming of Bones* 246), reiterating a point made earlier in the chapter that the version of history promoted by dictatorial regimes is intrinsically distorted by the national agenda. Instead, Yves pours his energy into cultivating and expanding his family land in order to avoid the "dead season" (263). He works to forget while Amabelle fights amnesia. It is unclear whether re-appropriating Haiti and "cultivating his garden" helps Yves overcome his trauma in the same way as Simone Schwarz-Bart's Télumée.

Danticat writes Amabelle's story in several chapters, detailing the recollections of her life before, during, and after the 1937 events. The novel's structure highlights the importance of the act of recollection for the heroine but also for Danticat, who seeks to testify to this violent history. Danticat recounts in a structured manner Amabelle's life before she was forced to flee the killings. The writer alternates between short chapters printed in bold and longer chapters presented in regular font. In the latter, Danticat gives a linear recounting, in the past tense, of Amabelle's life before, during, and after the events. The bold chapters, written in the present tense, capture the intensity of Amabelle's effort to remember her past. The fragmented recollections and thoughts concern events linked to the violence. The heroine repeatedly analyzes what she calls her "shadows" because, she explains, "when you have so few remembrances, you cling to them tightly and repeat them over and over in your mind so time will not erase them" (Danticat, *The Farming of Bones* 45).

Fear of forgetting is something she has in common with Sebastien and other Haitians living in the Dominican Republic who are "an orphaned people," belonging nowhere (Danticat, *The Farming of Bones* 56). Amabelle and Sebastien, like their fellow *vwayajè*, the term used for migrant workers, support each other in their resistance to falling into oblivion. Their priest, Father Romain, regularly reminds the Haitian workers "how remembering – though sometimes painful – can make you strong" (73). Amabelle clearly desires to reconnect with her shadows, which have multiple sources. We learn that they include her parents, who drowned during a storm while crossing the Massacre River, located between Haiti and the Dominican Republic. Amabelle survives the natural violence, and her Dominican rescuers, Papi and his motherless girl Valencia, take her with them. When Amabelle loses her parents, she also loses her country, her people, and her identity. She becomes Valencia's childhood companion, and when Valencia eventually marries, she is progressively transformed into a faithful domestic helper. Her parents, childhood memories, and homeland become her shadows. Sebastien will become her shadow as well when he disappears. His story bears similarities to Amabelle's. He loses his father to a hurricane, which subsequently leads him to leave Haiti and find work in the Dominican cane fields. He loses his homeland in the process because, like so many *vwayajè*, he could never afford to go back. These losses connect him and Amabelle, and at night they help each other remember. Because Danticat writes the story from Amabelle's perspective, we read more about Sebastien's role in helping her remember and reveal the true shape of her "shadows."

The novel opens with a chapter in bold in which Amabelle recounts – in a dream-like sequence – a story about a woman who is the victim of a nightmare. Sebastien, who is lying next to her, asks Amabelle to undress because, he says, "your clothes cover more than your skin . . . you become this uniform they make for you.

Now you are only you, just the flesh" (2). He encourages her to remove the identity given to her by others. Nakedness becomes a symbol for the return to nature, meaning her homeland. In a way, Danticat configures Sebastien as Amabelle's last link to Haiti and to her true self. In fact, Amabelle declares that she is afraid she will "cease to exist when he's not there" and that she knows no one "and no one knows" her (2). Reconnecting with her shadows is a matter of survival.

Sebastien is "a night talker," a figure that reappears in *The Dew Breaker*, meaning a person who can only talk away their trouble during their sleep. He continuously encourages Amabelle to remember. Thanks to him, she remembers aspects of her cultural heritage that she had thought forgotten, like her parents' profession as healers. This helps explain to her why she knows how to heal in her new life in the Dominican Republic. Sebastien's encouragement enables her to "night talk" and to remember events long lost in her memory. In these bold chapters, Amabelle revisits sites of memory, mostly tragic but also positive, like when she first made love with Sebastien. These recollections help chase away the nightmares, turning her shadows into positive memories. These memories accompany her through life and help explain who she is (119). Amabelle slowly recognizes that the shadows are "people walking ahead of me, people I cannot see, but whose form I hope will emerge again once the air is cleared" (139). In this image, she sees herself as a child with someone holding her hands. When Sebastien is no longer present, Amabelle is left with memories that will help her overcome the loneliness. The bold chapters stop during the segments that tell the story before her flight to Haiti, when the two lovers are separated with hope of reuniting later. Only two of the bold chapters emerge later, when Amabelle acknowledges Sebastien's demise and her role as a witness to the massacre. In these last bold chapters, however, Danticat continues to demonstrate that Amabelle's ability to survive depends on her connection to her "shadows." The theme of nakedness returns at the end, when Amabelle removes her dress to swim in the Massacre River, interacting with the shadows of her parents, who had been killed along with so many others at the same river. Danticat reconstructs Amabelle's memory and her identity through that contact.

Witness to Massacre

Unlike Danticat's young characters in *The Dew Breaker* and *Breath, Eyes, Memory*, Amabelle is within the site of war, making her a direct witness to massacre. Renée Larrier rightly defines Danticat's novel as a text that functions as oral testimony, just as other Caribbean female writers have positioned their heroines as witnesses at "important historical junctures." Larrier cites several examples, including *Pluie et vent sur Télumée Miracle*. She also reads Danticat's novels as part of a larger effort in Caribbean literature to bear witness to history, something that is particularly significant for a formerly enslaved people historically denied the right to "offer testimony" (Larrier, "'Girl by the shore'" 51). Amabelle is, however, a rather frustrating witness at times, especially when she remains quiet about what she "saw" even though Danticat's heroine was in the middle of the massacre. In the hospital at the border, many survivors share their stories, but Amabelle remains quiet and only listens. In Haiti, as she waits in line, she observes other survivors who practice telling their stories to the justice of the peace (230–32). The latter hears the stories and then gives the survivors monetary compensation. While others feel "a hunger to tell" or "the imperative to tell" (Laub 63), Amabelle is apparently paralyzed by her single mission to find out what happened to her lover. In other words, she is more interested in recovering the story of her loved one than giving her own. Because Danticat describes in detail her harrowing journey during the massacre in the novel's second part, we know what Amabelle knows. Danticat shows Amabelle witnessing the killings directly, being threatened with her road companions, and failing to rescue one of her friends from the Massacre River. Still, listening to survivors after the fact deepens her understanding of the events.

Amabelle's initial silence may well be attributable to the fact that she is a woman who has a single mission, but she is also a different kind of victim. Unlike other Haitians, she grew up in the Dominican Republic and is not a temporary worker. In fact, she acknowledges later that she "knew as well how to say 'pesi' [parsley in Haitian creole] as to say it 'perejil'" in Spanish (265). Here, Danticat adopts a historical anecdote about Trujillo's men, who supposedly used the term *parsley* in Spanish to identify Haitians who could not pronounce the word well. Amabelle enjoys, to a certain extent, protection from her Dominican adoptive family, including Valencia's husband Pico, Trujillo's henchman. Danticat creates a character that is not personally threatened, but because Amabelle is following her lover, she finds herself embroiled in the events. The absence of bold chapters during her flight means that Amabelle's subjective voice is also absent. Amabelle is more an observer than a participant, a listener more than a talker, which certainly mirrors Danticat's role as a listener and observer during her research. It is not until she realizes the finality of Sebastien's disappearance that Amabelle acknowledges her role as a witness to the massacre.

In the two bold chapters toward the end of the novel, Amabelle reveals that she "saw things" (265). Not only was she a witness to a massacre, but she also saw it coming. She acknowledges that she knew "the river of blood might come to [my] doorstep, that it has always been in our house, that it is in all our houses" (265). Amabelle dreams of giving her "testimony" (264): like the dead who leave their words as "inheritance" (265), she vows to "pass on" (266) her story of the slaughter. She appropriates the story, which she hopes to "lay down now and again, a sage nest where it will neither be scattered by the winds, nor remain forever buried beneath the sod" (266). In these last confessional chapters, Amabelle comes to terms with her status as witness to the massacre. She acknowledges that she "was never naïve, or blind" (265). The things she saw compose the anatomy of the massacre, which she feels and sees happening.

Amabelle is a witness to the evolving history of the massacre. While it is unclear whether she initially understands the sources of the animosity between Haitians and Dominicans, reading the novel and reviewing the story with her at the end, we see the evolution of events leading to massacre. Signs of war – fear, rumors, and a general atmosphere of doom and vigilance against Haitians – are precursors to the massacre. When she states that the river of blood was always in "our house," Amabelle is speaking literally of the home where she lived as a child with her rescuers Papi and Valencia. The household in which she grows up is a microcosm of the prejudice against Haitians. She experiences racism under the roof of the very people who raised her. Valencia later marries Pico, a military man who works for Trujillo and who will later carry out the first massacres of Haitians in Allegria, where they live. Pico is Trujillo's foot soldier, the one who implements the law of the dictator. In him, Danticat reveals the face of the military state terror, which she emphasizes in her later novels through the figure of the Haitian Tonton Macoute. Pico and Valencia name their son Rafi in honor of Rafael Trujillo, and a prominent painting of Trujillo done by Valencia herself dominates the wall of the living room, symbolizing how in effect Amabelle lives under Trujillo's roof. She becomes simultaneously an insider and outsider. On the one hand, she is an insider because, unlike other Haitians in the Dominican Republic, she was raised there and understands and speaks Spanish. On the other, Papi and Valencia both refer to dark-complexioned Haitians like her as *her people*, the outsiders. When Valencia's daughter is born with a darker complexion than her twin brother, she tells Amabelle that she would not like her baby girl to be mistaken "for one of *your people*" (emphasis added; 12). For the reader and later Amabelle herself, the relationship between Amabelle and her adoptive family unravels and becomes representative of racism against Haitians.

In *The Farming of Bones*, Danticat depicts militarized brutalization of men and women both in the Dominican Republic and Haiti. As stated earlier, Pico symbolizes the quintessential henchman for the dictator Trujillo. Danticat develops this figure — a loyal soldier — and his impact on women in the appropriately titled novel *The Dew Breaker*. The title signifies the Macoute who awakes at daybreak to go on violent missions that include the arrest, torture, and murder of people who are perceived to be enemies of the state. Several female characters in the novel that are living in exile testify to being raped by these Macoutes, even as young children. Mariselle is forced into exile after her artist husband was shot for having painted "an unflattering portrait of the president" (Danticat, *The Dew Breaker* 172). Like several characters in Danticat's fiction, Freda loses her father to dictatorship. In her texts, the Macoute is generally a man. He is presented as aggressive and violent, one who betrays the people and is extremely loyal to his boss, the dictator who becomes a father figure to him. As a representative of the police, he wields a lot of power over the populace. Danticat portrays the Macoute as a cowardly rapist who violates women and children while hiding his face. In *The Dew Breaker*, Danticat builds her poetics of war around female characters' attempts to uncover the Macoute's typically masked face.

Indeed, characters endeavor to uncover Macoutes who might be living in New York, such as the real-life Macoute Emmanuel "Toto" Constant. In the character Bienaimé, Danticat creates a generalized composite figure of such an individual. *The Dew Breaker* tells the stories of several Haitian immigrants in ex/isle conditions who are linked to the ex-prison guard Bienaimé, who has been hiding in New York with his wife Anne and their American-born daughter Kâ. In building the character of Bienaimé, Danticat removes the mask from the Macoute by imagining a complete physical and psychological portrait of a man capable of perpetrating torture. Danticat reveals him as a family man whose name literally means "well-loved." He manages to leave behind his life as a torturer to be reincarnated as a regular barber. She imagines him with a face that was scarred by his last victim's act of resistance. It is thanks to the scar that Bienaimé is able to blend in to his new community in New York because so many survivors of Duvalier's dictatorships bear similar scars on their bodies. The Macoute constitutes a nightmare and a constant shadow over his victims' lives. He haunts women such as the seamstress mentioned earlier. Ironically, he also suffers from constant nightmares, forced to constantly hide his real identity even from his own daughter. Kâ attempts to sculpt her father, who she thinks was a victim of dictatorship. The masquerade continues until the father confesses to her that he "was the hunter" and "not the prey" (20). By learning and demystifying the father's true role, she loses her subject as well as the sculpture she made of him. Bienaimé throws it away because he knew it did not represent him.

Danticat uses a comical tone to describe the Macoute, who is young and often wears a recognizable blue-denim uniform. She imagines details about him such as his likes and dislikes and reveals unflattering physical characteristics: he is vain, lazy, and looks like "a pig in a calabash" (184). Danticat's daunting task is, however, not to linger on the Macoute's physical identity, because these individuals were easily recognized in every community. The writer's challenge is to enter the Macoute's head and provide us with a mental and psychological profile. Bienaimé rationalizes his job because "he liked to work on people" (188). The nature of his job is to "follow order and prove his loyalty" (190). He is a man who wants to do his job well and does so. He likes to torture people and understands "the greatest hazard of the job," which is, paraphrasing the Haitian novelist Jacques Alexis, becoming "un véritable gendarme, un bourreau" [a true policeman, an executioner] (197–98). He works methodically, operating in full view of the people and punctuating everyday life with violence. Hence, he has no remorse and no regrets.

Danticat sketches Bienaimé's biography in order to understand how one becomes a Macoute. Bienaimé is a victim of Papa Doc himself. He joins the militia at age nineteen after military officers seize the family land. As a consequence, his mother leaves the family and his father grows mad. Bienaimé blindly enlists after listening to a mesmerizing speech by the dictator, even though the young man could hardly understand the dictator's "perfect nasal French," suggesting his lack of education (193). He is fascinated by rifle-toting men "dressed in uniforms with golden rope" (192). Later, he uses the power for a personal vendetta by avenging his family loss. Ironically, he does his job well to avoid becoming prey himself, a consequence for a fallen Macoute. Danticat follows Bienaimé to New York, where he flees after having botched his last mission. His life thereafter becomes a question of hiding his real identity.

Hiding is part of Macoute's life. In *Breath, Eyes, Memory*, Danticat describes the Macoute's appearance as that of a man whose face is hidden away from his victims. Though he operates openly, Bienaimé prefers to work without the uniform. In exile, he takes his secrecy even further. He loses weight, changes his behavior, and becomes an unassuming but respected barber (often referred to as Mr. Bienaimé). In addition, Bienaimé's hiding is made easier by the fact that he is married to his "angel" Anne, depicted as an innocent, devout woman. Similar to her husband, Anne must live a lie, a particularly difficult situation because Bienaimé's last victim happens to be her own brother. Danticat's literary representation of the Macoute establishes the link between militarized violence and women's daily lives.

Militarization and Sexual Violence

In *Breath, Eyes, Memory*, Danticat establishes the strongest connection between militarized and gendered violence. In particular, she shows how the state's use of military and paramilitary forces to control its people is closely linked to patriarchal domination. As discussed at the beginning of this chapter, feminist scholars across disciplines have studied the connections between war, militarization, and gendered violence. Gendered aspects of violence include the employment of women as "sexual slaves" during wars and the use of rape of women as a weapon of war. In some conflicts, rape has been used as a "systematic" and "strategic" tool to enable the troops to fight better and to humiliate and demoralize the enemy (Barstow 2–3). But it is the connection between patriarchal and political domination that is of interest to feminists. Echoing Chris Cuomo, Liz Kelly states that rape, as one of the "extreme and effective forms of patriarchal control . . . is connected in a range of ways to sexual violence in all other contexts" (Kelly 45). Like Cuomo, Kelly urges feminists to pay attention to everyday violence and to question the distinction between rape that occurs during conflicts and rape that is committed during so-called peacetime. Madeleine Morris pushes the theory further to suggest that the military culture itself encourages a higher incidence of rape. This culture, she argues, is built on "standards of masculinity that emphasize dominance, assertiveness, aggressiveness, independence, [and] self-sufficiency," and it features a greater propensity for "sexual promiscuity" and the general acceptance of violence against women (Morris 181). Hence, military development, whether in the context of war or during peacetime, is directly connected to patriarchal domination. The violence continuum that goes back and forth between gendered public and private violence is therefore visible during both war and women's everyday life in militarized states.

Women's testimonials in human rights reports reveal similar experiences around the world, including those of Haitian women who become victims of the military or paramilitary culture whether or not a civil war has been declared. Women are arrested, killed, and maimed. Rape and sexual violence continue to be used in Haiti as a weapon of political repression during the many bouts of violence. Miriam Chancy links violence against women to periods in which Haiti is highly militarized (316), whereas Carolle Charles argues that during the Duvalier dictatorships, state violence was gendered as women were subjugated to rape in addition to other forms of political violence (136). Military and paramilitary organizations that were supposed to protect the country against outside invaders were turned into a state force that waged war against the Haitian people.

In *Breath, Eyes, Memory*, Danticat explores women's postcolonial war story and its ongoing repercussions for younger generations that did not experience war firsthand yet suffer heavily from its consequences. The author presents three female generations of the Caco family as the quintessential victims of the dictatorship. They are Sophie, the narrator; her mother Martine; her grandmother; and Atie, her maternal aunt, who is also Sophie's surrogate mother. They constitute a family united by a strong bond and tragic stories. Martine is raped at age sixteen by a faceless Macoute. She is eventually forced to leave Haiti for the United States, like many other Haitians who have tried to escape their traumatic past. Sophie later joins her and will continue the female lineage with her own daughter, Brigitte. Danticat tells the story mostly from Sophie's point of view.

The name *Caco* is a reference to the armed Haitian peasants who contributed to numerous revolutionary uprisings. We get a sense that Martine and Atie Caco are no longer living the true Caco womanhood. Atie has become an alcoholic. And while Martine fled Haiti, Sophie notices upon meeting her that her past seems to have followed her. Martine has a "scrawny body", her face is long and hollow with dark circles under the eyes, and her fingers are scarred and sunburned as "though she has never stopped working in the cane fields after all" (42). A third of the way through the novel, we learn that Sophie is the product of Martine's rape. Though Martine never saw the rapist's face, she insists that Sophie looks like her father. She states, "when I look at your face I think it is true what they say. A child out of wedlock always looks like its father" (61). Not only did Martine suffer this violation in the public area, she and Atie also had to endure their mother's virginity tests, which Martine interpreted as another violation. Here, we have rape as a weapon of political violence superimposed on another type of sexual violence used to reinforce patriarchy. Danticat, like Beyala and Pineau, reveals a continuum of violence that extends from the public to the private sphere and vice-versa. In *Breath, Eyes, Memory*, Danticat depicts this continuum as follows: the police use rape to control and terrorize the people, and, at the same time, families police young girls' sexuality in private life. The methods are alike because both the rape and virginity test involve not only forms of patriarchal domination but also unwanted sexual penetration. Martine, the victim of Macoute rape, clearly sees the rape as the most problematic because she subjects Sophie to the patriarchal virginity tests while knowing their effect on the female psyche. Additionally, as we have seen in other novels, repetitive violations converge into self-violence. When Martine continues to test her daughter, Sophie eventually decides to uses a pestle to tear her "flesh" in order to fail and thereby end her mother's tests. This is similar to the attempt by Tanga's mother, discussed in chapter 3, to "dévancer le malheur" [stay ahead of misfortune] (Beyala, *Tanga* 45).

Sophie resorts to self-violence in order to free herself from her mother's terror. At the same time, it is ironic that Martine would choose to perpetrate this violence on her own daughter, even as she cannot acknowledge the rape by the Macoute without mentioning her own mother's tests on her. When Sophie asks why she put her through the tests, Martine admits that she was following the precedent set by her mother; she now realizes that "the two greatest pains of [her] life are related." She adds: "The one good thing about me being raped was that it made the *testing* stop. The testing and the rape. I live both every day" (170). Martine's statement links patriarchal domination to political domination.

Martine's suicide at the end is the ultimate form of self-violence. Pregnant again by her boyfriend in New York, she cannot help but remember her own victimization, seemingly reliving her sexual violation through this new pregnancy. Martine rejects the new baby just as she had Sophie, who, despite efforts to abort her, "wouldn't go away" (190). To have the new baby means "to have it at the expense of her sanity" (192). Unlike her mother, Sophie manages to confront and overcome her pain, thanks in part for her desire to spare her own daughter Brigitte from patriarchal violence. Sophie's healing begins when she understands how pain and violence link her to the mother. She discovers this after making multiple trips to Haiti to revisit the sites of her inherited pain. Speaking of the pain caused by her own mother, Sophie states: "I knew my hurt and hers were links in a long chain and if she hurt me, it was because she was hurt, too" (203). Danticat's poetics of recovery presents exiled women who adapt to new strategies of survival. For instance, in both *Breath, Eyes, Memory* and *The Dew Breaker*, Danticat includes descriptions of exiled women from different nations who rely on therapists and group therapy sessions to confront their private and political pain. Yet women like Aunt Atie who remain in Haiti do not have such resources and continue on the path of self-destruction.

At the end of the novel, Danticat chooses to depict two different endings for two women from different generations. Sophie is able to understand the source of her pain and face her painful heirloom, while Martine dies. Through Sophie's words in the last pages, however, Danticat is able to demonstrate that both women are free. Sophie surmises that her mother wanted "to live like a butterfly" (234). Sophie recalls a popular tale about a woman who asked Erzulie, one of the Vodun goddesses, to transform her into a butterfly so she could free herself from a body that was constantly bleeding. Sophie considers herself "ou liberé" because of therapy but also as a result of having faced her shadows, namely her father, a faceless Macoute.

Danticat creates a postcolonial war story in which stories and types of violence form, to borrow Antonio Benítez-Rojo's terms, a "discursive network" whereby several "discourses stay in touch/in contact" (163), or as Maryse Condé states, a story in which "it is almost impossible to separate one's personal life from the life of the country" (*La parole* 82). The women's discourse of war necessary enters the intimate space of the body in sexual violation; if nationalistic discourses associate the women's body with the land, this discourse considers rape as a weapon of war. The female body bears the brunt of the violation of war since "[w]ar violence rejects the body because it rejects life" (Marx-Scouras 179).

Literature of the Genocide of Tutsi in Rwanda: Monique Ilboudo's Murekatete

Most recent literary works by African and Caribbean women have been reactions not only to natural disasters like the one seen in Gisèle Pineau's *L'éspérance macadam* but also to human-made disasters, as exemplified by recent writings on the only African genocide to be recognized formally by the international community: the genocide of Rwandan Tutsi. These works by both Rwandan and non-Rwandan writers explore themes associated with war and conflicts. As testimonials of genocide, however, the authors focus on trying to understand how humans are capable of such horrors. In this section, I discuss the Burkina Faso writer Monique Ilboudo's literary response to the genocide in *Murekatete* (2000).

In 1994 the world watched a live broadcast of the genocide of Rwandan Tutsi while world leaders and the United Nations debated what to call the massacres. The event has since generated numerous fictional and nonfictional books and films from Rwandan survivors and foreign writers, scholars, and filmmakers alike. The success of films such as *Hotel Rwanda* and *Sometimes in April* is indicative of the universality of the Rwandan story, which needs to be re/told in order to preserve meaning in the phrase "never again." *Murekatete* is Ilboudo's contribution to this growing literature. She was part of the project "Rwanda: Ecrire par devoir de mémoire" [Rwanda: Writing as a Duty to Remember], in which African writers journeyed to postgenocide Rwanda with the intention of producing works of fiction.[5] *Murekatete* is a short novel that recounts the genocide's aftermath, focusing on the story of a heroine of the same name. Murekatete is a genocide survivor who has lost her entire family and witnessed her own children's massacre. She later marries her rescuer Venant, a soldier from the Rwandan Patriotic Front (RPF), the liberating army that is credited with ending the genocide.

Like many novels from the project "Rwanda: Ecrire par devoir de mémoire," Ilboudo attempts to understand the unspeakable act of genocide, in which people are targeted for who they are. Through the development of her character, the writer explains the origin of the hatred that led neighbors and even family members to dehumanize and then proceed to kill other human beings in horrific ways. Ilboudo dispels a notion widely publicized by the media that the decision to exterminate Tutsis and carry out genocide happened overnight. Through Murekatete's imagined biography, Ilboudo reconstructs the history of Rwanda and attempts to explain how Rwandan society reached the "the final solution" by implementing a politics of identification aimed at creating an internal enemy.[6] Like Danticat, Ilboudo links war and genocide to militarization — a nation's development of an army and a militia with the goal of engaging in war against its own people. The state slowly inculcates in its citizens the idea that their common enemy, in this case the Tutsi, must be destroyed. Indeed, genocide as defined by article 2 of the United Nations' *Convention on the Prevention and Punishment of the Crime of Genocide* means various acts of violence "committed with intent to destroy, in whole or in part, a national, ethnical, racial or religious group." The 1937 massacre of Haitians in the Dominican Republic, which Danticat describes in *The Farming of Bones*, has never been recognized as genocide. However, it can be argued that Haitians were indeed victims of genocide as they were clearly targeted because of their national and racial origins.

As a witness to massacre, Murekatete gives a first-person account that reveals to the reader the anatomy of genocide. At times the

"I" in the novel is that of Ilboudo herself, who wrote the book after making the journey to postgenocide Rwanda. For instance, after a visit to the Murambi site, one of the most horrific memorials of genocide — even today, visitors can see remnants of corpses including those of children clinging to their mothers — the "I" declares: "Murambi a profondément ébranlé ma foi en l'humain" [Murambi deeply destabilized my faith in humanity] (Ilboudo 63). Having experienced and witnessed the killings of people including her own children, Murekatete would hardly make such a declaration. Instead, here we see Ilboudo the writer-witness who traveled to postgenocide Rwanda and in the process of writing her experience identifies completely with the fictive victim/witness she has created.[7]

In *Murekatete*, Ilboudo explores questions similar to those found in other narratives of trauma examined in this book. How does a traumatized woman live following a massacre? Like Danticat's Amabelle or Pineau's Eliette, Murekatete leads an existence on the edge of life and death. She states, "I died. A long time ago" (Ilboudo 10). Like the body of Amabelle in *The Farming of Bones*, Murekatete's body is the site of her trauma. She describes her body as "mutilated" and "dislocated." Though she never states that she was a victim of sexual violence, she indicates that she is incapable of loving again and that she has lost sexual desire. At the end of the novel, Ilboudo also depicts Murekatete's body as it dies slowly from AIDS. Her description of Murekatete illustrates the ambivalence in victims' experience of genocide. Survivors agonize between forgetting the origin of their trauma and the inevitable desire to confront one's ghosts, between silence and "the imperative to tell." They find themselves in a liminal space between life and death.

Similar to Danticat's female characters, Murekatete's salvation arrives when she revisits the painful places to confront the genocide. In this case, Ilboudo puts the protagonist in the many real-life "sites of genocide" that survivors established as memorials to their loved ones. While Murekatete is "cured" by her confrontation with the reality of what happened in 1994, her husband Venant, who saved her, becomes unglued by the experience. Having not been a survivor but rather a rescuer of many victims of genocide, he never truly confronted what happened in 1994. In the end, perhaps illustrating the dire situations in which female survivors find themselves, Venant ironically becomes his wife's tormentor, raping her and contaminating her with the AIDS virus. Like many other authors of works and testimonials regarding catastrophe, Ilboudo felt an urgent need to respond and react to real events, especially because what happened in Rwanda was either initially trivialized or denied by many world authorities. The novel ends with a sense of impasse about the future of Rwanda in general and of survivors in particular, with "their questions without answers, with their love, with their dreams" (Ilboudo 75).

Conclusion

As African and Caribbean writings become ever more *intimistes* (intimist) – as authors present more intimate and deeply private topics – an examination of the subject of violence and particularly its gendered form in literature is crucial to the understanding of Francophone women writers. Reading violence in postcolonial women's literatures entails understanding the tension between public and private violence that results in gendered violence. While it can be argued that gendered violence is a corollary to imperialism and colonialism, women writers show how their societies contribute to gendered violence.

In the present study, I have attempted to answer questions about the uniqueness of women's experience of violence. Certainly, novels whose main protagonists are exclusively female constitute a composite of forms of violence, some of which are also experienced by their male counterparts. One of the main purposes of this work has been to situate the specificity of women's perspectives as victims of major sources of gendered violence. I have established that while some forms of gendered violence are public and others private, women writers prefer to represent them on a continuum. This work offers contributions in three areas: Fanon and sexual politics, women's responses to Fanon and his contemporaries regarding the issue of external and internal forms of violence, and a reading of contemporary representations of gendered violence.

First, I show that Fanon, as a voice of authority in decolonization and the future of the colonized, provided scholars with essential tools that can be applied to understanding women's plight but did not fairly explore the woman's point of view. My reading of Fanon's texts on sexual politics demonstrates that he at least considered the woman question, even though his conclusions did not correctly measure her impact on decolonization. His discourses on violence have been useful in my analyses. I have, however, taken exception to two of his conclusions. The first is that the woman of color represents a lost case of severe alienation and endeavors to whiten herself instead of remaining with her people — black men. Second, Fanon explained how the woman of color has the potential to become an important ally in decolonization efforts but neglected to question the social inequalities between men and women that existed in precolonial and colonial Africa and the colonial Caribbean.

My second contribution lies in my examination of women's reactions and responses to the conclusions of Fanon and his peers. Literature by some male writers, specifically by Fanon's peers, portrayed women as either the most assimilated colonized subjects or those who were the least affected by colonization (see Léopold Sédar Senghor's poetry). The analysis of works by Michele Lacrosil, Ken Bugul, and Sembène Ousmane demonstrates that the protagonists' self-exploration is a necessary step to counteract such views. Their characters experience extreme cases of colonial violence as they engage in a battle to recover their elusive black ancestry. Aside from the difficult task of deploring the colonial legacy of negative identification, Bugul, through her character Ken, for instance, directly accuses the black male elite of distorting the realities of black women. The autobiographical narrative explains how early African writers failed to understand the impact of colonialism on colonized women. Indeed, I argue that Lacrosil and Bugul, in particular, purposefully engage in a dialogue with previous male writers in order to complete the discourse on colonial violence.

The book also contributes to the study of the violence continuum as represented in women's writings on domestic and familial violence and on war and political violence. In the last three chapters of the book, I argue that Simone Schwarz-Bart, Calixthe Beyala, Gisèle Pineau, Nadine Bari, Edwidge Danticat, and Monique Ilboudo effectively capture the complexities of gendered contemporary violence. Their novels establish how intimate and domestic violence intermingles with public and political violence as a result of patriarchy. This book elucidates how women use writing as a medium to deconstruct traditional discourses on women and reveal how patriarchy fails and contradicts itself. The effect of patriarchal violence is no longer confined within intimate spaces but spills over into the public space. This is especially true for gendered aspects of war and political conflicts. The police and militia that violated women are indeed the products of the very patriarchal system that excludes and violates women.

These writers portray women who must resist violence and its consequences. For many of their characters, however, this resistance has ambiguous results. Self-violence and auto-destructive behavior seem the norm. As noted in the general introduction, Teresa de Lauretis insists that, by nature, violence is "en-gendered."[1] She goes further and scrutinizes the importance given to resistance in power relations. If Foucault contends, as quoted by de Lauretis, that "power relations depends on multiplicity of points of resistance," de Lauretis herself argues that it is, rather, "power not resistance or negativity, that is the positive condition of knowledge" (242). While I have interpreted self-destructive behaviors as symptoms of trauma, unusual forms of resistance, or even as an exercise of freedom, de Lauretis' argument reminds us that while women resist they still, in the end, hold less power in patriarchal societies. In my view, women writers who create such tragic characters are cognizant that power is still out of reach unless patriarchy is destroyed. Hence, writing serves to deconstruct the system as a first step toward empowerment.

Finally, reading and studying representations of gendered violence is an unsettling endeavor because it forces us to confront death, destruction, horror, and especially the corporeality and materiality of violence as well as subjects that are rather taboo in most cultures. Reading violence, as Laura E. Tanner puts it, implicates the reader, who becomes intimately linked with the story. As readers, we are forced to identify with one or more of the uncomfortable positions of victim, violator, and observer (Tanner 3). We risk becoming not only witnesses to but also part of horrific acts of violence. Despite the moral and ethical implications, there is a growing desire on the part of writers to react in narrative forms to violence and human catastrophe.

Notes

INTRODUCTION

1. In "Geographies of Pain: Captive Bodies and Violent Acts in the Fictions of Myriam Warner-Vieyra, Gayl Jones, and Bessie Head," Françoise Lionnet studies the reasons behind the use of violence such as murder by female protagonists.

2. All unattributed translations throughout this book are my own. When published translations from the French are used, page numbers from both versions are provided, starting with the original.

3. In this essay, Césaire exposes the contradiction in the so-called equation of colonization with civilization. He then proposes a new equation, colonization with thingification.

4. In her article "Fanon and the Role of Violence in Liberation: A Comparison with Gandhi and Mandela," Gail M. Presbey shows how Gandhi's nonviolence can be seen as feminine since it is usually women who are groomed to endure violence in silence.

1. EXCLUSION AS VIOLENCE

1. Some of the critics I refer to in this study are Carole Boyce Davies, the author of books and numerous articles on women's writings and the co-editor of two major collections of essays on African and Caribbean women writers: *Out of the Kumbla* (1991) and, with the collaboration of the leading African feminist Anne Adams Graves, *Ngambika* (1986); Irène D'Alméida, *Francophone African Women Writers* (1994); Odile Cazenave, *Femmes rebelles: naissance d'un nouveau roman africain au féminin* (1996); and Christopher Miller, *Theories of Africans* (1991). In the past few years, more book-length projects on Francophone female literatures have appeared, although most focus solely on African women writers.

2. In the essay "Remembering Fanon," Bhabha summarizes his position on women of color and Fanon in a note at the end of the essay in which he states that "Fanon's use of the word 'man' usually connotes a phenomenological quality of humanness, inclusive of man and woman

and, for that very reason, ignores the question of gender difference." I examine his position more closely later in this chapter.

3. There are additional examples of critics who have attempted to include women of color. Several essays address "L'Algérie se dévoile" in discussions on Maghrebian or Arab feminist issues. On the inclusion of black women, Rey Chow's article "The Politics of Admittance: Female Sexual Agency, Miscegenation, and the Formation of Community in Frantz Fanon," is by far the most useful, though she repeats some of the arguments regarding Fanon found in Doane's or Bergner's essays.

4. In "Of Mimicry and Man: The Ambivalence of Colonial Discourse," Bhabha defines "mimicry" within the colonial experience as "a representation of a difference that is itself a process of disavowal"; mimicry *repeats* rather than *re-presents* (128). The Algerian woman alternates between her veil and her European attire in order to accomplish a specific objective. She just plays her role and tries to convince either interested party that she is what they want her to become.

5. On the topic of object and subject, it is interesting to note the effect of the title's translation from the original "L'Algérie se dévoile" to the English title "Algeria Unveiled." The title in French points to the fact that Algeria (or the woman) is the subject of the action of unveiling, whereas the English title points to the objectification of Algeria (or the woman).

6. Here, Fanon is referring to the opposition originating from colonialism between the city and the up-country. The city is associated with civilization, and most of the city dwellers were the colonizers and a few African males who worked for them. The rural areas were associated with the uncivilized. Amina Mama has demonstrated in her essay "Sheroes and Villains: Conceptualizing Colonial and Contemporary Violence against Women in Africa" that women were not allowed to go to the city before the colonial mission needed to create a class of bourgeois women who might be suitable wives for "civilized" African men.

7. Fanon quotes from Michel Cournot, "Sur la Martinique," *Les Temps Modernes*, Février 1950.

8. *Loving v. Commonwealth of Virginia*, 388 U.S. 1, 87 S. Ct. 1817, 1967.

9. As an example, the female protagonist in Ken Buguls' *Le baobab fou* asks the following question: "Pourquoi n'avoir pas prévu la réaction de la femme noire au colonialisme" (113). Phrased by a woman experiencing a nervous breakdown because of colonial and postcolonial trauma, the

question testifies in my opinion to her agonizing realization that decolonization was mainly a male project for colonized men. See chapter 2 for further analysis of this quote.

2. REPRESENTING COLONIAL VIOLENCE

1. The discourse of racial categories is always complicated, especially in geographical areas such as South Africa, India, Thailand, and the Caribbean where possessing lighter skin complexions confers more prestige on their owners. In the Caribbean, there are different shades between whites or *békés* (dark-skinned blacks). Robert Smith Jr. identifies "mulattos" (those born of a white and a black parent), "câpres" (born of mulattoes and blacks), and "chabins" (born of câpres and mulattoes). Critics such as Beverly Ormerod (*Introduction to the French Caribbean Novel*, 1985) have located the origin of such racial stratification in the era of slavery. This racial stratification did not depend solely on skin color; social class also influenced it. Ormerod quotes a common proverb that expresses the interconnection between skin color and class: "Every rich black man is a mulatto; every poor mulatto is a black" (84). This quote is also found in Creole in Michel Leiris' *Contacts de civilisation en Martinique et en Guadeloupe* as "Nèg riche cé mulat', mulat' pauv' cé nèg'" (31).

2. Translations of *Le baobab fou* are from *The Abandoned Baobab, the Autobiography of a Senegalese Woman*, trans. Marjolijn de Jager (Chicago: Lawrence Hill Books, 1991).

3. See chapter 1 for a discussion of Frantz Fanon's critique of Mayotte Capecia's *Je suis martiniquaise* and the Caribbean woman's desire to whiten herself.

4. Clearly, Lacrosil was heavily influenced by psychoanalytic models of analysis. The triangular relationships, for instance, are reminiscent of the Freudian Oedipus complex between the mother, child, and father. In *Cajou*, the father is embodied by the white psychiatrist. He enters the dyadic relationship composed of the mother and the child in the pre-Oedipal phase. The child emerges from the Oedipus complex as a split subject. At the end of this chapter, in a study of Cajou's neurosis, I demonstrate Fanon's influence on Lacrosil, particularly through his belief that the colonized is incapable of the Oedipus complex. This assertion allows Lacrosil to explore unusual dyadic and triangular relationships.

For instance, a white female at times occupies the position of the Oedipal father, a fact that complicates Freud's contention that girls never quite resolve this Oedipus complex. This is also a reflection of the complication involving the combination of race and gender.

5. As noted in the introduction, Aimé Césaire defines the principal lie as the dishonest colonial premise equating colonization with civilization (see his *Discours sur le colonialisme*).

6. See Madeleine Cottenet-Hage and Kevin Meehan, "'Our Ancestors the Gauls . . .' Schools and Schooling in Two Caribbean Novels," *Callaloo* 15.1 (1992): 75–89. In this article, the authors point out that there is no shortage of Francophone novels that portray school experiences as a "strategy for exploring the crises and tensions of the protagonists' psychological development" (76). Lacrosil's first novel focuses on the acquisition of Western knowledge while exploring the progressive education of a colonial subject.

7. In chapter 3, I analyze the relationship between intergenerational violence — violence inherited through the female lineage — and the importance of familial communication.

8. The image of the female Caribbean female subject leaving for or living in the "mother country," France, has been analyzed in critical studies, but apart from current immigrant literature in Europe, little work has been done on the continental African woman's post/colonial metropolitan experience. The Caribbean and France have a special fifty-year-old relationship that dates from the establishment of the Départements d'outre-mer. Female characters typically want to leave the native island for the more desirable Métropole. For instance, Mayotte in *Je suis martiniquaise* narrates from France. In *Cajou* the protagonist lives in Paris and no longer yearns for an escape to the Métropole like Sapotille, the title character in Lacrosil's first novel. If anything, Cajou wants to leave the alienating "mother country." Several critics have analyzed the Caribbean female in Europe including Maryse Condé in her seminal study *La parole aux femmes*. My work focuses on the African female protagonist in Europe because such critical studies are scarce.

9. Césaire's use of the term *Négritude* not only reveals the awareness of being "other" but is also a positive affirmation of the black self.

10. See, for example, Senghor's poem "femme noire," in which the

woman's body is represented erotically. At the same time, the body represents the poet's homeland, Africa, and Senghor uses it to praise the African woman much in the tradition of French poets such as Ronsard.

11. The word *esclave* here can be interpreted in different ways. In the movie, Diouana refers most likely to how she is treated in France as opposed to Dakar. For instance, in France she is no longer a "bonne," or maid, the job she was hired for in Dakar, but "une bonne à tout faire" — a do-it-all-maid.

12. Ken Bugul's second novel, *Cendres et braises*, details her second detour, this time in Paris, France, where she once again tries unsuccessfully to integrate the West.

13. The protagonist evolves near closed spaces. Cajou is either in the enclosed garden, the site of her childhood games with Stéphanie; in the room in Paris; or in the enclosed space of the chemical laboratory where she works. In these spaces, Cajou undergoes psychological self-torture. The torture continues in the present because the objective of the narration is to revisit her past, which exists exclusively in her mind.

14. The theme of homosexuality is present in *Le baobab fou* as well. In this novel, Ken is sexually involved with a young Italian woman who is going through an identity crisis of her own. In addition, Ken lives with François, a gay man who will become violently jealous when he suspects that his male lover might have slept with her. In *Cajou*, Germain confesses to having had homosexual relations. These relationships appear to be either genuine (François) or a mere phase (Ken and Germain). The latter considers it to be a coming of age phase.

15. This subject of problematic and abusive family relations is developed further in other chapters.

16. Lacrosil writes "outsider" in English, probably to emphasize Cajou's otherness by using a foreign word. While many have praised Lacrosil's capacity to use the French language, she has been criticized for not using a proper Caribbean language, such as Creole sayings as found in Capécia's *Je suis martiniquaise*.

3. WRITING FAMILIAL VIOLENCE

1. Translations of *Pluie et vent sur Télumée Miracle* are from *The Bridge of Beyond*, trans. Barbara Bray (Portsmouth NH: Heinemann, 1974).

Translations of *Tu t'appelleras Tanga* are from *Your Name Shall Be Tanga*, trans. Marjolijn de Jager (Portsmouth NH: Heinemann, 1996).

2. Senghor writes in "Femme noire": "Femme nue, femme noire / Vêtue de ta couleur qui est vie, de ta forme qui est beauté! / J'ai grandi à ton ombre; la douceur de tes mains bandait mes yeux. / Et voilà qu'au cœur de l'Eté et de Midi, je te découvre Terre promise, du haut d'un haut col calciné/ . . . "

3. Some examples are the poems of Léon Gontran Damas such as "Hoquet" (see chapter 1) and the figure of the woman in Aimé Césaire's *Le cahier*. Women's novels such as Myriam Warner-Vieyra's *Le quimboiseur l'avait dit* present the black mother as the traitor who turns against her daughter in order to be admitted to, and preserve her status in a white community.

4. My study of Gisèle Pineau's *L'espérance macadam* in chapter 4 demonstrates how nature and its unstable temper is closely linked to the past, present, and future of the Caribbean peoples.

5. There is an important exception here with Ahmadou Kourouma's novel *Le soleil des indépendances*, discussed later.

6. Chapter 4 elaborates another correlation between nature's temper and violence against women.

7. The definition is taken from the 1987 edition of the *Diagnostic and Statistical Manual of Mental Disorders* (DSM III-Revised, 1987) of the American Psychiatric Association. It is important to note that the last two editions (1994 and 2000) have been more specific about the sources of stressors for this particular disorder.

8. The American Psychiatric Association excludes from its definition of dissociation meditative and trance practices that occur in many religions and cultures. See the diagnostic criteria from *DSM-IV* (Washington DC: 1994): 231–32. Dissociation should not be assumed to be a disorder unless it is accompanied by distress and impairment, which are considered manifestations of pathology in a given culture or society. There are no instances of voluntary or involuntary trances in the novel *Tanga*.

9. Sociologists do not agree on what causes family violence but have discovered that a high percentage of abusers have themselves been victims of violence in their childhoods. In addition, trauma disorders can be passed from generation to generation, as demonstrated by essays in the

second part of Cathy Caruth's *Trauma Explorations in Memory* (1995). One reason for this intergenerational transmission is the silence that accompanies trauma, either because it is difficult for the survivors to share their experience with their children or because they do not want to revisit the trauma in the process of telling the story. In *Tanga* it is clear that Daba is affected by her mother's original trauma. For instance, she adopts self-mutilation, one of the symptoms of dissociation, and exhibits numerous sexual disorders.

10. In 1996, upon receiving the prestigious "Prix de l'Académie française" for her novel *Les honneurs perdus*, Calixthe Beyala was plagued by several accusations of plagiarism. Pierre Assouline, director of the review magazine *Lire* and one of Beyala's firm accusers, has since identified several incidents of plagiarism in her novels. While they acknowledge that some of the accusations seem well founded, Beyala's supporters argue that she has produced an unparalleled body of creative work. For a literature review of the case against Beyala, see Rangira Béatrice Gallimore's postscript to her 1997 book *L'œuvre romanesque de Calixthe Beyala: le renouveau de l'écriture féminine en Afrique francophone sub-saharienne*.

11. See Julien, "Rape, Repression and Narrative Form in *Le Devoir de violence* and *La Vie et demie*," in *Rape and Representation*. She studies the symbolism of sexual violence in some African Francophone novels and concludes that sexual violence becomes a trope that refers to an aspect of torture and barbarism in fictional communities.

12. Clearly, contemporary issues of violence are at the forefront of world affairs, forming the basis for grass roots movements, and inform novels like Gisèle Pineau's *L'espérance macadam*.

13. A *pagne* is a traditional wrap worn by women like a skirt.

14. In "Order, Disorder, Freedom, and the West Indian Writer," Maryse Condé makes a point I develop in chapter 2 — that the West Indian woman writer is viewed as an agent for disorder in the tradition of written Caribbean literature. The conventional protagonist is usually male and considered to be a Christ-like character, the savior of the people. For example, Manuel in Jacques Roumain's *Gouverneurs de la rosée* and the poet in Aimé Césaire's *Le cahier* are messianic characters.

15. While the description of the house sounds negative, according to Elizabeth Wilson, Simone Schwarz-Bart "reverses the connotations of the closed space and emphasizes only its positive, nurturing aspects" (53).

16. Here, I am referring not only to the general imbalance in interest between male texts and female texts but also to the tendency, among scholars and publishers, to dismiss the importance of the so-called women's universe. I comment on this issue in chapter 2, concluding that critics often overlook the complexity of women's problems and therefore miss the crucial components of the story.

17. In *Discours sur le colonialisme*, Césaire labels the phenomenon in which the colonized is dehumanized "chosification" (*thingification*). In the article "Objects into Subjects," Michelle Cliff uses the term *objectification* to refer to "the process by which people are dehumanized, made ghostlike, given the status of other – an image created by the oppressor replaces the actual being. The actual being is denied speech; denied self-definition, self-realization, and overarching all this, denied selfhood" (272).

18. Incidentally, *Les yeux baissés* is the title of a novel by Tahar Ben Jelloun in which he criticizes patriarchal expectations of girls in his culture. While in many African cultures, boys are not allowed to look adults in the eye (see Ferdinand Oyono's *Une vie de boy*), females are not allowed to do so even as adults.

19. The deafness and blindness of Tanga's grandmother are reminiscent of the condition of Ken and her father in *Le baobab fou*, where they are unable to communicate because he is blind and she is metaphorically deaf.

20. The series of images in the sentence "J'aurai ma maison, le jardin, le chien, la pie au bout du pré, des enfants," ironically shows the protagonist's idealization of the clichéd aspirations of the French bourgeoisie.

4. SITES OF VIOLENCE

1. For the meaning of "geographies of pain," see note 1 in the general introduction.

2. In his notion of "Poétique de la Relation," Edouard Glissant delineates the dynamic and essential processes of "le Retour" (Return) and "le Détour" through which Caribbean people attempt to situate themselves "l'ailleurs" (elsewhere). As many critics have remarked, these processes are comparable to deterritorialization and reterritorialization, which Gilles Deleuze and Félix Guattari describe in relation to language in *Kafka: pour une littérature mineure*.

3. In her article "Presque un siècle de différence amoureuse: Simone Schwarz-Bart (1972), Gisèle Pineau (1996)," Christiane Makward compares the two novels but limits her discussion to the theme of love.

4. Though Creole dictionaries indicate that *Zeb* is the term for *zèbre* (zebra), Pineau uses it in its more contemporary sense as *les herbes* (grass), connoting illegal drugs.

5. The female protagonists studied in this book descend toward madness not only because of violence done to them but also because they cannot speak out against it.

6. In her article "Sheroes and Villains: Conceptualizing Colonial and Contemporary Violence against Women in Africa," Amina Mama describes how during colonial times, women who lived in town were either forced to marry within a few days of their arrival or taken back to the villages. If they did not find husbands, or if they refused to go back to their villages, they were simply labeled prostitutes.

7. In chapter 5, I discuss the theme of virginity tests in Edwidge Danticat's novel *Breath, Eyes, Memory*.

8. Chapter 3 delineates the differences between the trope of sexual violence in novels such as *Le devoir de violence* and *Les soleils des indépendances* and the narration of sexual and domestic violence in Beyala's *Tu t'appelleras Tanga* and Simone Schwarz-Bart's *Pluie et vent sur Télumée miracle*.

5. WAR AND POLITICAL VIOLENCE

1. Here is a partial list of female writers who have evoked wars and national conflicts in Africa: Léonie Abo, Nadine Bari, Calixthe Beyala, Tanella Boni, Maryse Condé, Marie Claire Dati, Nafissatou Diallo, Simone Kaya, Tita Mandeleau, Nadine Nyangoma, Michèle Rakotoson, Aminata Sow Fall, Véronique Tadjo, Marie-Léontine Tsibinda, Werewere Liking, and Marie Vieux Chauvet (partially compiled by Jean-Marie Volet, "La Guerre chez les romancières," http://www.arts.uwa.edu.au/MotsPluriels/MP497jvindex.html). It is important to note, however, that most contemporary African women writers have focused on current conflicts; see, most notably, testimonials by Rwandan women survivors of the genocide.

2. See works by Jean-Paul Atala, Sidiki Kobélé Keita, Camara Kaba,

Abdoulaye Conté, Mamadou Kaly Bah, and Ardo Ousmane Bâ, and novels by Tierno Monénembo and William Sassine.

3. The quote is a reference to Robert Debs Heinl's book *Written in Blood: The Story of Haitian People, 1492–1995*.

4. The 2007 documentary *Edwidge Danticat Visits her Haitian Roots* illustrates her desire to rediscover her land.

5. Several texts were published in the context of this project, including Jean-Marie Vianney Rurangwa's *Le génocide des Tutsi expliqué à un étranger*, Véronique Tadjo's *L'ombre d'Imana: voyages jusqu'au bout du Rwanda*, Koulsy Lamko's *La phalène des collines*, Abdourahman A. Waberi's *Moisson de crânes: textes pour le Rwanda*, Tierno Monénembo's *L'Aîné des orphelines*, and Boubacar Boris Diop's *Murambi: le livre des ossements*.

6. In his book *Récits fondateurs du drame rwandais: discours social, idéologies et stéréotypes* (1998), Josias Semujanga examines the politics of identification in Rwanda from the colonial period until the execution of the genocide in 1994.

7. In her article "*Murekatete*, un témoignage (im)possible, Monique Gasengayire analyses the converging roles of a writer-witness and a fictive-witness.

CONCLUSION

1. See the general introduction for Teresa de Lauretis' complete argument.

Works Cited

Barber-Williams, Patricia. "Images of the Self: Jean Rhys and Her French West Indian Counterpart." *Journal of West Indian Literature* 3.2 (1989): 9–19.

Bari, Nadine. *Chroniques de Guinée: essai sur la Guinée des années 90*. Paris: Editions Karthala, 1994.

———. *Grain de sable: les combats d'une femme de disparu*. Paris: Centurion, 1983.

———. *Noces d'absence*. Paris: Centurion, 1986.

Bar On, Bat Ami. "Teaching (About) Genocide." *Twenty-First-Century Feminist Classrooms: Pedagogies of Identity and Difference*. Ed. Amie A. MacDonald and Susan Sánchez-Casal. New York: Palgrave Macmillan, 2002. 233–49.

Barstow, Anne Llewellyn, ed. *War's Dirty Secret: Rape, Prostitution, and Other Crimes Against Women*. Cleveland OH: Pilgrim Press, 2000.

Benítez-Rojo, Antonio. *The Repeating Island: the Caribbean and the Postmodern Perspective*. Trans. James Maraniss. Durham NC: Duke University Press, 1996.

Benjamin, Walter. *Reflections: Essays, Aphorisms, Autobiographical Writings*. Trans. Edmund Jephcott. New York: Harcourt Brace Jovanovich, 1978.

Bergner, Gwen. "Who is That Masked Woman? Or, The Role of Gender in Fanon's *Black Skin, White Masks*." PMLA 110.1 (1995): 75–88.

Bernabé, Jean, Patrick Chamoiseau, and Raphaël Confiant. *Eloge de la créolité*. Paris: Gallimard, 1989.

Beyala, Calixthe. *C'est le soleil qui m'a brûlée*. Paris: Stock, 1987.

———. *The Sun Hath Looked Upon Me*. Trans. Marjolijn de Jager. African Writers Series. Portsmouth NH: Heinemann, 1996.

———. *Tu t'appelleras Tanga*. Paris: Stock, 1988.

———. *Your Name Shall Be Tanga*. Trans. Marjolijn de Jager. African Writers Series. Portsmouth NH: Heinemann, 1996.

Bhabha, Homi. "Of Mimicry and Man: The Ambivalence of Colonial Discourse." *October* 28 (Spring 1984): 125–33.

——. "The Other Question: Stereotype, Discrimination and the Discourse of Colonialism." *The Location of Culture*. New York: Routledge, 1994. 66–84.

——. "Remembering Fanon." *Colonial Discourse and Post-colonial Theory: A Reader*. Ed. Patrick Williams and Laura Chrisman. New York: Columbia University Press, 1994. 112–23.

Brière, Eloise A. *Le roman camerounais et ses discours*. Ivry: Editions Nouvelles du Sud, 1993.

Brown, Laura S. "Not Outside the Range: One Feminist Perspective on Psychic Trauma." *Trauma: Explorations in Memory*. Ed. Cathy Caruth. Baltimore: Johns Hopkins University Press, 1995. 100–112.

Bugul, Ken. *The Abandoned Baobab: The Autobiography of a Senegalese Woman*. Trans. Marjolijn de Jager. Chicago: Lawrence Hill Books, 1991.

——. *Le baobab fou*. Abidjan: Nouvelles éditions africaines, 1983.

Bunch, Charlotte, and Roxanna Carillo. *Gender Violence: A Development and Human Rights Issue*. New Brunswick NJ: Center for Women's Global Leadership, 1991.

Butler, Judith. "Burning Acts: Injurious Speech." *University of Chicago Law School Roundtable: A Journal of Interdisciplinary Legal Studies* 3.1 (1996): 199–221.

Capécia, Mayotte. *Je suis martiniquaise*. Paris: Editions Corrêa, 1948.

Caruth, Cathy, ed. *Trauma: Explorations in Memory*. Baltimore: Johns Hopkins University Press, 1995.

——. *Unclaimed Experience: Trauma, Narrative, and History*. Baltimore: Johns Hopkins University Press, 1996.

Case, Frederick Ivor. *The Crisis of Identity: Studies in the Guadeloupean and Martiniquan Novel*. Québec: Editions Naaman, 1985.

Cazenave, Odile. *Rebellious Women: The New Generation of Female African Novelists*. Boulder CO: Lynne Riener Publishers, 2000.

Césaire, Aimé. *Cahier d'un retour au pays natal*. Paris: Présence africaine, 1971.

——. "From Discourse on Colonialism." *Colonial Discourse and Post-Colonial Theory: A Reader*. Ed. Patrick Williams and Laura Chrisman. New York: Columbia University Press 1994. 172–80.

Chancy, Miriam. "'No Giraffes in Haiti': Haitian Women and State Terror." *Ecrire en pays assiégé-Haïti-Writing Under Siege*. Ed. Marie-Agnès Sourieau and Kathleen M. Balutansky. New York: Rodopi, 2004. 303–21.

Charles, Carolle. "Gender and Politics in Contemporary Haiti: The Duvalierist State, Transnationalism, and the Emergence of a New Feminist (1980–1990)." *Feminist Studies* 21.1 (1995): 135–64.

Chevrier, Jacques. "Les romans coloniaux: Enfer ou Paradis." *Notre Librairie* 90 (1987): 61–72.

Chow, Rey. "The Politics of Admittance: Female Sexual Agency, Miscegenation, and the Formation of Community in Frantz Fanon." *UTS Review* 1.1 (1995): 5–29.

Cixous, Hélène. "Le rire de la méduse." *L'Arc* 61 (1975): 39–54.

Cliff, Michelle. "Object Into Subject: Some Thoughts on the Work of Black Women Artists." *Making Face, Making Soul/Haciendo Caras: Creative and Critical Perspectives by Feminists of Color*. Ed. Gloria Anzaldúa. San Francisco: Aunt Lute Foundation Books, 1990. 271–90.

Condé, Maryse. "Order, Disorder, Freedom, and the West Indian Writer." *Yale French Studies* 83.2 (1993): 121–35.

———. *La Parole des femmes: essai sur les romancières des Antilles de langue française*. Paris: L'Harmattan, 1979.

Cooke, Miriam. *Women and the War Story*. Berkeley: University of California Press, 1996.

Corzani, Jack. "La littérature face à la violence. Le cas des Antilles-Guyane." *La Deriva delle francofonie, atti dei seminari annuali de Letterature Francophone: Figures et fantasmes de la violence dans les littératures francophones de l'Afrique subsaharienne et des Antilles*. II: Les Antilles. Ed. Franca Marcato-Falzoni. Bologna: Cooperativa Lib. Univ. Editrice, 1991. 13–38.

Cottenet-Hage Madeleine and Kevin Meehan. "'Our Ancestors the Gauls . . .' Schools and Schooling in Two Caribbean Novels." *Callaloo* 15.1 (1992): 75–89.

Cuomo, Chris. "War Is Not Just an Event: Reflections on the Significance of Everyday Violence." *Hypatia* 11.4 (1996): 30–45.

Dadié, Bernard Binlin. *Un nègre à Paris*. Paris: Présence africaine, 1959.

D'Alméida, Irène. *Francophone African Women Writers: Destroying the Emptiness of Silence*. Gainesville: University Press of Florida, 1994.

Danticat, Edwidge. *Breath, Eyes, Memory*. New York: Vintage Books, 1995.

———. *The Dew Breaker*. New York: Knopf, 2004.

———. *The Farming of Bones*. New York: Penguin, 1999.

Davies, Carol Boyce, and Elaine Savory Fido, eds. *Out of the Kumbla: Caribbean Women and Literature*. Trenton NJ: Africa World Press, 1990.

Dayan, Joan. "Haiti's Unquiet Past: Katherine Dunham, Modern Dancer, and her Enchanted Island." *Women At Sea: Travel Writing and the Margins of Caribbean Discourse*. Ed. Lizabeth Paravisini-Gebert and Ivette Romero-Cesareo. New York: Palgrave Macmillan, 2001. 281–91.

de Lauretis, Teresa. "The Violence of Rhetoric." *The Violence of Representation: Literature and the History of Violence*. Ed. Nancy Armstrong and Leonard Tennenhouse. London: Routledge, 1989: 239–57.

Deleuze, Gilles, and Félix Guattari. *Kafka: pour une littérature mineure*. Paris: Éditions de Minuit, 1975.

Doane, Mary Ann. *Femmes Fatales: Feminism, Film Theory, Psychoanalysis*. New York: Routledge, 1991.

Domenach, Jean-Marie, et al. *Violence and Its Causes*. Paris: UNESCO, 1981.

Donadey, Anne. "Between Amnesia and Anamnesis: Re-Membering the Fractures of Colonial History." *Studies in 20th Century Literature*. 23.1 (1999): 111–16.

Fanon, Frantz. "L'Algérie se dévoile." *Sociologie d'une révolution*. Paris: Libraire François Maspero, 1968.

———. "Algeria Unveiled." *Studies in a Dying Colonialism*. Trans. Haakon Chevalier. New York: Grove Press, 1965. 35–67.

———. *Black Skin, White Masks*. Trans. Charles Lam Markmann. New York: Grove Press, 1967.

———. *Les damnés de la terre*. Paris: Librairie François Maspero, 1968.

———. *Peau noire, masques blancs*. Paris: Editions du Seuil, 1952.

———. *The Wretched of the Earth*. Pref. Jean-Paul Sartre. Trans. Constance Farrington. New York: Grove Weidenfeld, 1991

Foucault, Michel. "Space, Power and Knowledge." *The Foucault Reader*. Ed. Paul Rabinow. New York: Pantheon Books, 1984. 239–56.

François, Irline. "Confinement to Freedom: Jan J. (Gigi) Dominique's *Mémoire d'une amnésique*." *Ecrire en pays assiégé-Haïti-Writing Under Siege*. Ed. Marie-Agnès Sourieau and Kathleen M. Balutansky. New York, 2004. 285–301.

Gallimore, Rangira Béatrice. *L'œuvre romanesque de Calixthe Beyala: le renouveau de l'écriture féminine en Afrique francophone sub-saharienne*. Paris: L'Harmattan, 1997.

Gasengayire, Monique. "*Murekatete*, un témoignage (im)possible." *Dix ans après : Réflexions sur le génocide rwandais*. Ed. Rangira Béatrice Gallimore and Chantal Kalisa. Paris: L'Harmattan, 2005. 143–60.

Gates, Henry Louis, Jr. "Critical Fanonism." *Critical Inquiry* 17 (Spring 1991): 457–70.

Gelles, Richard, and Claire Pedrick Cornell. *International Perspectives on Family Violence*. Lexington MA: Lexington Books, 1983.

Girard, René. *La violence et le sacré*. Paris: B. Grasset, 1972.

Glissant, Edouard. *Caribbean Discourse: Selected Essays*. Trans. J. Michael Dash. Charlottesville: University Press of Virginia, 1989.

———. *Le discours antillais*. Paris: Gallimard, 1997.

Le grand Larousse illustré: dictionnaire encyclopédique en 3 volumes et 1 CD-Rom. Paris: Larousse, 2005.

Green, December. *Gender Violence in Africa: African Women's Responses*. New York: St. Martin's Press, 1999.

Gros, Isabelle. "Michèle Lacrosil: Liberation par l'écriture ou comment vomir le dégoût de soi." *Elles écrivent des Antilles: Haïti, Guadeloupe, Martinique*. Ed. Suzanne Rinne and Joëlle Vitiello. Paris: Editions L'Harmattan, 1997. 121–32.

Heinl, Robert Debs, and Nancy Gordon Heinl. *Written in Blood: The Story of Haitian People, 1492–1995*, 2nd ed. Lanham MD: University Press of America, 1996.

Herman, Judith. *Trauma and Recovery*. New York: Basic Books, 1992.

Hezekiah, Randolph. "Martinique and Guadeloupe Time and Space." *A History of literature in the Caribbean*. Ed. A. James Arnold. Vol. 1. Philadelphia: J. Benjamins, 1994. 379–87.

Higgins, Lynne A., and Brenda R. Silver, eds. *Rape and Representation*. New York: Columbia University Press, 1991.

Ilboudo, Monique. *Murekatete*. Bamako, Mali: Le Figuier, 2000.

Ippolito, Emilia. *Caribbean Women Writers: Identity and Gender*. Rochester NY: Camden House, 2000.

Jacobs, Susie, Ruth Jacobson, and Jen Marchbank, eds. *States of Conflict: Gender, Violence and Resistance*. New York: Zed Books, 2000.

Julien, Eileen. "Rape, Repression and Narrative Form in *Le Devoir de violence* and *La Vie et demie*." *Rape and Representation*. Ed. Lynn A. Higgins and Brenda R. Silver. New York: Columbia University Press, 1991. 160–81.

Kake, Ibrahima Baba. *Sékou Touré: le Héros et le Tyran*. Collection Destins, Jeune Afrique Livres 3. Paris: Groupe Jeune Afrique, 1987.

Kane, Cheick Hamidou. *L'aventure ambiguë*. Paris: Julliard, 1961.

Kelly, Liz. "Wars against Women: Sexual Violence, Sexual Politics and the Militarised State." *State of Conflict Gender, Violence and Resistance*. Ed. Susie M. Jacobs, Ruth Jacobson, and Jen Marchbank. New York: Zed Books, 2000. 45–65.

———. "When Does the Speaking Profit Us?: Reflections on the Challenges of Developing Feminist Perspectives on Abuse and Violence by Women." *Women, Violence, and Male Power: Feminist Activism, Research, and Practice*. Ed. Marianne Hester, Liz Kelly, and Jill Radford. Philadelphia: Open University Press, 1996. 34–49.

Kennedy, Ellen Conroy, ed. *The Negritude Poets: An Anthology of Translations from the French*. New York: Viking, 1975.

Kesteloot, Lilyan. "Turning Point in the Francophone/African Novel: The Eighties to the Nineties." *New Trends and Generations in African Literature*. Ed. Eldred Durosomi Jones and Marjorie Jones. Africa Literature Today 20. London: James Currey Ltd., 1996. 4–13.

Koné, Amadou. "Violence du pouvoir et pouvoir de la violence dans Monnè, outrages et défis de Ahmadou Kourouma." *La Deriva delle francofonie, atti dei seminari annuali de Letterature Francophone: Figures et fantasmes de la violence dans les littératures francophones de l'Afrique subsaharienne et des Antilles*. I: L'Afrique subsaharienne. Ed. Franca Marcato-Falzoni. Bologna: Cooperativa Lib. Univ. Editrice, 1991. 163–82.

Kourouma, Ahmadou. *Les soleils des indépendances*. Paris: Éditions du Seuil, 1970.

Lacrosil, Michèle. *Cajou*. Paris: Gallimard, 1961.

Larrier, Renée. *Francophone Women Writers of Africa and the Caribbean*. Gainesville: University Press of Florida, 2000.

———. "'Girl by the shore': Gender and Testimony in Edwidge Danticat's *The Farming of Bones*." *Journal of Haitian Studies* (Fall 2001): 50–60.

Lashgari, Deirdre, ed. *Violence, Silence, and Anger: Women's Writing as Transgression*. Charlottesville: University Press of Virginia, 1995.

Laub, Dori. "Truth and Testimony: The Process and the Struggle." *Trauma: Explorations in Memory*. Ed. Cathy Caruth. Baltimore: Johns Hopkins University Press, 1995. 61–75.

Leiris, Michel. *Contacts de civilisations en Martinique et en Guadeloupe*. Paris: UNESCO Gallimard, 1955

Lionnet, Françoise. "Geographies of Pain: Captive Bodies and Violent Acts in the Fictions of Myriam Warner-Vieyra, Gayl Jones, and Bessie Head." *Callaloo* 16.1 (1993): 132–52.

Makward, Christiane. "Presque un siècle de différence amoureuse: Simone Schwarz-Bart (1972), Gisèle Pineau (1996)," *Nottingham French Studies* 40.1 (2001): 41–51.

Mama, Amina. "Sheroes and Villains: Conceptualizing Colonial and Contemporary Violence against Women in Africa." *Feminist Genealogies, Colonial Legacies, Democratic Futures*. Ed. M. Jacqui Alexander, and Chandra Talpade Mohanty. New York: Routledge, 1997. 46–62.

Marcato-Falzoni, Franca, ed. *La Deriva delle francofonie, atti dei seminari annuali de Letterature Francophone: Figures et fantasmes de la violence dans les littératures francophones de l'Afrique subsaharienne et des Antilles*. II: Les Antilles. Bologna: Cooperativa Lib. Univ. Editrice, 1991–92.

Marx-Scouras, Danielle. "Muffled Screams/Stifled Voices." *Post/Colonial Conditions: Exiles, Migrations, and Nomadisms*. Spec. issue of *Yale French Studies* 1.82 (1993): 172–82.

Matateyou, Emmanuel. "Calixthe Beyala: entre le terroir et l'exil." *The French Review* 69.4 (1996): 603–15.

Minh-ha, Trinh T. *Woman, Native, Other: Writing Postcoloniality and Feminism*. Bloomington: Indiana University Press, 1989.

Mohanty, Chandra Talpade. "Under Western Eyes, Feminist Scholarship and Colonial Discourses." *Third World Women and the Politics of Feminism*. Ed. Chandra Talpade Mohanty, Ann Russo, and Lourdes Torres. Bloomington: Indiana University Press, 1991. 51–80.

Morgan, Paula, and Valerie Youssef. *Writing Rage: Unmasking Violence through Caribbean Discourse*. Kingston, Jamaica: University of West Indies Press, 2006.

Morris, Madeleine. "In War and Peace: Rape, War, and Military Culture." *War's Dirty Secret: Rape, Prostitution, and Other Crimes Against Women*. Ed. Ann Llewellyn Barstow. Cleveland OH: Pilgrim Press, 2000. 167–203.

Mudimbe-Boyi, Elizabeth. "Langue volée, langue violée: Pouvoir, écriture et violence dans le roman africain." *La Deriva delle francofonie, atti dei seminari annuali de Letterature Francophone: Figures et fantasmes de la violence dans les littératures francophones de l'Afrique subsaharienne et des Antilles*. II: Les Antilles. Ed. Franca Marcato-Falzoni. Bologna: Cooperativa Lib. Univ. Editrice, 1991–92. 101–18.

———. "The State, the Writer and the Politics of Memory." *Studies in 20th Century Literature* 23.1 (1999): 143–61.

Nfah-Abbenyi, Juliana Makuchi. *Gender in African Women's Writing: Identity, Sexuality, and Difference*. Bloomington: Indiana University Press, 1997.

Nkashama, Pius Ngandu. *Ruptures et écritures de violence: études sur le roman et les littératures africaines contemporaines*. Paris: L'Harmattan, 1997.

Nnaemeka, Obioma, ed. *The Politics of (M)othering: Womanhood, Identity, and Resistance in African Literature*. London: Routledge, 1997.

La noire de . . . Written and dir. Sémbène Ousmane. Co-produced by Les Actualités françaises and Films Domirev. New Yorker Films, 1987.

Ogundipe-Leslie, Molara. *Re-creating Ourselves: African Women and Critical Transformations*. Trenton NJ: Africa World Press, 1994.

Orlando, Valérie. *Of Suffocated Hearts and Tortured Souls: Seeking Subjecthood through Madness in Francophone Women's Writing of Africa and the Caribbean*. Lanham MD: Lexington Books, 2003.

Ormerod, Beverley. *An Introduction to the French Caribbean Novel*. London: Heinemann, 1985.

Ouologuem, Yambo. *Le devoir de violence*. Paris: Éditions du Seuil, 1968.

Oxford English Dictionary Online. Oxford University Press. 13 February 2009. http://www.oed.com.

Oyono, Ferdinand. *Une vie de boy*. Paris: Juillard, 1956.

Paravisini-Gebert, Lizabeth. "Feminism, Race and Difference in the works of Mayotte Capécia, Michèle Lacrosil, and Jacqueline Manicom." *Callaloo* 15.1 (1992): 56–62.

——. "Women against the Grain: Theorizing Caribbean Women's Writings." *Winds Of Change: The Transforming Voices of Caribbean Women Writers and Scholars*. Ed. Adele S. Newson and Linda Strong-Leek. New York: P. Lang, 1998. 161–68.

Perinbam, Marie. *Holy Violence: The Revolutionary Thought of Frantz Fanon. An Intellectual Biography*. Washington DC: Three Continents Press, 1982.

Pfaff, Françoise. *The Cinema of Ousmane Sembène, a Pioneer of African Film*. Westport CT: Greenwood Press, 1984.

Pineau, Gisèle. *Le cyclone Marilyn*. Illus. Béatrice Favereau. Montréal: Montréal Hurtubise HMH, 1998.

——. *L'espérance-macadam*. Paris: Stock, 1995.

——. *Macadam Dreams = L'espérance-macadam*. Trans. C. Dickson. Lincoln: University of Nebraska Press, 2003.

——. *Un papillon dans la cité*. Saint-Maur-des-Fossés: Sépia, 1992.

Presbey, Gail M. "Fanon and the Role of Violence in Liberation: A Comparison with Gandhi and Mandela." *Fanon: A Critical Reader*. Ed. and trans. Lewis R. Gordon, T. Denean Sharpley-Whiting, and Renée T. White. Cambridge MA: Blackwell Publishers, 1996. 283–96.

Quayson, Ato. "Symbolisation Compulsions: Freud, African Literature and South Africa's Process of Truth and Reconciliation." *The Cambridge Quarterly* 30.3 (2001): 191–214.

Rich, Adrienne. "Resisting Amnesia: History and Personal Life." *Blood,*

Bread, and Poetry: Selected Prose 1979–1985. New York: Norton, 1986. 136–55.

Rosello, Mireille. "Pluie et vent sur Télumée Miracle. *Présence Francophone: Revue Internationale de Langue et de Littérature* 36 (1990): 73–90.

Rupesinghe, Kumar, and Marcial C. Rubio, eds. *The Culture of Violence*. New York: United Nations University Press, 1994.

Russell, Diana E. H. *The Secret Trauma: Incest in the Lives of Girls and Women*. New York: Basic Books, 1986.

Savory, Elaine. "Ex/Isle: Separation, Memory, and Desire in Caribbean Women's Writing." *Winds of Change: The Transforming Voices of Caribbean Women Writers and Scholars*. Ed. Adele S. Newson and Linda Strong-Leek. New York: P. Lang, 1998. 169–77.

Scarry, Elaine. *The Body in Pain: The Making and Unmaking of the World*. New York: Oxford University Press, 1985.

Scharfman, Ronnie. "Mirroring and Mothering in Simone Schwarz-Bart's *Pluie et vent sur Télumée Miracle* and Jean Rhys's *Wide Sargasso Sea*." *Yale French Studies* 62 (1981): 88–106.

——. "Theorizing Terror: The Discourse of Violence in *Amour colère folie*." *Postcolonial Subjects: Francophone Women Writers*. Ed. Mary Jean Green, et al. Minneapolis: University of Minnesota Press, 1996. 229–45.

Schipper, Mineke. *Unheard Words: Women and Literature in Africa, the Arab World, Asia, the Caribbean and Latin America*. Trans. Barbara Potter Fasting. London: Allison & Busby, 1985.

Schwarz-Bart, Simone. *The Bridge of Beyond*. Trans. Barbara Bray. Portsmouth NH: Heinemann, 1974.

——. *Pluie et vent sur Télumée Miracle*. Paris: Éditions du Seuil, 1972.

Semujanga, Josias. *Récits fondateurs du drame rwandais: Discours social, idéologies et stéréotypes*. Paris: L'Harmattan, 1998.

Sharpley-Whiting, T. Denean "Anti-black Femininity and Mixed-race identity: Engaging Fanon to Reread Capécia." *Fanon: A Critical Reader*. Ed. and trans. Lewis R. Gordon, T. Denean Sharpley-Whiting, and Renée T. White. Cambridge MA: Blackwell Publishers, 1996. 155–62.

Shelton, Marie-Denise. "A New Cry from the 1960s to the 1980s." *A*

History of Literature in the Caribbean. Ed. A. James Arnold, et al. Vol. 1. Philadelphia: J. Benjamins, 1994. 427–33.

Sielke, Sabine. *Reading Rape: The Rhetoric of Sexual Violence in American Literature and Culture, 1790–1990*. Princeton NJ: Princeton University Press, 2002.

Smith, Robert P., Jr. "Michèle Lacrosil: Novelist with a Color Complex." *The French Review* 47.4 (March 1974): 783–90.

Sorry, Charles E. *Sékou Touré: l'ange exterminateur: un passé à dépasser*. Paris: L'Harmattan, 2000.

Spivak, Gayatri Chakravorty. "Can the Subaltern Speak?" *Colonial Discourse and Post-Colonial Theory: A Reader.* Ed. Patrick Williams and Laura Chrisman. New York: Columbia University Press, 1994. 66–111.

Stoler, Ann Laura. "Carnal Knowledge and Imperial Power, Gender, Race and Morality in Colonial Asia." *Gender at the Crossroads of Knowledge: Feminist Anthropology in the Postmodern Era*. Ed. Micaela di Leonardo. Berkeley: University of California Press, 1991. 51–101.

Stratton, Florence. *Contemporary African Literature and the Politics of Gender*. New York: Routledge, 1994.

Tal, Kalí. *Worlds of Hurt: Reading the Literatures of Trauma*. New York: Cambridge University Press, 1996.

Tanner, Laura E. *Intimate Violence: Reading Rape and Torture in Twentieth-Century Fiction*. Bloomington: Indiana University Press, 1994.

Vickroy, Laurie. *Trauma and Survival in Contemporary Fiction*. Charlottesville: University of Virginia Press, 2002.

Vieyra, Paulin Semanou. *Ousmane Sembène, cinéaste; première période, 1962–1971*. Paris: Présence Africaine, 1972.

Volet, Jean-Marie. "La Guerre chez les romancières." http://www.arts.uwa.edu.au/MotsPluriels/MP497jvindex.html.

Warner-Vieyra, Myriam. *Juletane*. Paris: Présence africain, 1982.

Whitmer, Barbara. *The Violence Mythos*. Albany: State University of New York, 1997.

Wilson, Elizabeth. "Le voyage et l'espace clos: Island and Journey as Metaphor: Aspects of Woman's Experience in the Works of

Francophone Women Novelists." *Out of the Kumbla: Caribbean Women and Literature*. Ed. Carol Boyce Davies and Elaine Savory Fido. Trenton NJ: Africa World Press, 1990. 45–57.

Woodhull, Winifred. *Transfigurations of the Maghreb: Feminism, Decolonization, and Literatures*. Minneapolis: University of Minnesota Press, 1993.

Zabus, Chantal J. *The African Palimpsest: Indigenization of Language in the West African Europhone Novel*. Atlanta GA: Rodopi, 1991.

Index